why we stay together

why we stay together

20 writers on marriage and its rewards

Edited by

Jennifer Schwamm Willis

Marlowe & Company
New York

WHY WE STAY TOGETHER: 20 WRITERS ON MARRIAGE AND ITS REWARDS

Compilation copyright © 2002 by Jennifer Schwamm Willis
Introductions copyright © 2002 by Jennifer Schwamm Willis

Published by
Marlowe & Company
An Imprint of Avalon Publishing Group Incorporated
161 William Street, 16th floor
New York, NY 10038

A Balliett & Fitzgerald book

Book design: Sue Canavan

Library of Congress Catalog-in-Publication Data is available.

ISBN: 1-56924-540-1

9 8 7 6 5 4 3 2 1

Printed in the United States of America
Distributed by Publishers Group West

For Clint Willis

who has helped open my heart to love and compassion

Contents

Introduction

Why and how, once married, should we work to stay together even in the face of moments of great unhappiness, frustration and often anger? This question arises in good and bad marriages alike. We all have moments, days, weeks and even years when we struggle to understand why we stay.

The work of reading and selecting pieces for this collection conjured up an image which hovered before me. When I looked closely at it, I saw myself— not a reflection, but a materialization of my deeper feelings and thoughts. I discovered there a set of new questions about the importance of love and commitment in our lives beyond the marital relationship. These questions drew me into a deeper spiritual inquiry.

Reading about marriage and thinking about my own 20-year marriage, I have come to understand marriage as a model for my relationship not just with my spouse, but with the human community at large. I recently attended my uncle's funeral. As I stood at his graveside I saw husbands, wives, children, aunts, uncles, grandparents, friends; a community of people—some happy, some unhappy, some close to one another, some estranged. The question of why we stay together in marriage took on a greater dimension. It struck me that love and commitment should extend to those around us in ever-widening circles. Love is work, work is essential for wisdom, and wisdom circles back to love, bringing with it the range of human emotions from joy to despair.

We make the choice to marry a particular individual, but marriage is part of a process that begins at birth—a coming-to-terms with love. This process is an evolving understanding of love and what it means, with love's definition changing and expanding as we grow. The mother of the bride in Anne Morrow Lindbergh's novel *Dearly Beloved* considers her own long and imperfect marriage as she looks at her husband across the table around which are gathered bride, groom and guests:

> The phrase "community of marriage" came to her from the old-fashioned past. Community was what they had together. And perhaps this was the meaning of marriage, not the communication she was forever looking for. Community-communion-communication: the words might be closer than she knew. All this they had made, shared, held together—wasn't it a form of communication? At the moment it seemed enough. It

compensated for all the humdrum grocery-string length of days. It gave meaning to her life.

Was this then "real life"—the life she was always wondering about and looking for; life stripped to its naked core, for once clear and vivid, not embedded in a chaotic lava flow? The ore of life was suddenly visible, not covered as it usually was, to be dug out with difficulty, but on the surface, exposed and gleaming.

All relationships, including marriage, change. It also is in the nature of life to ask us to continually revisit the fundamental issues each of us faces: love, death and truth. Each time I do so I return to my marriage with a different, deeper understanding of its meaning and value. As I have passed through the stages of first infatuation, marriage, children and mid-life, with old age still to come, I have learned that my wisdom and love will continue to grow—and that they will grow to incorporate more and more of the people and indeed the world around me. Difficult periods of transition will inevitably arise. I had to let go of my first, intensely exclusive love for my husband to include children in the circle; as they grow up, becoming dear to me in new ways, the circle widens yet again to include friends, community and work—and I find new and deeper ways to include myself in it.

The writers whose work I've included in this collection have approached the subject of marriage with seriousness and compassion; with intelligence, humor and grace. Each writer has a unique voice and perspective, but all of the writers find value in the idea of embracing marriage as a way to understand not only one's spouse and family, but also oneself and one's essential connection to the rest of humanity.

—JENNIFER SCHWAMM WILLIS

respect

from

Teachings on Love
by Thich Nhat Hanh

Vietnamese Monk Thich Nhat Hanh is a Zen Master, poet and activist for world peace. He lives in Plum Village, an international meditation community in southern France. This passage explores the idea of nghiā—a state of profound connection arrived at by "sharing difficulties and joys over a long period of time."

Tr"rue love contains respect. In the Vietnamese tradition, husband and wife always respect each other as honored guests. When you practice this, your love will last for a long time. In Vietnamese, the words *tinh* and *nghiā* both mean love. Tinh contains a lot of passion. Nghiā is calmer, more understanding, more faithful. You are not as passionate, but your love is deeper and more solid. You are more willing to sacrifice to make the other person happy. Nghiā is the result of sharing difficulties and joys over a long period of time.

You begin with passion, but, living with each other, you learn to deal with difficulties, and your love deepens. The passion diminishes, but nghiā increases all the time. You understand the other person better, and you feel a lot of gratitude: "Thank you for being my husband (my wife), for having chosen me as your companion to share your best qualities, as well as your suffering. While I was having difficulty and remained awake deep into the night, you took care of me. You showed me that my well-being is your own well-being. You did the impossible to help me get well. I am deeply grateful." When a couple stays together for a long time, it is because of nghiā. Nghiā is the kind of love we really need for our family and for our society. With nghiā, you are sure the other person will love you and take care of you "until your hair becomes white and your teeth fall out." Nghiā is built by both of you in your daily life.

Look deeply to see which of these elements are in your love. You cannot say love is one hundred percent tinh or one hundred percent nghiā. Both are in it. Look into the eyes of your beloved and ask deeply, "Who are you, my love, who has come to me and taken my suffering as your suffering, my happiness as your happiness, my life and death as your life and death? Who are you whose self has become my self? Why aren't you a dewdrop, a butterfly, a bird, a pine tree?" Ask with your whole body and mind. Later, you will have to ask the person who causes you the most suffering the same questions: "Who are you who brings me such pain, who makes me feel so much anger and hatred?" To understand, you have to become one with your beloved, and also one with your so-called enemy. You have to worry about what they worry about, suffer their suffering, appreciate what they appreciate. You and the object of your love cannot be two. They are as much you as you are yourself.

Continue until you see yourself in the cruelest person on Earth, in the child starving, in the political prisoner. Practice until you recognize yourself in everyone in the supermarket, on the street corner, in a concentration camp, on a leaf, in a dewdrop. Meditate until you see yourself in a speck of dust in a distant galaxy. See and listen with the whole of your being. If you are fully present, the rain of the Dharma will water the deepest seeds in your store consciousness, and tomorrow, while you are washing the dishes or looking at the blue sky, that seed will spring forth, and love and understanding will appear as a beautiful flower.

> *Being rock, being gas, being mist, being mind,*
> *being the mesons traveling among the galaxies*
> *at the seed of light,*
> *you have come here, my beloved.*
> *And your blue eyes shine, so beautiful, so deep.*
> *You have taken the path traced for you*
> *from the non-beginning and the never-ending.*
> *You say that on your way here*
> *you have gone through*
> *many millions of births and deaths.*
> *Innumerable times you have been transformed*
> *into firestorms in outer space.*
> *You have used your own body*
> *to measure the age of the mountains and rivers.*
> *You have manifested yourself*
> *as trees, grass, butterflies, single-celled beings,*
> *and as chrysanthemums.*
> *But the eyes with which you look at me this morning*
> *tell me that you have never died.*

Your smile invites me into the game
whose beginning no one knows,
the game of hide-and-seek.

O green caterpillar, you are solemnly using your body
to measure the length of the rose branch that grew up last
*   Summer.*
Everyone says that you, my beloved, were just born this
*   Spring.*
Tell me, how long have you been around?
Why wait until this moment to reveal yourself to me,
carrying with you that smile which is so silent and so
deep?
O caterpillar suns, moons, and stars flow out
each time I exhale.
Who knows that the infinitely large must be found
in your tiny body?
Upon each point on your body,
thousands of Buddha fields have been established.
With each stretch of your body, you measure time
from the non-beginning to the never-ending.
The great mendicant of old is still there on Vulture Peak,
contemplating the ever-splendid sunset.

Gautama, how strange!
Who said that the Udumbara flower blooms
only once every 3,000 years?

The sound of the rising tide—you cannot help hearing it
if you have an attentive ear.

If you really love someone, you have to be fully present for him or her. A ten-year-old boy I know was asked by his father what he wanted for his birthday, and he said, "Daddy, I want you!" His father was too busy. He had no time for his family. His son knew that the greatest gift his father could offer was his true presence.

When you are concentrated—mind and body at one—anything you say can be a mantra. It does not have to be spoken in Sanskrit. It can be uttered in your own language: "Darling, I am here for you." If you are fully present, this mantra will produce a miracle. You become real, the person you say it to becomes real, and life becomes real in that moment. You bring happiness to yourself and to the other person. This is the greatest gift you can offer your loved one. To love is to be there for him, for her, and for them.

"I know you are there, and I am very happy" is a second mantra. When I look deeply at the moon, I breathe in and out deeply and say, "Full moon, I know you are there, and I am very happy." I do the same when I see the morning star. Walking among the beautiful spring magnolia trees in Korea, I looked at the beautiful flowers and said, "I know you are there, and I am very happy." To be truly present and know that the other is also there is a miracle. Whenever you are really there, you are able to recognize and appreciate the presence of the other—the full moon, the morning star, the magnolia flowers, the person you love the most. First practice breathing in and out mindfully to recover yourself. Then sit close to the one you love and, in that state of deep concentration, pronounce the second mantra. You will be happy, and the person you love will be happy at the same time. These mantras can be practiced in daily life. To be a true lover, you have to practice mindful breathing in order to produce your true presence.

There is a third mantra: "Darling, I know you are suffering. That is why I am here for you." If you are mindful, you will notice when your beloved is suffering. Sit close to him and say, "Darling, I know you are suffering. That is why I am here for you." That alone will bring a lot of relief.

There is a fourth mantra you can practice when you yourself suffer: "Darling, I am suffering. Please help." Only six words, but sometimes they are difficult to say because of the pride in our hearts, especially if it was the person we love whom we believe caused us to suffer. If it had been someone else, it would not be so hard. But because it was him, we feel deeply hurt. We want to go to our room and weep. But if we really love him, when we suffer like that, we have to ask for help. We must overcome our pride.

There is a story that is well-known in my country about a young couple who suffered deeply because of pride. The husband had to go off to war, and he left his pregnant wife behind. Three years later, when he was released from the army, his wife came to the village gate to welcome him, and she brought along their little boy. When the young couple saw each other, they could not hold back the tears of joy. They were thankful to their ancestors for protecting them, and the young man asked his wife to go to the marketplace to buy some fruit, flowers, and other offerings to place on the ancestors' altar.

While she was shopping, the young father asked his son to call him Daddy, but the little boy refused. "Sir, you are not my daddy! My daddy used to come every night, and my mother would talk to him and cry. When mother sat down, daddy also sat down. When mother lay down, my daddy lay down." Hearing these words, the young father's heart turned to stone.

When his wife returned, he could not even look at her. The young man offered fruit, flowers, and incense to the ancestors, made prostrations, and then rolled up the bowing mat and did not allow her to do the same. He believed that she was not worthy to present herself in front of the ancestors. Then he walked out of the house and spent his days drinking and walking about the village. His wife could not understand why he was acting like that. Finally, after three days, she could bear it no longer, and she jumped into the river and drowned herself.

The evening after the funeral, when the young father lit the kerosene lamp, his little boy shouted, "There is my daddy!" He pointed to his father's shadow projected on the wall and said, "My daddy used to come every night just like that, and my mother would talk to him and cry a lot. When my mother sat down, he sat down. When my mother lay down, he lay down." "Darling, you have been away for too long. How can I raise our child alone?" she cried to her shadow. One night the child asked her who and where his father was. She pointed to her shadow on the wall and said, "This is your father." She missed him so much.

Suddenly the young father understood, but it was too late. If he had gone to his wife and asked, "Darling, I suffer so much. Our little boy said a man used to come every night and you would talk to him and cry with him, and every time you sat down, he also sat down. Who is that person?" she would have had an opportunity to explain and avert the tragedy. But he did not because of the pride in him.

The lady behaved the same. She was deeply hurt because of her husband's behavior, but she did not ask for his help. She should have practiced the fourth mantra, "Darling, I suffer so much. Please help. I do not understand why you will not look at me or talk with me. Why didn't you allow me to prostrate before the ancestors? Have I done anything wrong?" If she had done that, her husband could have told her what the little boy said. But she did not, because she, too, was caught in pride.

In true love, there is no place for pride. When you are hurt by the person you love, when you suffer and believe that your suffering has been caused by the person you love the most, remember this story. Do not act like the father or the mother of the little boy. Do not let pride stand in your way. Practice the fourth mantra: "Darling, I am suffering. Please help." If you really consider him to be the one you love the most in this life, you have to do that.

When he hears your words, he will come back to himself and practice looking deeply. Then the two of you will be able to sort things out, reconcile, and dissolve the wrong perception.

Buddhist meditation aims, first of all, at restoring communication with ourselves. We are seldom there for ourselves. We run away from ourselves, because we are afraid to go home and face the fear and suffering in our wounded child who has been ignored for such a long time. But it is wonderful to return home and say, "Little boy or little girl, I am here for you. Don't worry. I will take care of you." This is the first step. You are the deeply wounded child waiting for you to come home. And you are the one who has run away from home, who has neglected your child.

Go back and take care of yourself. Your body needs you, your feelings need you, your perceptions need you. The wounded child in you needs you. Your suffering, your blocks of pain need you. Your deepest desire needs you to acknowledge it. Go home and be there for all these things. Practice mindful walking and mindful breathing. Do everything in mindfulness so you can be really there, so you can love.

transformation

from

Gift from the Sea
by Anne Morrow Lindbergh

American writer and aviator Anne Morrow Lind-bergh (1906–2001) was married to pilot Charles Lindbergh for 45 years. She wrote *Gift From the Sea* in 1955, during a solitary stay in a small seaside cottage. She uses seashells she found on the beach as metaphors for the various stages of life.

But surely we *do* demand duration and continuity of relationships, at least of marriage. That is what marriage is, isn't it—continuity of a relationship? Of course, but not necessarily continuity in one single form or stage; not necessarily continuity in the double-sunrise stage. There are other shells to help me, to put in the row on my desk. Here is one I picked up yesterday. Not rare; there are many of them on the beach and yet each one is individual. You never find two alike. Each is fitted and formed by its own life and struggle to survive. It is an oyster, with small shells clinging to its humped back. Sprawling and uneven, it has the irregularity of something growing. It looks rather like the house of a big family, pushing out one addition after another to hold its teeming life—here a sleeping porch for the children, and there a veranda for the play-pen; here a garage for the extra car, and there a shed for the bicycles. It amuses me because it seems so much like my life at the moment, like most women's lives in the middle years of marriage. It is untidy, spread out in all directions, heavily encrusted with accumulations and, in its living state—this one is empty and cast up by the sea—firmly imbedded on its rock.

Yes, I believe the oyster shell is a good one to express the middle years of marriage. It suggests the struggle of life itself. The oyster has fought to have that place on the rock to which it has fitted itself perfectly and to which it clings tenaciously. So most couples in the growing years of marriage struggle to achieve a place in the world. It is a physical and material battle first of all, for a home, for children, for a place in their particular society. In the midst of such a life there is not much time to sit facing one another over a breakfast table. In these years one recognizes the truth of Saint Exupéry's line: "Love does not consist in gazing at each other (one perfect sunrise gazing at another!) but in looking outward together in the same direction." For, in fact, man and woman are not only *looking* outward in the same direction; they are *working* outward. (Observe the steady encroachment of the oyster bed over the rock.) Here one forms ties, roots, a firm base. (Try and pry an oyster from its ledge!) Here one makes oneself part of the community of men, of human society.

Here the bonds of marriage are formed. For marriage, which is always spoken of as a bond, becomes actually, in this stage, many bonds, many strands, of different texture and strength, making up a web that is taut and firm. The web is fashioned of love. Yes, but many kinds of love: romantic love first, then a slow-growing devotion and, playing through these, a constantly rippling companionship. It is made of loyalties, and interdependencies, and shared experiences. It is woven of memories of meetings and conflicts; of triumphs and disappointments. It is a web of communication, a common language, and the acceptance of lack of language, too; a knowledge of likes and dislikes, of habits and reactions, both physical and mental. It is a web of instincts and intuitions, and known and unknown exchanges. The web of marriage is made by propinquity, in the day to day living side by side, looking outward and working outward in the same direction. It is woven in space and in time of the substance of life itself.

But the bond—the bond of romantic love is something else. It has so little to do with propinquity or habit or space or time or life itself. It leaps across all of them, like a rainbow—or a glance. It is the bond of romantic love which fastens the double-sunrise shell, only one bond, one hinge. And if that fragile link is snapped in the storm, what will hold the halves to each other? In the oyster stage of marriage, romantic love is only one of the many bonds that make up the intricate and enduring web that two people have built together.

I am very fond of the oyster shell. It is humble and awkward and ugly. It is slate-colored and unsymmetrical. Its form is not primarily beautiful but functional. I make fun of its knobbiness. Sometimes I resent its burdens and excrescences. But its tireless adaptability and tenacity draw my astonished admiration and sometimes even my tears. And it is comfortable in its familiarity, its homeliness, like old garden gloves which have moulded themselves perfectly to the shape of the hand. I do not like to put it down. I will not want to leave it.

But is it the permanent symbol of marriage? Should it—any

more than the double-sunrise shell—last forever? The tide of life precedes. The house, with its bulging sleeping porches and sheds, begins little by little to empty. The children go away to school and then to marriage and lives of their own. Most people by middle age have attained, or ceased to struggle to attain, their place in the world. That terrific tenacity to life, to place, to people, to material surroundings and accumulations—is it as necessary as it was when one was struggling for one's security or the security of one's children? Many of the physical struggles have ceased, due either to success or to failure. Does the shell need to be so welded to its rock? Married couples are apt to find themselves in middle age, high and dry in an outmoded shell, in a fortress which has outlived its function. What is one to do—die of atrophy in an outstripped form? Or move on to another form, other experiences?

Perhaps, someone will suggest, this is the moment to go back to the simple self-enclosed world of the sunrise shell? Alone at last again over the muffins and the marmalade! No, one cannot go back to that tightly closed world. One has grown too big, too many-sided, for that rigidly symmetrical shell. I am not sure that one has not grown too big for any shell at all.

Perhaps middle age is, or should be, a period of shedding shells; the shell of ambition, the shell of material accumulations and possessions, the shell of the ego. Perhaps one can shed at this stage in life as one sheds in beach-living; one's pride, one's false ambitions, one's mask, one's armor. Was that armor not put on to protect one from the competitive world? If one ceases to compete, does one need it? Perhaps one can at last in middle

age, if not earlier, be completely oneself. And what a liberation
that would be!

It is true that the adventures of youth are less open to us. Most
of us cannot, at this point, start a new career or raise a new family.
Many of the physical, material, and worldly ambitions are less
attainable than they were twenty years ago. But is this not often a
relief? "I no longer worry about being the belle of Newport," a
beautiful woman, who had become a talented artist, once said to
me. And I always liked that Virginia Woolf hero who meets
middle age admitting: "Things have dropped from me. I have outlived certain desires . . . I am not so gifted as at one time seemed
likely. Certain things lie beyond my scope. I shall never understand the harder problems of philosophy. Rome is the limit of my
travelling . . . I shall never see savages in Tahiti spearing fish by the
light of a blazing cresset, or a lion spring in the jungle, or a naked
man eating raw flesh . . ." (Thank God! you can hear him adding
under his breath.)

The primitive, physical, functional pattern of the morning of
life, the active years before forty or fifty, is outlived. But there is
still the afternoon opening up, which one can spend not in the
feverish pace of the morning but in having time at last for those
intellectual, cultural, and spiritual activities that were pushed aside
in the heat of the race. We Americans, with our terrific emphasis
on youth, action, and material success, certainly tend to belittle
the afternoon of life and even to pretend it never comes. We push
the clock back and try to prolong the morning, overreaching and
overstraining ourselves in the unnatural effort. We do not succeed,

of course. We cannot compete with our sons and daughters. And what a struggle it is to race with these over-active and under-wise adults! In our breathless attempts we often miss the flowering that waits for afternoon.

For is it not possible that middle age can be looked upon as a period of second flowering, second growth, even a kind of second adolescence? It is true that society in general does not help one accept this interpretation of the second half of life. And therefore this period of expanding is often tragically misunderstood. Many people never climb above the plateau of forty-to-fifty. The signs that presage growth, so similar, it seems to me, to those in early adolescence: discontent, restlessness, doubt, despair, longing, are interpreted falsely as signs of decay. In youth one does not as often misinterpret the signs; one accepts them, done rightly, as growing pains. One takes them seriously, listens to them, follows where they lead. One is afraid. Naturally. Who is not afraid of pure space—that breath-taking empty space of an open door? But despite fear, one goes through to the room beyond.

But in the middle age, because of the false assumption that it is a period of decline, one interprets these life-signs, paradoxically, as signs of approaching death. Instead of facing them, one runs away; one escapes—into depressions, nervous breakdowns, drink, love affairs, or frantic, thoughtless, fruitless overwork. Anything, rather than face them. Anything, rather than stand still and learn from them. One tries to cure the signs of growth, to exorcise them, as if they were devils, when really they might be angels of annunciation.

Angels of annunciation of what? Of a new stage in living when, having shed many of the physical struggles, the worldly ambitions, the material encumbrances of active life, one might be free to ful-fill the neglected side of one's self. One might be free for growth of mind, heart, and talent; free at last for spiritual growth; free of the clamping sunrise shell. Beautiful as it was, it was still a closed world one had to outgrow. And the time may come when—comfortable and adaptable as it is—one may outgrow even the oyster shell.

There are in the beach-world certain rare creatures, the "Argonauta" (Paper Nautilus), who are not fastened to their shell at all. It is actu-ally a cradle for the young, held in the arms of the mother argonaut who floats with it to the surface, where the eggs hatch and the young swim away. Then the mother argonaut leaves her shell and starts another life. I am fascinated by this image of the argonaut, whose temporary dwelling I have seen only as the treasure of a spe-cialist's collection. Almost transparent, delicately fluted like a Greek column, this narcissus-white snail shell is feather light as some cor-acle of ancient times, ready to set sail across unknown seas. It was named, the book tells me, for the fabled ships of Jason that went in search of the Golden Fleece. Sailors consider these shells a sign of fair weather and favorable winds.

Lovely shell, lovely image—I am tempted to play with it in my mind. Is this the symbol for another stage in relationships? Can we middle-aged argonauts when we outgrow the oyster bed, look forward to the freedom of the nautilus who has left its shell for the open seas? But what does the open sea hold for us? We cannot believe that the second half of life promises "fair weather and favorable winds." What golden fleece is there for the middle-aged?

In speaking of the argonauts one might as well admit one has left the usual shell collections. A double-sunrise shell, an oyster bed— these are common knowledge to most of us. We recognize them; we know about them; they are part of our daily life and the lives of others around us. But with this rare and delicate vessel, we have left the well-tracked beaches of proven facts and experiences. We are adventuring in the chartless seas of imagination.

Is the golden fleece that awaits us some kind of new freedom for growth? And in this new freedom, is there any place for a relationship? I believe there is, after the oyster bed, an opportunity for the best relationship of all: not a limited, mutually exclusive one, like the sunrise shell; and not a functional, dependent one, as in the oyster bed; but the meeting of two whole fully developed people as persons. It would be, to borrow a definition of the Scottish philosopher, Mac-Murray, a fully personal relationship, that is, "a type of relationship into which people enter as persons with the whole of themselves." "Personal relationships," he goes on to explain, ". . . have no ulterior motive. They are not based on particular interests. They do not serve partial and limited ends. Their value lies entirely in themselves and for the same reason transcends all other values. And that is because they are relations of persons as persons." This relationship of "persons as persons" was prophetically hinted at by the German poet, Rilke, almost fifty years ago. He foresaw a great change in the relationships between men and women, which he hoped in the future would no longer follow the traditional patterns of submission and domination or of possession and competition. He described a state in which there would be space and freedom for growth, and in which each partner would be the means of releasing the other. "A relation," he concludes, "that is meant to be of one human being to another. . . . And this more human love (that will fulfill itself, infinitely considerate and gentle, and good and clear in binding and releasing) will resemble that which we are with struggle and endeavor preparing, the love that consists in this, that two solitudes protect and touch and greet each other."

But this new relationship of persons as persons, this more human love, this two solitudes conception is not something that comes easily. It must have grown, like all firm-rooted growth, slowly. It perhaps can only follow a long development in the history of human civilization and individually in each human being's life. Such a stage in life, it would seem to me, must come not as a gift or a lucky accident, but as part of an evolutionary process, an achievement which could only follow certain important developments in each partner.

It cannot be reached until woman—individually and as a sex—has herself come of age, a maturing process we are witnessing today. In this undertaking she must work alone and cannot count on much help from the outsider, eager as he may be in pointing out the way. There are many signs of interest in the new woman today, chiefly in the form of mechanistic studies of her as a female animal. Of course it is necessary and helpful for woman to understand and accept her sexual needs and habits but it is only one side of a very complex problem. One cannot expect statistics on her physical reactions to add much knowledge or nourishment to her inner life, to her basic relation to herself, or to her long postponed hope and right, as a human being, to be creative in other ways besides the purely physical one.

Woman must come of age by herself. This is the essence of "coming of age"—to learn how to stand alone. She must learn not to depend on another, nor to feel she must prove her strength by competing with another. In the past, she has swung between these two opposite poles of dependence and competition, of Victorianism and Feminism. Both extremes throw her off balance; neither is the center, the true center of being a whole woman. She must find her true center alone. She must become whole. She must, it seems to me, as a prelude to any "two solitudes" relationship, follow the advice of the poet to become "world to oneself for another's sake."

In fact, I wonder if both man and woman must not accomplish this heroic feat. Must not man also become world to himself? Must he not also expand the neglected sides of his personality; the art of inward looking that he has seldom had time for in his active outward-going life; the personal relationships which he has not had as much chance to enjoy; the so-called feminine qualities, aesthetic, emotional, cultural and spiritual, which he has been too rushed to fully develop. Perhaps both men and women in America may hunger, in our material, outward, active, masculine culture, for the supposedly feminine qualities of heart, mind and spirit— qualities which are actually neither masculine nor feminine, but simply human qualities that have been neglected. It is growth along these lines that will make us whole, and will enable the individual to become world to himself.

And this greater wholeness in each person, this being "world to oneself," does this not mean greater self-sufficiency and therefore, inevitably, greater separation between man and woman? With growth, it is true, comes differentiation and separation, in the sense that the unity of the tree-trunk differentiates as it grows and spreads into limbs, branches, and leaves. But the tree is still one, and its different and separate parts contribute to one another. The two separate worlds or the two solitudes will surely have more to give each other than when each was a meager half. "A complete sharing between two people is an impossibility," writes Rilke, "and whenever it seems, nevertheless, to exist, it is a narrowing, a mutual agreement which robs either one member or both of his fullest freedom and development. But, once the realization is accepted that, even between the closest human beings, infinite distances continue to exist, a wonderful living side by side can grow up, if they succeed in loving the distance between them which makes it possible, for each to see the other whole and against a wide sky!"

This is a beautiful image, but who can achieve it in actual life? Where has one seen such a marriage except in a poet's correspondence? It is true that Rilke's two solitudes or MacMurray's fully personal relationship are as yet somewhat theoretical concepts. But theory precedes exploration; we must use any signposts that exist to help us through the wilderness. For we are, actually, pioneers trying to find a new path through the maze of tradition, convention and dogma. Our efforts are part of the struggle to mature the conception of relationships between men and women—in fact all relationships. In such a light, every advance in understanding has value. Every step, even a tentative one, counts. And though we may seldom come upon a perfect argonauta life cycle, we have all had glimpses of them, even in our own lives for brief periods. And these brief experiences give us insight into what the new relation might be.

On this island I have had such a glimpse into the life of the argonauta. After my week alone I have had a week of living with my sister. I will take from it one day. I shall examine it, set it before me as I have set the shells on my desk. I shall turn it around like a shell, testing and analyzing its good points. Not that my life will ever become like this day—a perfect one plucked out of a holiday week; there are no perfect lives. The relation of two sisters is not that of a man and a woman. But it can illustrate the essence of relationships. The light shed by any good relationship illuminates all relationships. And one perfect day can give clues for a more perfect life—the mythical life, maybe, of the argonauta.

We wake in the same small room from the deep sleep of good children, to the soft sound of wind through the casuarina trees and the gentle sleep-breathing rhythm of waves on the shore. We run barelegged to the beach, which lies smooth, flat, and glistening with fresh wet shells after the night's tides. The morning swim has the nature of a blessing to me, a baptism, a rebirth to the beauty and wonder of the world. We run back tingling to hot coffee on our small back porch. Two kitchen chairs and a child's tale between us fill the stoop on which we sit. With legs in the sun we laugh and plan our day.

We wash the dishes lightly to no system, for there are not enough to matter. We work easily and instinctively together, not bumping into each other as we go back and forth about our tasks. We talk as we sweep, as we dry, as we put away, discussing a person or a poem or a memory. And since our communication seems more important to us than our chores, the chores are done without thinking.

And then to work, behind closed doors neither of us would want to invade. What release to write so that one forgets oneself, forgets one's companion, forgets where one is or what one is going to do next—to be drenched in work as one is drenched in sleep or in the sea. Pencils and pads and curling blue sheets alive with letters heap up on the desk. And then, pricked by hunger, we rise at last in a daze, for a late lunch. Reeling a little from our intense absorption, we come back with relief to the small chores of getting lunch, as if they were lifelines to reality—as if we had indeed almost drowned in the sea of intellectual work and welcomed the firm ground of physical action under our feet.

After an hour or so of practical jobs and errands we are ready to leave them again. Out onto the beach for the afternoon where we are swept clean of duties, of the particular, of the practical. We walk up the beach in silence, but in harmony, as the sandpipers ahead of us move like a corps of ballet dancers keeping time to some interior rhythm inaudible to us. Intimacy is blown away. Emotions are carried out to sea. We are even free of thoughts, at least of their articulation; clean and bare as whitened driftwood; empty as shells, ready to be filled up again with the impersonal sea and sky and wind. A long afternoon soaking up the outer world.

And when we are heavy and relaxed as the seaweed under our feet, we return at dusk to the warmth and intimacy of our cottage. We sip sherry at leisure in front of a fire. We start supper and we talk. Evening is the time for conversation. Morning is for mental work, I feel, the habit of school-days persisting in me. Afternoon is for physical tasks, the out-of-door jobs. But evening is for sharing, for communication. Is it the uninterrupted dark expanse of the night after the bright segmented day, that frees us to each other? Or does the infinite space and infinite darkness dwarf and chill us, turning us to seek small human sparks?

Communication—but not for too long. Because good communication is stimulating as black coffee, and just as hard to sleep after. Before we sleep we go out again into the night. We walk up the beach under the stars. And when we are tired of walking, we lie flat on the sand under a bowl of stars. We feel stretched, expanded to take in their compass. They pour into us until we are filled with stars, up to the brim.

This is what one thirsts for, I realize, after the smallness of the day, of work, of details, of intimacy—even of communication, one thirsts for the magnitude and universality of a night full of stars, pouring into one like a fresh tide.

And then at last, from the immensity of interstellar space, we swing down to a particular beach. We walk back to the lights of the cottage glowing from the dark mist of trees. Small, safe, warm and welcoming, we recognize our pinpoint human match-light against the mammoth chaos of the dark. Back again to our good child's sleep.

• • •

What a wonderful day, I think, turning it around in my hand to its starting point again. What has made it so perfect? Is there not some clue here in the pattern of this day? To begin with, it is a pattern of freedom. Its setting has not been cramped in space or time. An island, curiously enough, gives a limitless feeling of both. Nor has the day been limited in kinds of activity. It has a natural balance of physical, intellectual and social life. It has an easy unforced rhythm. Work is not deformed by pressure. Relationship is not strangled by claims. Intimacy is tempered by lightness of touch. We have moved through our day like dancers, not needing to touch more than lightly because we were instinctively moving to the same rhythm.

A good relationship has a pattern like a dance and is built on some of the same rules. The partners do not need to hold on tightly, because they move confidently in the same pattern, intricate but gay and swift and free, like a country dance of Mozart's. To touch heavily would be to arrest the pattern and freeze the movement, to check the endlessly changing beauty of its unfolding. There is no place here for the possessive clutch, the clinging arm, the heavy hand; only the barest touch in passing. Now arm in arm, now face to face, now back to back—it does not matter which. Because they know they are partners moving to the same rhythm, creating a pattern together, and being invisibly nourished by it.

The joy of such a pattern is not only the joy of creation or the joy of participation, it is also the joy of living in the moment. Lightness of touch and living in the moment are intertwined. One cannot dance well unless one is completely in time with the music, not leaning back to the last step or pressing forward to the next one, but poised directly on the present step as it comes. Perfect poise on the beat is what gives good dancing its sense of ease, of timelessness, of the eternal. It is what Blake was speaking of when he wrote:

> *He who bends to himself a joy*
> *Doth the wingèd life destroy;*
> *But he who kisses the joy as it flies*
> *Lives in Eternity's sunrise.*

The dancers who are perfectly in time never destroy "the wingèd life" in each other or in themselves.

But how does one learn this technique of the dance? Why is it so difficult? What makes us hesitate and stumble? It is fear, I think, that makes one cling nostalgically to the last moment or clutch greedily toward the next. Fear destroys "the wingèd life." But how to exorcise it? It can only be exorcised by its opposite, love. When the heart is flooded with love there is no room in it for fear, for doubt, for hesitation. And it is this lack of fear that makes for the dance. When each partner loves so completely that he has forgotten to ask himself whether or not he is loved in return; when he only knows that he loves and is moving to its music—then, and then only, are two people able to dance perfectly in tune to the same rhythm.

But is this all to the relationship of the argonauta—this private pattern of two dancers perfectly in time? Should they not also be in tune with a larger rhythm, a natural swinging of the pendulum between sharing and solitude; between the intimate and the abstract; between the particular and the universal, the near and the far? And is it not the swinging of the pendulum between these opposite poles that makes a relationship nourishing? Yeats once said that the supreme experience of life was "to share profound thought and then to touch." But it takes both.

First touch, intimate touch of the personal and particular (the chores in the kitchen, the talk by the fire) then the loss of intimacy in the great stream of the impersonal and abstract (the silent beach, the bowl of stars overhead). Both partners are lost in a common sea of the universal which absorbs and yet frees, which separates and yet unites. Is this not what the more mature relationship, the meeting of two solitudes, is meant to be? The double-sunrise stage was only intimate and personal. The oyster bed was caught in the particular and the functional. But the argonauta, should they not be able to swing from the intimate and the particular and the functional out into the abstract and the universal, and then back to the personal again?

And in this image of the pendulum swinging in easy rhythm between opposite poles, is there not a clue to the problem of relationships as a whole? Is there not here even a hint of an understanding and an acceptance of the wingèd life of relationships, of their eternal ebb and flow, of their inevitable intermittency? "The life of the spirit," said Saint-Exupéry, "the veritable life, is intermittent and only the life of the mind is constant. . . . The spirit . . . alternates between total vision and absolute blindness. Here is a man, for example, who loves his farm—but there are moments when he sees in it only a collection of unrelated objects. Here is a man who loves his wife—but there are moments when he sees in love nothing but burdens, hindrances, constraints. Here is a man who loves music—but there are moments when it cannot reach him."

The "veritable life" of our emotions and our relationships also is intermittent. When you love someone you do not love them all the time, in exactly the same way, from moment to moment. It is an impossibility. It is even a lie to pretend to. And yet this is exactly what most of us demand. We have so little faith in the ebb and flow of life, of love, of relationships. We leap at the flow of the tide and resist in terror its ebb. We are afraid it will never return. We insist on permanency, on duration, on continuity; when the only continuity possible, in life as in love, is in growth, in fluidity—in freedom, in the sense that the dancers are free, barely touching as they pass, but partners in the same pattern. The only real security is not in owning or possessing, not in demanding or expecting, not in hoping, even. Security in a relationship lies neither in looking back to what it was in nostalgia, nor forward to what it might be in dread or anticipation, but living in the present relationship and accepting it as it is now. For relationships, too, must be like islands. One must accept them for what they are here and now, within their limits—islands, surrounded and interrupted by the sea, continually visited and abandoned by the tides. One must accept the security of the wingèd life, of ebb and flow, of intermittency.

Intermittency—an impossible lesson for human beings to learn.

How can one learn to live through the ebb-tides of one's existence? How can one learn to take the trough of the wave? It is easier to understand here on the beach, where the breathlessly still ebb-tides reveal another life below the level which mortals usually reach. In this crystalline moment of suspense, one has a sudden revelation of the secret kingdom at the bottom of the sea. Here in the shallow flats one finds, wading through warm ripples, great horse-conchs pivoting on a leg; white sand dollars, marble medallions engraved in the mud; and my myriads of bright-colored cochina-clams, glistening in the foam, their shells opening and shutting like butterflies' wings. So beautiful is the still hour of the sea's withdrawal, as beautiful as the sea's return when the encroaching waves pound up the beach, pressing to reach those dark rumpled chains of seaweed which mark the last high tide.

Perhaps this is the most important thing for me to take back from beach-living: simply the memory that each cycle of the tide is valid; each cycle of the wave is valid; each cycle of a relationship is valid. And my shells? I can sweep them all into my pocket. They are only there to remind me that the sea recedes and returns eternally.

consciousness

from

Journey of the Heart
by John Welwood, Ph.D.

Therapist and clinical psychiatrist John Welwood integrates eastern religious and psychological traditions with western psychotherapy. He suggests that marriage can support the growth of "love's urge toward greater awareness, freedom and truth."

Marriage throughout history has been primarily a worldly institution, designed to provide family cohesion and social stability and, more recently, personal happiness. Yet marriage no longer functions very well at delivering these "worldly goods." Given the fickleness of romantic feelings, the difficulty of getting along with another person, and the ease of divorce, it offers little guarantee of stability or happiness anymore. Nor does it confer any special status or cachet; for many people, even the words *husband* and *wife* have acquired a stodgy, boring ring. Thus marriage has become a major focal point of dissatisfaction. Some people complain that it no longer provides the security they seek, while others attack it as a faded relic from another era, an instrument of oppression, or a stifling arrangement that inhibits the natural appetites.

This situation brings up important questions: Why marry at

all? Is marriage just an outdated artifact? Or does it serve some deeper human need and purpose? Apart from conventional social and religious beliefs, does marriage have a larger sacred function or meaning? Can marriage serve love's urge toward greater awareness, freedom, and truth, instead of being an instrument of torture, suppression, or deadening routine? What new source of inspiration can we find for marriage, beyond childrearing and hopes for perpetual romance or security?

The Container of Marriage

Marriage is not just a pragmatic worldly arrangement. It also reflects a larger imperative of human life—which is to realize love's full potential by giving it an earthly form. Human nature is the intersection of inspiration and practicality, consciousness and matter, heavenly passion and earthly discipline. And marriage as a path provides continual opportunities to bring these two sides of life into fruitful union. Love without marriage is all inspiration, all passion. Marriage without love is all perspiration, all discipline. Neither of these situations allows us to realize the larger possibilities of the man/woman relationship. When a man and a woman blend the inspiration of love with the hard work of putting that inspiration into practice, their marriage becomes a sacred alchemy, joining heaven and earth.

Marriage involves the discipline of forging a container in which the love and passion between a man and a woman can ripen and bear fruit. Discipline always involves working with form. Form provides a vehicle through which we can put our passion and inspiration to work for creative purposes, so that we do not just squander these energies aimlessly. We may have great talent, but unless we cultivate a form of expression—such as writing, drawing, speaking, or playing a musical instrument—it will lack a creative outlet. Similarly, passion cannot be a creative path unless it is grounded in earthly form.

A couple I knew once wrote a book in which they argued that marriage involves a commitment to a *process,* rather than to any *form.* With this "process commitment," as they called it, if a couple is no longer growing, they should not feel obliged to stay together. Yet this approach is somewhat naive. If two people stay together only because their growth feels inspiring, then when that inspiration ebbs, going on together will become a problem. Commitment to growth without commitment to form is only a partial truth. The larger truth is that growth frequently brings two people up against extremely difficult issues that threaten to tear them apart as individuals and as a couple. Inspiration is essential, for it provides energy to work through these difficulties. Yet unless two people can also take on the practice of giving their love form, they are unlikely to go very far with each other.

This does not mean fitting a relationship into some preconceived mold. Rather, marriage gives love form by serving as an alchemical vessel in which two people's natures are steadily refined through the heat of their loving commitment to stand by each other: "We will not abandon or harm each other. We will not let our energetic connection leak or drain away, through carelessness or neglect. We will work out our conflicts within the container of our marriage, rather than letting them tear us apart. We intend to help each other develop our finest human qualities." This kind of intention and commitment helps us trust that it is all right to be completely open and exposed with our partner.

For this kind of trust to develop, we need a structure that can *contain* and *protect* the process of opening. If we turn to other lovers when things get hard, or complain to friends about problems in the relationship instead of confronting those problems with our partner, the container will be too leaky. And the potency of the connection cannot build. Marriage is a way of creating and sealing a container, so that the energies cooking within the relationship do not drain away.

By bringing all the different parts of ourselves into alignment with our highest intention, the marriage vow establishes the boundaries of this container. We all have parts of ourselves that do not want to bother with things that are difficult. Especially in our affluent society, we want to feel free to walk away from anything at any time. Yet because marriage is about the *realization* of love, not just its inspiration, it calls on us to deal with our fears of the earth—of becoming tied down, losing our freedom, having to deal with limitation and necessity. In taking a vow, we begin to subdue these fears and bring them under the yoke of our higher intelligence. We pledge that when things get hard, we will bring our combined energy to bear on the difficulties and see them through.

Of course, vowing to face whatever comes up in a marriage does not mean that we will always execute this vow perfectly. How could we possibly do that? We cannot really discover what such a vow means until we have already been married for some time. We can learn about it only through practice, trying out new ways of being, making mistakes and giving ourselves tremendous room to learn. While the marriage vow cannot guarantee that we will always handle everything that comes up, it does signal our intention to make the attempt.

This kind of commitment is important because marriage is not just a connection between two people's beings, but also a juncture where, in the words of a Zen marriage ceremony, "two streams of karma become joined." When we marry someone, we also say, "I'm willing to take on your karma as part of what I am working with." Loving our partners "in sickness and in health" means not only accepting their larger being, but also staying open to them in the midst of all their karmic obstructions, even those that create pain and conflict.

Indeed, a marriage is unlikely to be transformative without a certain measure of pain and strife. Often only forceful confrontation can touch deeply ingrained patterns of fear and aggression, which rarely give up without a fight. When the heat of a couple's strife is contained by their commitment to marriage as a practice and a path, it can generate greater consciousness instead of blowing their relationship apart. A couple's willingness to work with each other "in sickness and in health" creates a sacred context for their conflicts, so that their fights can act on them, touch them, soften them, make them see new things about themselves they might not otherwise have seen, and thus deepen their connection.

When contained in this way, even our fights have a sacred

quality, since they boil up out of the alchemical exchange that is happening between us. As the Tantric traditions suggest, when a man and a woman dedicate themselves to developing greater consciousness, then "the emotional vicissitudes of their personal relationship, the love and hate, the pride and jealousy, *are* the dakini's fine ornaments." The dakini, as discussed earlier, represents the forceful quality of wakefulness that shakes us up and rouses us from our delusions. So when turbulence arises between two people who are using it as a tool to wake up, that chaos can be regarded as awakening mind in action.

Fortunately, the practice involved in working with form is not just hard work. It also helps us relax, give birth to new qualities of being, and realize new inner freedom. The more a musician practices his instrument, for instance, the more fully and freely his talent can express itself, without having to struggle with the limitations of technique. Through his practice and devotion, he masters not just technique, but, more importantly, *himself,* developing the inner confidence and sensitivity that will allow him to interpret his music in a masterful way. Similarly, the practice of meditation can help us realize the intrinsic wisdom and freedom of the mind— this, the very same mind that can drive us crazy when allowed to run on in an undisciplined way.

The practice of marriage works in the same way. Choosing to create a life and a path together helps my partner and I relax with each other; we no longer have to try so hard to win each other's approval, prove ourselves, or defend our separate territories. This frees up our energy to explore new areas, to cultivate deeper qualities of our being and see how to bring these more fully into our daily life.

Marriage as Mandala

Whenever two halves of life come together—consciousness and form, passion and discipline, male and female, heaven and earth—a new world of possibilities comes into being. In this sense, two people joining their lives in marriage are engaging in a sacred activity because they are creating a cosmos in miniature—where all the different sides of themselves, personal and transpersonal, can be included. Before marriage, a couple's association is still loose and informal because it lacks clear boundaries. Taking a marriage vow creates a formal boundary, establishing the relationship as a sacred space where all the elements of life can interact and find expression.

The Eastern traditions use the term *mandala* to describe this kind of sacred microcosm. Mandalas have been portrayed visually in many different times and cultures as circles with four directions and a strong central focus. These symbols of totality and integration turn up in Paleolithic drawings, in Hindu and Buddhist sacred rituals, in sand paintings of the Pueblo Indians, as well as in medieval paintings of Christ surrounded by the four Evangelists. C. G. Jung also found mandala-like images spontaneously appearing in his patients' dreams as they were moving toward greater wholeness. A mandala portrays the conquest of oppositional mind, by bringing together life's polarities around a central unifying principle.

A mandala is a "cosmos" (literally, an "orderly world") because it is large enough to contain and handle chaos; thus it is "orderly chaos," in Chögyam Trungpa's words. When a man and a woman join their lives in marriage, they bring together a mix of many different, often contradictory influences; thus what comes up between them is bound to be chaotic. Marriage as a mandala is a formal practice of containing this chaos, so that it can enlarge, rather than destroy, their relationship. The chaos of relationship can become workable when a couple creates a sacred context around it, by setting boundaries and agreeing on a central governing principle—such as opening the heart or waking up to their deeper potential—to guide their life together.

In this way, the practice of marriage is akin to meditation. As you sit still and become more present to your experience, all the chaos of the mind arises. A flood of thoughts, feelings, fantasies passes through you. Your whole life passes before your eyes. It's total chaos. Yet the form of sitting practice—maintaining an upright posture and following the breath—creates a boundary that allows this chaos to be contained. And returning to the still, sane presence of awareness provides a central focus, which differentiates this practice from just letting the mind go wild. Because your mental chaos is contained in a formal setting, you can bring your attention and consciousness to bear on it, see through it, and learn to tame it. Without such a form, you are simply subject to the vagaries and wanderings of the mind.

Similarly, marriage, as a sacred microcosm, both invites all our chaos to come up and enables us to work with it more consciously. This allows a man and a woman to draw on all the turbulent energies arising out of their interaction as fuel for their journey. So instead of trying to make marriage fit some conventional image of harmony, we could welcome its power to expand our world. Regarding marriage as a mandala helps us take heart: If all kinds of wild energies and karmic eruptions arise in this space, that is not a problem. It is all part of the dance.

Sacred Order

So far we have seen that the formal commitment to marriage creates a boundary and a container that helps two people work and play with the energies arising between them. Yet something more is needed to create a mandala—a central governing principle. What is the central principle in the marriage mandala that can help make the chaos contained within it workable? In the Tibetan Buddhist tradition, the focal point of a mandala is always enlightened wisdom, symbolized by a deity at the center, surrounded by all the elements of the universe. This suggests that if two people are to make good use of the chaos arising between them, and not become overwhelmed by it, they must accord wisdom and truth a central place in their relationship. Then the natural order of things can unfold, for a sacred order has been established.

The original term for sacred order is hierarchy (from the Greek hieros, sacred, and arche, order). When most of us hear the term hierarchy, we think of a vertical pecking order, with a big boss at the top. Such a structure represents a debased form of hierarchy, however, because wisdom is not the organizing principle. For instance, in the patriarchal family, the wife and children had to submit to the decisions of the father or grandfather who was in charge, whether he was wise or foolish, right or wrong. For obvious reasons, that kind of "domination hierarchy" has been tremendously destructive and no longer works.

To establish sacred order in today's egalitarian marriages, we need a more flexible kind of arrangement, one that encourages both partners to realize their larger potential. For this, we could draw on the pattern found in all life forms—where more evolved structures (such as bodily organs) govern and integrate the functions of simpler structures (such as cells), thus promoting a higher level of overall functioning. This kind of "actualization hierarchy" is what we find in a mandala, which, like a cell, contains a strong center around which peripheral elements organize themselves. How might this kind of life-affirming hierarchy work in a marriage?

First, a couple would recognize some form of wisdom or wakefulness as a central principle governing their union. Second, they would acknowledge that neither of them has exclusive access to this larger sanity; instead, each of them has different areas where they are strong or weak, clear or confused, insightful or blind. Third, recognizing and respecting each other's natural strengths, they would be willing to let the partner who has greater wisdom or clarity in a given area take the lead. For instance, if a woman has greater emotional flexibility than her man, then he would recognize her as his teacher in this area. He would let himself learn from her wisdom, instead of trying to force her to go along with his emotional rigidity. This is what it means to recognize her as his *consort,* someone who is in his life to help him grow. In this way, by recognizing, respecting, and learning from each other's natural strengths, two partners establish sacred order in their marriage.

When a man and a woman do not honor and respect each other's innate wisdom and strength, they disrupt natural hierarchy in their relations. For instance, a man who does not express appreciation for his wife's feminine qualities, who scorns the ways she is not like a man, who uses his yang power to dominate and criticize her, undermines the woman in her, thus destroying any possibility of a creative alliance between them. Or if a woman tries to cut down her husband's male power, she is undermining his yang and diminishing the real juice in their connection. When natural hierarchy is destroyed, the resulting disharmony will adversely affect every member of the family.

Surrender

Honoring each other's wisdom and strength means that both partners must be willing to surrender when the occasion calls for it. Indeed, marriage teaches us a great deal about the importance of surrender in our life as a whole.

The notion of surrender is widely misunderstood in our culture, and, like commitment and intimacy, often brings up fear. It conjures up images of "come out with your hands up"—waving a white flag, admitting defeat, losing power. Yet, if we understand it rightly, surrender does not have to mean giving up power or freedom. As an act of putting wisdom and truth above our personal ambitions or beliefs, it helps us align ourselves with the natural order of things.

The ability to surrender is central to any graceful or creative activity. Whether we are appreciating the sights, sounds, and tastes of the world, dancing, making love, or simply listening to another person, life continually calls on us to yield control and to open to what is beyond us. We cannot ultimately control what happens to us or have our way on this earth, if only because we must eventually give up everything and return to the great unknown from which we spring. Surrender involves letting go—of what we already know or have—and letting be—opening to the situations that life presents.

Many people distrust the notion of surrender because they confuse it with *submission* to another's will—which can in fact have disastrous consequences in a relationship. Submission means giving over power to someone else, putting that person above us while putting ourselves down. People often do this when they feel unworthy and in need of validation. An employee submits to his boss in order to gain recognition, favor, or a promotion. In a relationship, one partner might sacrifice his or her true direction or path in life to win approval, acceptance, or simply peace and quiet.

Of course, marriage does require real sacrifices. We cannot be as free and independent as we were before, and we are continually called upon to give, often at the most inconvenient times. Yet we should distinguish between two very different kinds of sacrifice. When we knowingly choose to give up something for a greater good, this is *conscious sacrifice,* which helps us grow and thus empowers us. However, when we try to please or placate by blindly going along with someone or bending ourselves out of shape, this is *neurotic sacrifice*—a form of submission that only debilitates.

In marriage, we can distinguish one from the other in the following way: Submission involves distorting who we are in order to win something in return. When we submit to someone, we give away our power and hope for the best. Surrender, on the other hand, requires discriminating awareness—recognizing a larger truth or following a direction that leads toward greater aliveness—rather than blind hope. When we surrender to what life situations call for, real power, which comes from beyond our personality, can enter us. While submission occurs out of inner weakness, genuine surrender can happen only out of feeling strong enough to take a risk.

The essential surrender in marriage is not *to our partner* as a finite personality. Instead, it involves opening ourselves to what the relationship has to teach us from day to day. As a marriage grows and develops, it provides continual opportunities to practice surrendering: by yielding to our partners' wisdom and opening ourselves to learning from them in areas where they are more wise or healthy; by giving ourselves more fully to the relationship; or by letting go of fixed attitudes and positions that prevent love from flowing freely. We can usually tell that some kind of surrender is called for when our standard operating procedure is not working, and our partner or the situation itself is calling on us to give it up. This might involve something as simple as recognizing that we have acted in a hurtful or stubborn way and saying, "I'm sorry." Such moments provide rare and powerful opportunities to break out of old karmic patterns.

The following examples illustrate three different kinds of surrender.

Eric felt awkward in social situations, while his wife, Robin, was more socially adept. At first, Eric tried to make his shyness the guideline for their relations with the outside world. As a result, they spent very little time as a couple with other people. By forcing Robin to submit to his fears in an area where she was more evolved than he was, Eric upset the natural hierarchy in their relationship, eventually creating a breach between them. After many fights, Eric finally saw that he needed to surrender control and let her be his teacher in this area. Although yielding to her guidance brought up anxiety and uncertainty, it also forced him to extend himself in new ways. This broadened him and enriched their relationship.

After twenty years of marriage, when a new depth of feeling opened up between Laura and her husband following a tragic family incident, she began to see that she had never given herself fully to their relationship. Yet she was unsure whether she could take the risk involved in becoming more open to him. In her words:

> I feel scared now that we have a new opportunity to be more open and loving together. I sense an immensity there that I almost don't want to see or touch. It feels so immense that I could get carried away or lose myself in it. Talking about it makes it sound wonderful, but the actual feeling isn't. . . . It's like a joy I almost don't want to permit myself. If I had that kind of joy, I'd be afraid it could get taken away. If I open to Daniel, how could I rely on him to be there? What if he died? How could I bear to let myself be that vulnerable?

• • •

These are the questions of someone on the razor's edge, feeling both the fear and the excitement of opening to unknown possibilities. Laura had no guarantee that opening up more with her husband would be safe. Yet she made the choice to move in this direction because it led toward greater aliveness.

Late one night Alex and his wife reached an impasse in a fight they were having. She just wanted to go to bed, while he was desperately worrying, "How can we work this out? If we love each other, why can't we solve this disagreement? If we can't resolve this, something must be wrong with our relationship. She should stick with this and not just go to bed." Yet the more he pressed for a resolution, the worse everything felt. In his words:

> I didn't know what to do. So I just let the situation be, and waited to see what would come of it, instead of trying to push through it—which was my usual style. This put me in a place where nothing made sense, where my ideas about how things should be were blown: "I thought Donna was like this, and she's not. I thought our relationship was like that, and it's not. I thought I could resolve anything between us, and I can't." This was one of those rare times when I had to admit that I couldn't understand, that life is bigger than what I could make out of it. Something snapped inside me. There was a moment of just letting go. Later it was followed by a sense of gratitude: "Our

relationship is big enough to handle this. I'm so glad that I don't have to try to make everything right." I had discovered a new kind of trust. We went to bed, and the next day things felt much better between us.

Surrendering for Alex in this situation meant not trying to push ahead with his customary way of resolving differences, no matter how well it had worked before. Since the situation did not fit his usual logic, it was calling on him to back off and just let things be.

Surrendering does not mean always going along with whatever is happening. Nor does it mean that if a situation makes us angry, we should say to ourselves, "I shouldn't be angry, I should surrender." That would be suppressing ourselves, which could be a form of submission. If our usual pattern is to suppress our feelings, then maybe we need to surrender to our experience of anger. However, if our habitual style is to vent anger or use it to control others, then surrendering might mean putting aside our anger and approaching the situation in a more gentle way.

In each of these examples, one partner's act of surrendering opened up a stuck point in their relationship. Eric, Laura, and Alex were each being called on to let go of their standard operating procedures—which was frightening because it brought them to the edge of the unknown. Yet their willingness to open at those moments invited a certain natural wisdom into the situation, revealing new directions just when things seemed most scary. New order was born from seeming chaos.

Dimensions of Marriage

Appreciating marriage as a mandala helps us understand that it is more than just a worldly arrangement. The Buddhist tradition recognizes mandalas as having three dimensions—outer, inner, and secret. The outer aspect of a mandala is how it manifests its structure and form. The inner aspect of a mandala is what goes on within it—its meaning and energetic qualities. And the secret aspect of a mandala is how it affects and acts on us in subtle, less visible ways. Similarly, marriage is not just unidimensional, but works on several different levels at once.

The outer dimension of marriage is its socially recognized form: man and woman joining together in a lifelong partnership. This form is sacred because it belongs to the whole human community and is part of the human search to create a wholesome way of life. Wendell Berry describes the outer marriage when he says, "Forms join generations together, the young and the old, the living and the dead. Thus, for a couple, marriage is an entrance into a timeless community."

The outer mandala also includes creating a home or living space that expresses the character of a couple's connection. When two people attend to the details of their environment, their home enriches both themselves and everyone else who enters it. However, if they neglect their environment and leave it in disarray, this will magnify the disorder in their relationship as well. How life proceeds in the home, how a couple set up the schedule of daily life, reflects and affects how they are with each other. Do they get up and run off to work, come home, throw some food together, turn on the TV, and jump in bed? Or does their way of life express more elegance and dignity? These are all important aspects of the outer dimension of marriage.

Traditionally, marriage has been defined solely in terms of these outer elements—as a social contract, as participation in a community, as the making of a home and family. Yet though the outer marriage is important and sacred in its own right, it is no longer enough by itself to bind two people together. What is more crucial today is the inner marriage—the nature and quality of a couple's connection and interaction. How do they regard and treat each other? How do they communicate with each other? How do they respect each other and honor their connection?

The inner marriage is like a garden; even though the outer circumstances, such as soil and weather, may be favorable, it must still be tended if it is to bear fruit. Unless two people tend to the quality of their relationship, it is likely to deteriorate from unintentional neglect. They become sloppy, little things slip by, and before they know it, they have built up tremendous antagonism and resentment. The garden has become choked with weeds.

Mutual respect is an essential ingredient of the inner mandala. Respect involves recognizing that a human being has a great spirit, which reaches far beyond the familiar facade of personality we may know or see. If my partner and I always treat each other in a casual, familiar manner, relating to each other primarily as known quantities, we block the larger mysteries from entering our relationship. This causes us to lose respect for one another. Since marriage taps into larger energies beyond personality, this relationship can never be merely casual.

Because we are representatives in marriage of the elemental male and female, we could even regard each other as king and queen. A king and a queen treat each other with great dignity and respect. That is part of their discipline. A little formality of this kind can wake us up from the cozy familiarity that tends to envelop a long-term relationship. For instance, since men and women wear very different clothes when dressing up, occasionally dressing more formally can be a way to express and emphasize the different principles we represent. Dressing up is like polishing our qualities, so that they shine forth brilliantly, unobscured by the dust of everyday casualness. Many of us in present generations have rebelled against any kind of formality, perhaps because our parents or elders were formal in a stiff or sterile way. Yet marriage is a formal rather than a casual relationship. So a certain amount of formality, as a display of elegance and respect, can fan the sacred fire of a couple's love and brighten up the inner mandala of their marriage.

Finally, the "secret" dimension of marriage is the inner transformation that occurs as a direct result of two people's interaction. Within each individual a marriage is going on between yin and yang, heaven and earth, power and gentleness, and countless other polarities. This inner alchemy often precisely mirrors what is happening in the external relationship. For instance, caring for my partner forces me to see that I must also care for myself; commitment to the growth of the marriage also requires a commitment to my own growth; joining my life with a woman I love forces me to bring my own inner masculine and feminine into balance. The secret marriage involves giving up our old ideas about who we are, so that the different elements inside us can come together in new ways and we can keep being born anew.

All three of these dimensions of marriage—outer, inner, and secret—mutually enhance one another. If any of them are missing, a couple's life together will be that much poorer. Some couples may have a strong inner connection, but be unable to create a healthy, vibrant environment or lifestyle on the outer plane. Other couples may make a beautiful home together, while their exchange with each other remains shallow. When a couple can create a world together, relate to each other with passion and respect, and continually refine their natures through their interaction, their life together will be fertile and creative.

Marriage as Realization

The easy part of any creative work is feeling inspired. The hard part is putting our inspiration into practice, embodying it in earthly form, for this brings us up against the limitations of the materials we are working with. A writer may have a grand vision of a book he wants to write, but finding the right words and format is always exacting and difficult. A pianist may know how he would like to sound, but getting his fingers to match his inspiration takes ongoing practice. Dealing with practical necessities and limitations is humbling. Yet it also gives birth to a richer kind of inspiration—which grows out of bringing vision into form.

The creative work of marriage is no different. It is easy to fall in love, but not so easy to put that love into practice. We keep coming up against the limitations of the raw materials—in this case, ourselves! The marriage commitment brings up levels of fear that we have never faced before. Yet in resolutely bringing our love to bear on the fears that threaten to constrict our hearts, we mine fresh sources of inspiration, much deeper than the first spontaneous sparks of falling in love. It is inspiring to see a man and a woman dancing with the energies contained in their chaos and helping each other open more fully to life. Just as an artist can affect others only through wrestling with his materials, similarly, a couple who can wrestle with the chaos arising between them develop a strength and humor that is heartening to others. Marriage, like a finished poem, is inspiration made manifest.

Many discussions of the difficulties of marriage today never go beyond the superficial and the mundane. They often focus on how hard it is for the modern couple to "have it all"—intimacy, commitment, children, two careers, child care, money, a home, and time enough to enjoy these things. Although these may be important practical concerns, merely finding a way to "have it all" will not save or renew marriage in these precarious times.

We can revitalize marriage only by re-visioning it as a sacred path. The sacredness of marriage is not handed down by family, society, or church. It arises out of two individuals' passionate devotion to bringing love into form. This involves taking each other on, no holds barred, in the spirit of "I accept you and am willing to bring my intelligence and heart to bear on all your rough edges; and I want you to do the same for me. Let us work on these things, and help each other realize the full range of our powers and possibilities." When a man and a woman join forces like this, all their ups and downs, their struggles and their joys, are held within a sacred context. Their marriage enables them to realize how "the two become one," how, despite all their differences and separateness, self and other, male and female, are of one spirit.

This vision of marriage as joining the two halves of life—the inspiration of heaven and the practicality of earth—has never been widely realized. The old model of marriage as a family duty was too earthbound, while modern attempts to "have it all" and "live happily ever after" are too naive and ungrounded. Perhaps only a small percentage of couples will be able to live marriage as an alchemical relationship that helps them give birth to their finest qualities. Nonetheless, both history and evolution have shown many times that even a few pioneers can forge a new direction, which points the way for countless others.

People generally consider an intimate relationship successful if it provides basic fulfillment in such areas as companionship, security, sex, and self-esteem. Describing such an arrangement, one of the characters in Woody Allen's film *Manhattan* provided what *Time* magazine called a "reasonable definition of modern love": "We have laughs together. I care about you. Your concerns are my concerns. We have great sex." Yet in regarding relationship as path, especially as a sacred path, we hold a larger vision, one that includes these needs, but is not limited to them. Our central concern is with cultivating a conscious love, which can inspire the development of greater awareness and the evolution of two people's beings.

Yet we should not be too idealistic about this, for intimate relationships never function entirely on a conscious level. We live on many levels simultaneously, all with different needs. The tender child, the adventurous youth, the seasoned adult, and the spiritual seeker are all simultaneously present in us. Intimate relationships reflect this multilevel quality of our existence and therefore never involve just one single kind of relatedness. To clarify the part that conscious love can play in a relationship, it helps to consider it in the context of the many different levels of connection that can exist between two people.

Levels of Connection

The most primitive bond that may form between intimate partners is the urge for symbiotic *fusion,* born out of a desire to obtain emotional nurturance that was lacking in childhood. Of course, it is common for many couples, when they first get together, to go through a temporary symbiotic phase, when they cut out other activities or friends and spend most of their free time together. This stage in a relationship may help two people establish close emotional bonding. Yet if symbiosis becomes the primary dynamic in a relationship or goes on for too long, it will become increasingly confining. It sets up a parent-child dynamic that limits two people's range of expression and interaction, undermining the male-female charge between them and creating addictive patterns.

Beyond the primitive need for symbiotic fusion, the most basic desire in an intimate relationship is for *companionship.* This can take more or less sophisticated forms. On a crude level, we might just want another body around, almost like a pet, to share our bed or keep us company. On a more sophisticated level, the child in us wants a playmate, someone we can laugh and romp with, and the adult in us enjoys sharing activities such as cooking or attending cultural events together. Basic companionship plays a part in all relationships, although some people do not seem to want anything more than this from an intimate partner.

A further level of connectedness can happen when two people share not only activities and each other's company, but also common interests, goals, or values. We could call this level, where a couple begins to create a shared world, *community.* Like companionship, community is a concrete, earthy form of relatedness.

Beyond sharing values and interests lies *communication.* On this level, we share what is going on inside us—our thoughts, visions, experiences, and feelings. Establishing good communication is much more arduous than simply creating companionship and community. It requires that a couple be honest and courageous enough to expose what is going on inside them, and be willing to work on the inevitable obstacles in the way of sharing their different truths with each other. Good communication is probably the most important ingredient in the everyday health of a relationship.

A further extension of communication is *communion.* Beyond just sharing thoughts and feelings, this is a deep recognition of another person's being. This often takes place in silence—perhaps while looking into our partner's eyes, making love, walking in the woods, or listening to music together. Suddenly we feel touched and seen, not as a personality, but in the depth of our being. We are fully ourselves and fully in touch with our partner at the same time. This kind of connection is so rare and striking that it is usually unmistakable when it comes along. While two people can work on communication, communion is more spontaneous, beyond the will. Communication and communion are deeper, more subtle forms of intimacy than companionship and community, taking place at the level of mind and heart.

The deeper intimacy of communion may stir up a longing to overcome our separateness altogether, a longing for total *union* with someone we love. Yet though this longing expresses a genuine human need, it is more appropriately directed to the divine, the absolute, the infinite. When attached to an intimate relationship, it often creates problems. Putting our whole longing for spiritual realization onto a finite relationship can lead to idealization, inflation, addiction, and death. The most appropriate way to address our longing for union is through a genuine spiritual practice, such as meditation, that teaches us how to go beyond oppositional mind altogether, in every area of our life. By pointing us in this direction, intimate relationship may inspire this kind of practice, but it can never be a complete substitute for it.

Every relationship will have different areas of strength along this continuum of connectedness. Some couples may share companionship and common interests, but have little real communication or communion; and some may have occasional moments of communion, but still find their strongest link at more basic levels. Others may share a deep soul-communion, yet have little in common on the earthly plane of community and companionship. Such couples might have a hard time creating a life together because they would lack simpler forms of relatedness to fall back on when the intensity of their communion wanes. Couples who share a deep being-connection, good communication, common interests and values, and a simple enjoyment of each other's company will have an ideal balance of heaven and earth connectedness. (Sexuality can operate at any of these levels—as a form of symbiotic fusion, as a body-companionship, as a shared sport, as a form of communication, or as a deeper communion.)

Conscious Love and Broken Heart

Conscious love begins to develop in a relationship where two people share a being-to-being communion. This is because it is love of being rather than love of personality. In moments of communion, I am in touch with the depth of my own being and my partner's being at the same time. From day to day our inner lives also begin to move in synchrony. Her face becomes more familiar to me than my own. I become as sensitive to her changing moods and feelings as to my own. I share her longings and cannot separate myself from her pain. We have interpenetrated too deeply for me ever to be able to stand entirely separate from her again.

And yet, I *am* separate. No matter how close she and I are, we can never fully share our different worlds: She can never really know what it is like to be me and I can never really know what it is like to be her. Although we may share fleeting moments of oneness when our beings touch, complete union remains forever just out of reach. The closer we are, the more even a hair's breadth of distance between us seems like a huge ravine.

Nor is there any way to hold on to each other or use our closeness to shield ourselves from the truth of our aloneness. We are on temporary loan to each other from the universe, and we never know when it will claim us back. Feeling this edge—where we are neither entirely separate, nor entirely one—puts me back in touch with the rawness of the heart. In realizing that I can never completely overcome my aloneness by melting into the one I love, I am left with a basic ache from which no one can ever save me. Part of me would like to save her from her pain and make everything right for her, yet there is nothing I can do to shield her from her life or from our death. Here, where the heart feels both full and empty, I find the answer to the question posed by the modern love song, "Why does love got to be so sad?"

Yet this kind of sadness is not a problem. In Chögyam Trungpa's words, it "is unconditioned. It occurs because your heart is completely exposed." Love songs are so often sad in tone because devotion to another stirs a deep longing to melt and give ourselves away. As Trungpa puts it, "You would like to spill your heart's blood, give your heart to others." The word *sad* is related etymologically to *satisfied* or *sated,* meaning "full." Love's sadness is the *fullness of feeling* that arises out of our longing to open and connect. Thus at the core of devotion to another is a sweet, sad fullness of heart, which longs to overflow.

Since my aloneness is also what makes me want to overflow, it need not isolate me. As a simple presence to life, it is what I share with all the creatures of the earth. It is an inner depth from which many treasures arise: a passion to reach out, extend myself, write a poem or a song, give something of substance or beauty that could touch the one I love in *her* magnificent aloneness. Out of it comes the greatest gift I can give: myself, the whole of who I am, in all my desire to live and die as fully as I can.

Thus when we appreciate our aloneness, we can be ourselves and give ourselves most fully, and we no longer need others to save us or make us feel good about ourselves. Instead, we want to help them become *themselves* more fully as well. In this way, conscious love is born as a gift from our broken heart.

All the great spiritual traditions teach that single-minded pursuit of one's own happiness cannot lead to true satisfaction, for personal desires multiply endlessly, forever creating new dissatisfaction. Real happiness, which no one can ever take away, comes from breaking our heart open, feeling it radiating toward the world around us, and rejoicing in the well-being of others. Cherishing the growth of those we love exercises the larger capacities of our being and helps us ripen. Since their unfolding calls on us to develop all our finest qualities, we know that we are being fully used.

In an essay written in the 1920s, Orage maintained that conscious love was something extremely rare. Since people do not generally regard wisdom, truth, or creativity as central to an intimate relationship, he argued, they will seek out relationships based primarily on companionship or mutual self-interest. Yet though conscious love may still be rare today, it is no longer such a remote possibility. This is because unconscious love no longer works very well. As more and more couples discover that a relationship is most exciting when it helps them develop their deepest resources and finest qualities, conscious love may be seen as more of a necessity than a luxury. Thus all the current difficulties of relationships present us with a rare opportunity: to discover love as a sacred path, which calls on us to cultivate the fullness and depth of who we are.

The Farther Shore of Love

In its final outreach, conscious love leads two lovers beyond themselves toward a greater connectedness with the whole of life. Indeed, two people's love will have no room to grow unless it develops this larger focus beyond themselves. The larger arc of a couple's love reaches out toward a feeling of kinship with all of life, what Teilhard de Chardin calls "a love of the universe." Only in this way can love, as he puts it, "develop in boundless light and power."

So the path of love expands in ever-widening circles. It begins at home—by first finding our seat, making friends with ourselves, and discovering the intrinsic richness of our being, underneath all our ego-centered confusion and delusion. As we come to appreciate this basic wholesomeness within us, we find that we have more to give to an intimate partner.

Further, as a man and a woman become devoted to the growth of awareness and spirit in each other, they will naturally want to share their love with others. The new qualities they give birth to— generosity, courage, compassion, wisdom—can extend beyond the circle of their own relationship. These qualities are a couple's "spiritual child"—what their coming together gives to the world. A couple will flourish when their vision and practice are not focused solely on each other, but also include this larger sense of community and what they can give to others.

From there, a couple's love can expand still further, as Teilhard suggests. The more deeply and passionately two people love each other, the more concern they will feel for the state of the world in which they live. They will feel their connection with the earth and a dedication to care for this world and all sentient beings who need their care. Radiating out to the whole of creation is the farthest reach of love and its fullest expression, which grounds and enriches the life of the couple. This is the great love and the great way, which leads to the heart of the universe.

communion

from

The Solace of Open Spaces
by Gretel Ehrlich

Gretel Ehrlich writes novels, short stories, poems and essays of startling clarity—often featuring her adopted home state, Wyoming. Here she discusses the connection between her marriage to her husband and her marriage to the West and its wildness.

I met my husband at a John Wayne film festival in Cody, Wyoming. The film series was a rare midwinter entertainment to which people from all over the state came. A mutual friend, one of the speakers at the festival, introduced us, and the next morning when *The Man Who Shot Liberty Valance* was shown, we sat next to each other by chance. The fact that he cried during sad scenes in the film made me want to talk to him so we stayed in town, had dinner together, and closed down the bars. Here was a man who could talk books as well as ranching, medieval history and the mountains, ideas and mules. Like me he was a culture straddler. Ten months later we were married.

He had planned to propose while we were crossing Cougar Pass—a bald, ten-thousand-foot dome—with twenty-two head of loose horses, but a front was moving through, and in the commotion, he forgot. Another day he loped up to me: "Want to get hitched?" he said. Before I could respond there was horse-trouble ahead and he loped away. To make up for the unceremonious interruption, he serenaded me that night with the wistful calls sandhill cranes make. A cow elk wandered into the meadow and mingled with the horses. It snowed and in the morning a choir of coyotes howled, "Yes."

After signing for our license at the county courthouse we were given a complimentary "Care package," a Pandora's box of grotesqueries: Midol, Kotex, disposable razors, shaving cream, a bar of soap—a summing up, I suppose, of what in a marriage we could look forward to: blood, pain, unwanted hair, headaches, and dirt. "Hey, where's the champagne and cigars?" I asked.

We had a spur-of-the-moment winter wedding. I called my parents and asked them what they were doing the following Saturday. They had a golf game. I told them to cancel it. "Instead of waiting, we've decided to get married while the bloom is still on," I said.

It was a walk-in wedding. The road crew couldn't get the snow plowed all the way to the isolated log cabin where the ceremony was to be held. We drove as far as we could in my pickup, chaining up on the way.

In the one hushed moment before the ceremony started, Rusty, my dog, walked through the small crowd of well wishers and lay down at my feet. On his wolfish-wise face was a look that said, "What about me?" So the three of us were married that day. Afterward we skated on the small pond in front of the house and drank from open bottles of champagne stuck in the snow.

"Here's to the end of loneliness," I toasted quietly, not believing such a thing could come true. But it did and nothing prepared me for the sense of peace I felt—of love gone deep into a friendship—so for a while I took it to be a premonition of death—the deathbed calm we're supposed to feel after getting our affairs in order.

A year later while riding off a treeless mountain slope in a rainstorm I was struck by lightning. There was a white flash. It felt as though sequins had been poured down my legs, then an electrical charge thumped me at the base of my skull as if I'd been mugged. Afterward the crown of my head itched and the bottoms of my feet arched up and burned. "I can't believe you're still alive," my husband said. The open spaces had cleansed me before. This was another kind of scouring, as when at the end of a painful appointment with the dentist he polishes your teeth.

Out across the Basin chips of light on waterponds mirrored the storm that passed us. Below was the end-of-the-road ranch my husband and I had just bought, bumped up against a nine-thousand-foot-high rockpile that looks like a Sung Dynasty painting. Set off from a series of narrow rambling hay fields which in summer are cataracts of green, is the 1913 poor-man's Victorian house—uninsulated, crudely plumbed—that is now ours.

A Texan, Billy Hunt, homesteaded the place in 1903. Before starting up the almost vertical wagon trail he had to take over the Big Horns to get there, he married the hefty barmaid in the saloon where he stopped for a beer. "She was tough as a piece of rawhide," one old-timer remembered. The ten-by-twenty cabin they built was papered with the editorial and classified pages of the day; the remnants are still visible. With a fresno and a team of horses, Hunt diverted two mountain creeks through a hundred acres of meadows cleared of sagebrush. Across the face of the mountain are the mossed-over stumps of cedar and pine trees cut down and axed into a set of corrals, sheds, gates, and hitchrails. With her first child clasped in front of the saddle, Mrs. Hunt rode over the mountains to the town of Dayton—a trip that must have taken fifteen hours—to buy supplies.

Gradually the whole drainage filled up with homesteaders. Twenty-eight children attended the one-room schoolhouse a mile down the road; there were a sawmill and blacksmith's shop, and once-a-month mail service by saddle horse or sleigh. Now the town of Cloverly is no more; only three families live at the head of the creek. Curiously, our friends in the valley think it's crazy to live in such an isolated place—thirty miles from a grocery store, seventy-five from a movie theater. When I asked one older resident what he thought, he said, "Hell almighty . . . God didn't make ranchers to live close to town. Anyway, it was a better town when you had to ride the thirty miles to it."

We moved here in February: books, tables, and a rack of clothes at one end of the stock truck, our horses tied at the back. There was a week of moonless nights but the Pleiades rose over the ridge like a piece of jewelry. Buying a ranch had sent us into spasms of soul-searching. It went against the bachelor lives we had grown used to: the bunkhouse-bedroll-barroom circuit; it meant our chronic vagrancy would come to an end. The proprietary impulse had dubious beginnings anyway—we had looked all that up before getting married: how ownership translates into possessiveness, protection into xenophobia, power into greed. Our idea was to rescue the ranch from the recent neglect it had seen.

As soon as the ground thawed we reset posts, restrung miles of barbed wire, and made the big ranch gates—hung eighty years ago between cedar posts as big around as my hips—swing again.

Above and around us steep canyons curve down in garlands of red and yellow rimrock: Pre-Cambrian, Madison, Chugwater formations, the porous parts of which have eroded into living-room-sized caves where mountain lions lounge and feast on does and snowshoe rabbits. Songbirds fly in and out of towering cottonwoods the way people throng office buildings. Mornings, a breeze fans up from the south; evenings, it reverses directions, so there is a streaming of life, a brushing back and forth like a massage. We go for walks. A friend told us the frosting of limestone that clings to the boulders we climb is all that's left of the surface of the earth a few million years ago. Some kinds of impermanence take a long time.

The seasons are a Jacob's ladder climbed by migrating elk and deer. Our ranch is one of their resting places. If I was leery about being an owner, a possessor of land, now I have to understand the ways in which the place possesses me. Mowing hayfields feels like mowing myself. I wake up mornings expecting to find my hair shorn. The pastures bend into me; the water I ushered over hard ground becomes one drink of grass. Later in the year, feeding the bales of hay we've put up is a regurgitative act: thrown down from a high stack on chill days they break open in front of the horses like loaves of hot bread.

Rules of the Game: Rodeo

Instead of honeymooning in Paris, Patagonia, or the Sahara as we had planned, my new husband and I drove through a series of blizzards to Oklahoma City. Each December the National Finals Rodeo is held in a modern, multi-storied coloseum next to buildings that house banks and petroleum companies in a state whose flatness resembles a swimming pool filled not with water but with oil.

The National Finals is the "World Series of Professional Rodeo," where not only the best cowboys but also the most athletic horses and bucking stock compete. All year, rodeo cowboys have been vying for the honor to ride here. They've been to Houston, Las Vegas, Pendleton, Tucson, Cheyenne, San Francisco, Calgary; to as many as eighty rodeos in one season, sometimes making two or three on a day like the Fourth of July, and when the results are tallied up (in money won, not points) the top fifteen riders in each event are invited to Oklahoma City.

We climbed to our peanut gallery seats just as Miss Rodeo America, a lanky brunette swaddled in a lavender pantsuit, gloves, and cowboy hat, loped across the arena. There was a hush in the audience; all the hats swimming down in front of us, like buoys, steadied and turned toward the chutes. The agile, oiled voice of the announcer boomed: "Out of chute number three Pat Linger, a young cowboy from Miles City, Montana, making his first appearance here on a little horse named Dillinger." And as fast as these words sailed across the colosseum, the first bareback horse bumped into the lights.

There's a traditional order to the four timed and three rough stock events that make up a rodeo program. Bareback riders are first, then steer wrestlers, team ropers, saddle bronc riders, barrel racers, and finally, the bull riders.

After Pat Linger came Steve Dunham, J. C. Trujillo, Mickey Young, and the defending champ, Bruce Ford on a horse named Denver. Bareback riders do just that: they ride a horse with no saddle, no halter, no rein, clutching only a handhold riveted into a girth that goes around the horse's belly. A bareback rider's loose style suggests a drunken, comic bout of lovemaking: he lies back on the horse and, with each jump and jolt, flops delightfully, like a libidinous Raggedy Andy, toes turned out, knees flexed, legs spread and pumping, back arched, the back of his hat bumping the horse's rump as if nodding, "Yes, let's do 'er again." My husband, who rode saddle broncs in amateur rodeos, explains it differently: "It's like riding a runaway bicycle down a steep hill and lying on your back; you can't see where you're going or what's going to happen next."

Now the steer wrestlers shoot out of the box on their own well-trained horses: there is a hazer on the right to keep the steer r-unning straight, the wrestler on the left, and the steer between them. When the wrestler is neck and neck with the animal, he slides sideways out of his saddle as if he'd been stabbed in the ribs and reaches for the horns. He's airborne for a second; then his heels swing into the dirt, and with his arms around the horns, he skids to a stop, twisting the steer's head to one side so the animal loses his balance and falls to the ground. It's a fast-paced game of catch with a thousand-pound ball of horned flesh.

The team ropers are next. Most of them hall from the hilly, oak-strewn valleys of California where dally roping originated. Ropers are the graceful technicians, performing their pas de deux (plus steer) with a precision that begins to resemble a larger clarity—an erudition. Header and heeler come out of the box at the same time, steer between them, but the header acts first: he ropes the horns of the steer, dallies up, turns off, and tries to position the steer for the heeler who's been tagging behind this duo, loop clasped in his armpit as if it were a hen. Then the heeler sets his generous, unsweeping loop free and double-hocks the steer. It's a complicated act which takes about six seconds. Concomitant with this speed and skill is a feminine grace: they don't clutch their stiff loop or throw it at the steer like a bag of dirty laundry the way I do, but hold it gently, delicately, as if it were a hoop of silk. One or two cranks and both arm and loop vault forward, one becoming an appendage of the other, as if the tendons and pulse that travel through the wrist had lengthened and spun forward like fishing line until the loop sails down on the twin horns, then up under the hocks like a repeated embrace that tightens at the end before it releases.

The classic event at rodeo is saddle bronc riding. The young men look as serious as academicians: they perch spryly on their high-kicking mounts, their legs flicking forward and back, "charging the point," "going back to the cantle" in a rapid, staccato rhythm. When the horse is at the high point of his buck and the cowboy is stretched out, legs spurring above the horse's shoulder, rein-holding arm straight as a board in front, and free hand lifted behind, horse and man look like a propeller. Even their dismounts can look aeronautical: springing off the back of the horse, they land on their feet with a flourish—hat still on—as if they had been ejected mechanically from a burning plane long before the crash.

Barrel racing is the one women's event. Where the men are tender in their movements, as elegant as if Balanchine had been their coach, the women are prodigies of Wayne Gretzky, all speed, bully, and grit. When they charge into the arena, their hats fly off; they ride brazenly, elbows, knees, feet fluttering and by the time they've careened around the second of three barrels, the whip they've had clenched between their teeth is passed to a hand, and on the home stretch they urge the horse to the finish line.

Calf ropers, are the whiz kids of rodeo: they're expert on the horse and on the ground, and their horses are as quick-witted. The cowboy emerges from the box with a loop in his hand, a piggin' string in his mouth, coils and reins in the other, and a network of slack line strewn so thickly over horse and rider, they look as if they'd run through a tangle of kudzu before arriving in the arena. After roping the calf and jerking the slack in the rope, he jumps off the horse, sprints down the length of nylon, which the horse keeps taut, throws the calf down, and ties three legs together with the piggin' string. It's said of Roy Cooper, the defending calf-roping champion, that "even with pins and metal plates in his arm, he's known for the fastest groundwork in the business; when he springs down his rope to flank the calf, the resulting action is pure rodeo poetry." The six or seven separate movements he makes are so fluid they look like one continual unfolding.

Bull riding is last, and of all the events it's the only one truly dangerous. Bulls are difficult to ride: they're broadbacked, loose-skinned, and powerful. They don't jump balletically the way a horse does; they jerk and spin, and if you fall off, they'll try to gore you with a horn, kick, or trample you. Bull riders are built like the animals they ride: low to the ground and hefty. They're the tough men on the rodeo circuit, and the flirts. Two of the current champs are city men: Charlie Samson is a small, shy black from Watts, and Bobby Del Vecchio, a brash Italian from the Bronx who always throws the audience a kiss after a ride with a Catskill-like show-manship not usually seen here. What a bull rider lacks in technical virtuosity—you won't see the fast spurring action of a saddle bronc rider in this event—he makes up for in personal flamboyance, and because it's a deadlier game they're playing, you can see the bel-ligerence rise up their necks and settle into their faces as the bull starts his first spin. Besides the bull and the cowboy, there are three other men in the ring—the rodeo clowns—who aren't there to make children laugh but to divert the bull from some of his dead-lier tricks, and, when the rider bucks off, jump between the two—like Secret Service men—to save the cowboy's life.

Rodeo, like baseball, is an American sport and has been around almost as long. While Henry Chadwick was writing his first book of rules for the fledgling ball clubs in 1858, ranch hands were

paying $25 a dare to a kid who would ride five outlaw horses from
the rough string in a makeshift arena of wagons and cars. The first
commercial rodeo in Wyoming was held in Lander in 1895, just
nineteen years after the National League was formed. Baseball was
just as popular as bucking and roping contests in the West, but no
one in Cooperstown, New York, was riding broncs. And that's
been part of the problem. After 124 years, rodeo is still misunderstood. Unlike baseball, it's a regional sport (although they do have
rodeos in New Jersey, Florida, and other eastern states); it's derived
from and stands for the western way of life and the western spirit.
It doesn't have the universal appeal of a sport contrived solely for
the competition and winning; there is no ball bandied about
between opposing players.

Rodeo is the wild child of ranch work and embodies some of
what ranching is all about. Horsemanship—not gunslinging—was
the pride of western men, and the chivalrous ethics they formu-
lated, known as the western code, became the ground rules for
every human game. Two great partnerships are celebrated in this
Oklahoma arena: the indispensable one between man and animal
that any rancher or cowboy takes on, enduring the joys and pun-
ishments of the alliance; and the one between man and man,
cowboy and cowboy.

Though rodeo is an individualist's sport, it has everything to do
with teamwork. The cowboy who "covers" his bronc (stays on the
full eight seconds) has become a team with that animal. The cowboys' competitive feelings amongst each other are so mixed with
western tact as to appear ambivalent. When Bruce Ford, the bare-

back rider, won a go-round he said, "The hardest part of winning this year was taking it away from one of my best friends, Mickey Young, after he'd worked so hard all year." Stan Williamson, who'd Just won the steer wrestling, said. "I just drew a better steer. I didn't want Butch to get a bad one. I just got lucky, I guess."

Ranchers, when working together, can be just as diplomatic. They'll apologize if they cut in front of someone while cutting out a calf, and their thanks to each other at the end of the day has a formal sound. Like those westerners who still help each other out during branding and roundup, rodeo cowboys help each other in the chutes. A bull rider will steady the saddle bronc rider's horse, help measure out the rein or set the saddle, and a bareback rider might help the bull rider set his rigging and pull his rope. Ropers lend each other horses, as do barrel racers and steer wrestlers. This isn't a show they put on; they offer their help with the utmost goodwill and good-naturedness. Once, when a bucking horse fell over backward in the chute with my husband, his friend H.A., who rode bulls, jumped into the chute and pulled him out safely.

Another part of the "westernness" rodeo represents is the drifting cowboys do. They're on the road much of their lives the way turn-of-the-century cowboys were on the trail, but these cowboys travel in style if they can—driving pink Lincolns and new pickups with a dozen fresh shirts hanging behind the driver, and the radio on.

Some ranchers look down on the sport of rodeo; they don't want these "drugstore cowboys" getting all the attention and glory. Besides, rodeo seems to have less and less to do with real ranch work. Who ever heard of gathering cows on a bareback horse with no bridle, or climbing on a herd bull? Ranchers are generalists—they have to know how to do many things—from juggling the futures market to overhauling a tractor or curing viral scours (diarrhea) in calves—while rodeo athletes are specialists. Deep down, they probably feel envious of each other: the rancher for the praise and big money; the rodeo cowboy for the stay-at-home life among animals to which their sport only alludes.

People with no ranching background have even more difficulty with the sport. Every ride goes so fast, it's hard to see just what happened, and perhaps because of the Hollywood mythologizing of the West which distorted rather than distilled western rituals, rodeo is often considered corny, anachronistic, and cruel to animals. Quite the opposite is true. Rodeo cowboys are as sophisticated athletically as Björn Borg or Fernando Valenzuela. That's why they don't need to be from a ranch anymore, or to have grown up riding horses. And to undo another myth, rodeo is not cruel to animals. Compared to the arduous life of any "using horse" on a cattle or dude ranch, a bucking horse leads the life of Riley. His actual work load for an entire year, i.e., the amount of time he spends in the arena, totals approximately 4.6 minutes, and nothing done to him in the arena or out could in any way be called cruel. These animals aren't bludgeoned into bucking; they love to buck. They're bred to behave this way, they're athletes whose ability has been nurtured and encouraged. Like the cowboys who compete at the National Finals, the best bulls and horses from all the bucking strings in the country are nominated to appear in Oklahoma, winning money along with their riders to pay their own way.

The National Finals run ten nights. Every contestant rides every night, so it is easy to follow their progress and setbacks.

One evening we abandoned our rooftop seats and sat behind the chutes to watch the saddle broncs ride. Behind the chutes two cowboys are rubbing rosin—part of their staying power— behind the saddle swells and on their Easter-egg-colored chaps which are pink, blue, and light green with white fringe. Up above, standing on the chute rungs, the stock contractors direct horse traffic: "Velvet Drums" in chute #3, "Angel Sings" in #5 "Rusty" in #1. Rick Smith, Monty Henson, Bobby Berger, Brad Gjermudson, Mel Coleman, and friends climb the chutes. From where I'm sitting, it looks like a field hospital with five separate operating theaters, the cowboys, like surgeons, bent over their patients with sweaty brows and looks of concern. Horses are being haltered; cowboys are measuring out the long, braided reins, saddles are set: one cowboy pulls up on the swells again and again, repositioning his hornless saddle until it sits just right. When the chute boss nods to him and says "Pull 'em UP, boys," the ground crew tightens front and back cinches on the first horse to go, but very slowly so he won't panic in the chute as the cowboy cases himself down over the saddle, not sitting on it, just hovering there. "Okay, you're on." The chute boss nods to him again. Now he sits on the saddle, taking the rein. In one hand, holding the top of the chute with the other. He flips the loose bottoms of his chaps over his shins, puts a foot in each stirrup, takes a breath, and nods. The chute gate swings open releasing a flood—not of water, but of flesh, groans, legs kicking. The horse lunges up and out in the first big jump like a wave breaking whose crest the cowboy rides, "marking out the horse," spurs well above the bronc's shoulders. In that first second under the lights, he finds what will be the rhythm of the ride. Once again he "charges the point," his legs pumping forward, then so far back his heels touch behind the cantle. For a moment he looks as though he were kneeling on air, then he's stretched out again, his whole body taut but released, free hand waving in back of his head like a palm frond, rein-holding hand thrust forward: *"En garde!"* he seems to be saying, but he's airborne; he looks like a wing that has sprouted suddenly from the horse's broad back. Eight seconds. The whistle blows. He's covered the horse. Now two gentlemen dressed in white chaps and satin shirts gallop beside the bucking horse. The cowboy hands the rein to one and grabs the waist of the other—the flank strap on the bronc has been undone, so all three horses move at a run—and the pickup man from whom the cowboy is now dangling slows almost to a stop, letting him slide to his feet on the ground.

Rick Smith from Wyoming rides, looking pale and nervous in his white shirt. He's bucked off and so are the brash Monty "Hawkeye" Henson, and Butch Knowles, and Bud Pauley, but with such grace and aplomb, there is no shame. Bobby Berger, an Oklahoma cowboy, wins the go-round with a score of 83.

By the end of the evening we're tired, but in no way as exhausted as these young men who have ridden night after night. "I've never been so sore and had so much fun in my life," one first-time bull rider exclaims breathlessly. When the performance is over we walk across the street to the chic lobby of a hotel chock full of cowboys. Wives hurry through the crowd with freshly ironed shirts for tomorrow's ride, ropers carry their rope bags with them into the coffee shop, which is now filled with contestants, eating mild midnight suppers of scrambled eggs, their numbers hanging crookedly on their backs, their faces powdered with dust, and looking at this late hour prematurely old.

We drive back to the motel, where, the first night, they'd never heard of us even though we'd had reservations for a month. "Hey, it's our honeymoon," I told the night clerk and showed him the white ribbons my mother had tied around our duffel bag. He looked embarrassed, then surrendered another latecomer's room.

The rodeo finals in Oklahoma may be a better place to honeymoon than Paris. All week, we've observed some important rules of the game. A good rodeo, like a good marriage or a musical instrument when played to the pitch of perfection, becomes more than what it started out to be. It is effort transformed into effortlessness; a balance becomes grace, the way love goes deep into friendship.

In the rough stock events such as the one we watched tonight, there is no victory over the horse or bull. The point of the match is not conquest but communion: the rhythm of two beings becoming one. Rodeo is not a sport of opposition; there is no scrimmage line here. No one bears malice—neither the animals, the stock contractors, nor the contestants; no one wants to get hurt. In this match of equal talents, it is only acceptance, surrender, respect, and spiritedness that make for the midair union of cowboy and horse. Not a bad thought when starting out fresh in a marriage.

fear

Ciudad Juàrez
by Elizabeth Tallent

Elizabeth Tallent is a distinguished novelist and short story writer. She writes with intelligence, grace and feeling about the dark and unexamined aspects of relationships. This story follows a young couple, traveling in Mexico with their infant son, as they stumble into that darkness.

The Subaru's air-conditioning purrs arduously, pitted against the one-hundred-and-one-degree radiance of Texas, turning the dust on its dash to platinum lint and burning twin suns into the big black lenses hiding Tom's wife's eyes. Tatters of orange peel, a Styrofoam cup whose crescent indentations are the repeated nickings of Tom's wife's thumbnail, a foxed map folded to the Rio Grande, a tiny quartz arrowhead—bird point—from the desert beyond the last rest stop: the litter, cumulatively somehow depressing, of five hours' conversationless travel. Her silence isn't aimed at him, Tom knows. They're not a couple to nurse mutual incomprehension in silence; they're more likely to expect too much of each other, and so, after a little oblique study, he decided to leave Nina alone.

Ten miles back, she'd caught his wrist and slanted it toward herself to read his watch, and then, he'd thought, she would say something; she'd say, "It's two o'clock," or "It's getting late," in the faintly marveling tone she reserves for that observation, but she'd said nothing after all. In essence, despite touching him, she had not felt compelled to acknowledge his existence. She'd simply taken possession of his wrist. For years they had done such things back and forth without their meaning anything. She had straightened his tie, or he had brushed strands of hair from the corner of her smile. He can remember using a fingertip to rub lipstick from one of her front teeth, the left, which minutely, endearingly, overlaps the other, his favorite imperfection in her body. Just now her clasp was too light to alter the peacefulness with which his hand lay on the wheel. Her touch was utterly familiar, light, practical, dismissive, quick. It made him nervous. Yet they can't make each other nervous; it's a possibility that vanished from their marriage long ago. They're so deeply unselfconscious with each other, in fact, that it's not even clear that she "borrowed" his wrist, or "took temporary possession" of it. It's as if she read her own watch, really, moving her own arm slightly to do so, thinking nothing of it. Her touch couldn't have been more neutral, so why did he experience it as so suddenly, exquisitely sexual? If a stranger, someone he'd never seen before, touched him unexpectedly, wanting only to learn the time, he would feel this intruded on, this moved. How can Nina's touch be as disturbing as a stranger's?

A generous interpretation: sex, sensing a vacuum, nimbly presents itself as a way of making contact.

Here, on the map, the Rio Grande's blue hairline intersects the black dashes of the Mexican border, but if the river's down there, it's lost in the glare of sunstruck sand. The American traffic slows for the bridge. On its far side the sentry boxes that should house Mexican Customs are boarded shut, spray-painted in slashes and scrawls naming couples and sexual acts. Nina asks, "Nobody stops us?"

"Hey, they want us," Tom says, relieved. Garbo talks. She goes further, twisting in her seat belt to report, of the baby behind them in his car seat, "Still out. Thumb in his mouth."

"Is he getting enough air-conditioning?"

She leans over the seat back to not-quite-touch the baby's forehead. "I think so."

The books say parents should spend time alone with each twin, but this is almost the first occasion Wills and Griffin have been separated. Griffin has been left in Santa Fe with the boys' sitter, Carmelita Diáz, who was hardly in the door before she cocked a confident hip for Griffin to straddle and told Nina to leave now, please, before the *hijito* knew what was happening. If Nina had only trusted her with Wills, too, this weekend would surely be easier.

Juárez is, first, a small park of dead grass edged with dying palms and an asphalt spur where drivers lean against their cabs, surveying the crush of tourist traffic. Tom could park the Subaru, safe in its shiny, uninsured Americanness, and bargain for a cab. Too late. Traffic carries him past the turnoff. His sunglasses are so clouded with baby fingerprints that he hands them to Nina to burnish on her skirt, hoping that her gesture will clear his mind as well.

What he wants wiped away is a scene: himself, growling like an airplane, aiming a spoon at Griffin's mouth, while in his high chair

Wills yelled, "Da! Da-da!" Nina came up behind, putting an arm around Tom's neck, weighing against him until he knew from the tightening helplessness of her hold that something was wrong and asked, "O.K., what?" She said, "I am," and he had to look from the brilliant blue slip of litmus paper into her eyes, also brilliant, reading there that until he too saw this proof, she had not believed it. "Oh, Nina, no," he said. "It can't be right."

"It is right. I knew anyway. I feel like before."

Griffin threw his bowl to the floor, and oatmeal splattered Nina's bare feet. She bent to wipe them clean with the sleeve of her sweatshirt, and he couldn't see her face for the fall of her hair when she said, "I can't have another baby."

"I know."

He was agreeing, but she went on as if he hadn't, her voice as furious as when they quarreled. "These two take everything. I'd be gone. I'd disappear. My life would be gone."

He turns his head briefly for Nina to slide his glasses back on. Her touch smarts on his nose, burned from the few desert minutes in which, walking away from the rest stop into an arroyo whose air had the sick shimmer of gasoline-tainted heat, past the inevitable charred tires and shattered glass, he'd found the quartz point. It had a fresh whiteness like salt's, and was weightless as a contact lens, ancient, intact, still pristinely sharp. He'd wished he could walk farther—an archaeologist's constant impulse—but Nina was waiting, and he hadn't worn his baseball cap. Usually he's pretty self-protective. The sun at his dig in Chaco Canyon has an X-ray intensity. He's in the sun a lot. Gone a lot. Nina's needed him, and he just hasn't been home. The sleepless intensity of the twins' first ten months fell almost entirely on her. This time there's anguish in the commonplace recognition that he could have been more careful.

"This traffic," Nina says vaguely.

"Want to stop?"

"Where? And it would wake Wills."

"How's he doing?"

Absurd to ask for the second time in five minutes, but again Nina reassures him, "He's really out. He's fine," the tenderness in her tone referring backward, as she assumes his anxiety does, to ten months ago, to a relief so pure that time has scarcely diluted it. His brother was fine, but Wills, too small, spent his first week in neonatal care, heels periodically pricked for blood, fists small as violin scrolls, chapped skin distressingly red against sterile cotton; even his mewing sounded raw, fetal, exposed. Nina would not touch him. The nurses said this was not an uncommon response. It wasn't unusual, even, that Nina didn't want to name him. Attachment, at this point, seemed too dangerous, but a touch or a name would be good signs. Under the heat lamp's mild aura the newborn waited, silver disks taped to his chest, wires flexing minutely with his breathing, illumined dials presiding, until one night Nina, stepping cautiously across the trailing wires, stroked his cheek. His head jerked, his eyes opened to her gaze. In a corner, there was a rocking chair. The nurses whispered back and forth. Wills gained two ounces—three—to weigh four and a half pounds. Rocking, Nina looked up at Tom as if she didn't remember him. The baby that might not make it was always crying, Nina's head bent until her lips grazed his hair, repeating the name she'd given him: Will, to add, with each repetition, a feather's weight to the side opposite death. Tom was stunned, when once a vial of the baby's blood was carried past him, by the wish to cry out.

Ten days, then two weeks. Their neighbor Carmelita Diáz had moved into their house, taking over Griffin. Though he needed a way to pass the time, there were only so many phone calls Tom could stand to make, so many quarters he could stand to send *chinging* into the pay phone in the corridor. Once as he waited there, about to dial his home number again, a nightgowned girl in labor approached, wheeling her IV stand, stopping to brace herself against a wall when a contraction hit. Tom found himself wanting to ask, as her breathing eased, if he could do something, get her something, but his T-shirt was sweated through under the arms; he probably smelled of his own sick tension. He hung up the phone. He went to the window: outside was a July evening, birds skimming past, cumulonimbus clouds boiling up over the Sangre de Cristos. Tom leaned his forehead and forearm against glass alive with the permanent, mute, scarcely perceptible tremor of air-conditioning, while the girl, with small moans, rode out another contraction.

In the end, they were lucky: Wills weighing five pounds, they went home, but the emotional constellation formed in neonatal care subversively persists. It's Wills whose hold on his parents is the more potent and infatuated, Griffin who chose to wean himself abruptly, biting Nina whenever she unbuttoned for him. Letting himself in one evening, wondering at the silence, Tom padded in stocking feet through the house to find Nina asleep in a pile of dirty laundry, the naked twins crawling around her. As Tom caught Wills, Griffin peed, crowing, on Tom's favorite shirt. It was an hour before Tom got both boys bathed and in bed, and still Nina lay dreaming in a welter of sheets and shirts and small overalls.

"Did we lose a dirty diaper in here?" Tom asks. "No," Nina says shortly. A lick of red hair, loosed from her chignon, clings to Nina's nape, and her freckles are out in force. Six lanes of idling American cars are the Avenida de la Revolución. Neon ice in cones: their vendor, a pretty girl ducking to Tom's window, smiles brightly to show missing front teeth. Nina shakes her head, and the girl is gone. Glacierlike, the glittering cars grind forward in concerted, decisive inches. Nina bites her thumbnail in rapid, critical clicks. What her ob-gyn in Santa Fe gently told Nina was that abortions are not considered safe before six weeks. She was—the sonogram proved—only four weeks along. The wait is now almost behind them. The abortion is scheduled for Monday, the day after tomorrow, in Santa Fe, but they couldn't have stood waiting at home.

When a street opens to their right, Tom tries it. "How hot do you think it is?" Nina says. "Do you know where we're going?"

"*Is* there a dirty diaper lost in here?" Tom demands, with such miserable rudeness that she scrabbles underfoot even as he chooses street after street for their increasing emptiness, and the buildings on either side grow smaller, meeker, older, and more foreign, their plaster no longer pink or turquoise but dusty ocher, no neon advertising *cerveza*, no iron flourishes. When Nina sits up, having found nothing, the world is poor and shut against them.

"I hate this," she says.

"Well, we're lost." Desperately, he's trying to reconstruct the turns he made, each on the spur of the moment, no logic linking them, when Nina says, "Look," and a bicycle whisks alongside agilely as a trotting dog. The bicycle's crouching child, a wing of black hair falling just shy of his eyes, asks Tom, "Where to?" This phrase exhausts the boy's English and he can only, pitched forward optimistically over the handlebars, wait on Tom's answer; he does this by gracefully, agreeably coasting, adding not a pedal's stroke of pressure to his sweet selling job.

Nina leans across Tom, her hand on his leg, and asks in Spanish to be led to the big shopping *mercado, por favor.* The bicycle flicks away, down an even narrower street, and Tom asks, "Did we have a deal?"

"He's showing off," Nina says, "but yes."

"What are you getting us into?" Tom wrenches the Subaru into the turn, but it's tight, and he's glancing back to check the fender when Nina cries "No!" in time for Tom to brake, the Subaru jolting to a stop, the boy inches before them, holding up his arms to show no harm was done. Nina calls, *"¡Oye, chico, demasiado cerca!"*

"Can you get him back? I'm going to get out and scream at him. That was fucking dangerous."

"In what language?"

"He'd get it."

"He thought he'd lost his rich customers," Nina says, "plus he's a little macho."

"Now where are we?" Tom asks, because this street is wider, opening into another, where spandex-legged girls balance on high heels

and iron arabesques guard shop windows. Here it is again, the blazing
Avenida, traffic locked tight, and Tom hammers the wheel with a fist.

"It's O.K., it's O.K.," Nina says.

"How is this O.K.?"

"So he made a mistake. He can't be more than ten."

"I should never have followed him," Tom says, and then, "Did
you notice his hand?"

"His hand?"

"He's got it bandaged in something filthy."

"All I saw was his face. His face is beautiful."

"I haven't given him a dime," Tom says, "and he's sitting out
there for us in that sun."

Tremors of movement run toward them through the traffic. The
boy waits for an opening to the right, taking it so fast that Tom pops
his turn signal and begs over his shoulder for a way in. Granted, by
an Isuzu pickup; Nina waves thanks, and the boy shoots away again,
another lane over, behind a refrigerator truck.

"I'm going to lose him if he's not careful."

"Pay attention."

"This is his fault," Tom insists, because it's infuriating, the adroit
bicycle, the blocked traffic unpredictably spurting ahead, the glare
he's squinting into when Nina cries out. Something thumps into
them and spills with a raggedly rolling momentum across the hood
and down. He has automatically slowed and stopped, he has even
assured himself from the rearview that he won't get hit from behind,
because while his fear is great, it has endowed Tom with the lucidity
of adrenaline, plowing him through a single vast thought at a time

as everything around him shudders, slows, and stalls, and the beautiful life he has lived until this moment breaks off and floats away.

Nina pleads, "Don't go," in a tone so passionate and clear that he listens to her; he stops, thinking she knows something he's missed, but of course she doesn't, and though he hates leaving her now he answers in a voice as clear as her own, "I killed him," and climbs from the car to crouch at what should be the body of the boy and is, instead, *instead,* a khaki duffel from which, by lifting and violently shaking, he spills five pairs of boots, their leather superheatedly slick in the sun, unreal, real. From nearby cars, he is called a whore's son, an idiot, a *chingal,* but he feels an exquisite high, setting each miraculous boot onto its sharp-toed shadow. Nina is squatting, asking, "Are you all right?"

"I'm wonderful."

"Please don't lose it. Not now."

They stand up together. He takes her sunglasses off for the first time that day to tell her eyes "I love you."

"I know."

"How are you? Are you O.K.?"

"I'm fine," she says, but the bearded guy who's climbing out of the Mercedes in front of them, having heard Tom's question, feels obscurely bound to repeat it, and when Nina doesn't answer, he tries Tom. "How are you? How is she?" He's wearing a Dodgers cap, and mirror shades; little of his expression shows. "I'm a doctor," he adds.

"What's with the boots?" Tom asks, over the symphony of horns and insults.

"I bring my boots down here to get them reheeled. A Mexican guy does it for me. Hospital floors wear them right down. We're having one hell of a fight, and she says she can't stand it, and chucks these boots out the window before I can stop her. Throws the back door right open. She's always throwing things of mine away. Sometimes I come home after a long day to find two dozen shirts on the lawn, flung all over, getting rained on by the sprinklers. Next time we come down to Juárez it's for a divorce." He shakes his head heavily. "My insurance is taking care of this." He flicks through a satiny black wallet for a card.

"Good," Tom says.

Nina says, "We're leaving. I'm driving," hooking her sunglasses; Tom had forgotten he had them. She tells the bearded doctor, "We never want to hear from you. Never, got it?"

The guy appeals to Tom—"You should take this"—but Nina drops the card into the street. Nina drives, and either Juárez does not confuse her or the accident has, oddly, cleared her mind. A small street with one pretty restaurant in its middle appears for her. They park under palms. Inside, the restaurant is wonderfully cold and dark. Nina deciphers the handwritten menu while Wills peels cellophane from a saltine. The waitress stops to admire Wills's corn-silk blondness before liberating him from his high chair and waltzing him away.

"I should trust this, but I don't," Nina says, and follows. From the kitchen comes high, ecstatic Spanish—a baby party. The fuss is even worse when both twins are together. Tom agrees with himself that he's light-headed and should eat. The waitress reappears, alone but bearing huge plates. Tom tarts up his Tecate with salt and lime. In the poster above him, the bull's head is lowered, the cape soars out, and the matador's golden backside is beautiful as a girl's.

"It's nice you didn't go crazy back there with that guy," Nina says, returning to buckle Wills into his chair.

"I was so scared it was that kid I hit."

"You told me, 'I killed him.'"

"I remember."

"I killed him."

"Well, didn't you think that?"

"I didn't think it was him you hit, no. You weren't being rational."

"So I'm the one who panics," he marvels, meaning he very slightly doubts her word. He doubts he went through those frantic emotions alone.

"Do you know that story Paula tells?" Paula is a friend of theirs, an anthropologist working in Cuzco; he nods, and she goes on. "The earthquake wakes her in the middle of the night, and she grabs her husband, and they're flat in the bed with fear, and it's this long, long time for them before they think of the baby in his crib across the room."

"And?"

"Don't be like that. Don't expect me to be like that."

"I still don't understand."

"I mean"—she sets her fork down—"Paula fears for herself. That's natural. You feared for that boy. That's natural. All I think of is Wills right behind us in his car seat, strapped in, safe, quiet, O.K., and my fear stops right there, and that's natural. I'm not going to judge the way any of us responds to things. In what people feel, they're alone."

"But that's so lonely," Tom says. "I couldn't stand to believe that."

"You want to know the first time I even remembered that boy? When we got back into the car and traffic had carried him away, I thought, 'He's not going to get paid.' Then I felt sorry for him."

Tom says, "His instinct would be not to hang around trouble. The cops could come."

Wills oils a piece of avocado with saliva and skates it around his tray. Nina says, "Eat it, Wills. Eat it. Eat it." Wills says, "Da fix," and sweeps it to the floor. He trades stares with his mother, angelic sweetness on his side, maternal inscrutability on hers. Nina says, "I want to go home *now*."

Under a half-moon, the border has backed up into a vast plain of taillights in which the only moving things are beggars. Tom hangs his hand out the window, but when a crippled girl lifts twenty dollars from his fingers and seesaws away on her crutches, he feels nothing, no more than if the wind had blown it away. U.S. Customs is the distant waist of the hourglass, letting a red grit of taillights tick through. In the seat behind him, Nina nurses Wills, being discreet because now and then a beggar leans right into the window, having observed that the driver is vulnerable, is guilty, will give. Though Tom empties his wallet, Nina says nothing. She doesn't say, "Save at least something." Nursing, Wills fools around, cooing to the breast. "I wish I was you," Tom tells Nina.

"Why?"

"Because all you do is sit there, and he gets what he needs."

Tom keeps the Subaru nuzzled up against the rear of an old Ford pickup. Four men are sleeping there, dirty straw hats slanted down. When the truck reaches Customs, the inspector lowers his clipboard and lets his flashlight wake the men. He orders them out. They clamber down, standing ashamed in the concentrated light of waiting cars.

"These guys could take forever," Tom tells Nina. "They're Mexican, crossing on a big night. I'd be suspicious."

"Of what?"

"Don't you worry that Carmelita's husband comes and goes this way?"

Carmelita's husband periodically disappears back to his Oaxacan hometown. "Sure," Nina says. "But he's paid somebody here. He knows how to get away with it. I'm not even sure she'd mind if he went to jail."

"The last time he was home, I could hear them making love," Tom says.

"What do you mean, you could hear them?"

She's not going to like this part. "It was when you had the flu and she stayed over. They were on the floor of the babies' room."

"My God," Nina says. "She's fired."

"They weren't loud. It was just their voices, talking."

"Were they happy?"

He thinks. "Yes, they were happy. I think so." He waits a moment. "Nina, we'll be happy again. We'll be fine."

"You don't wish you were me," she says.

She's still behind him, so he can't see her. "Why don't I?"

"You couldn't stand to feel what I'm feeling."

The four men swing themselves in, the pickup rolls forward, and Nina and Tom are asked what country they're citizens of. The flashlight splashes the backseat bright as daylight and starts Wills crying, and he cries as they're waved through, he cries all the way through an El Paso abandoned for Saturday night, he cries at the desk under the disapproving gaze of the clerk and up the elevator of the hotel, the first hotel Tom noticed, Nina holding Wills and humming against his head. Somebody, some drunk, has punched all the buttons, and Wills cries in gusting wails until finally, as the elevator doors break apart on a last genteelly lit and carpeted corridor, he quiets.

Tom lugs bags around and settles them in while Nina bathes Wills. When Tom looks in on them, the mother leaning into the tub, the baby standing up sucking a washcloth, Nina yawns. "I can't stay awake," she says. "Please stay awake," he says, "we have to talk," but once she's put Wills down, singing him through his resistance to yet another strange place, she drags her T-shirt off, her shoulder blades set tight with fatigue, her bare back brilliant in the moment before the bathroom door closes. Fresh water is run into the baby's leftover bath, a hairbrush clicks down against the sink, and then Tom hears her gratefulness as she enters the water, the skid of her bottom against porcelain, her chin tilted up, he imagines, so that her head can rest against the rim. While still distantly conscious of needing to stay awake, he's asleep. He's almost asleep. Wills whimpers and is shushed. Nina's in bed, then, and to his surprise she wants to make love. When they're done, she's still lying across him, breathing past his ear into the pillow; she says, "Sadness. Just such sadness"—answer to a question he can't remember asking. She kisses him before he can say "What?" His tongue finds the imprecision in her front teeth, that minute edge of overlap, and maybe because he's so tired he thinks something strange: if they were buried just like this, then someone unearthing Nina's skull could see that same flaw a hundred, a thousand, years from now, could even touch it, could be that far from now and not know what to feel.

children

from

Everyday Blessings
by Myla and Jon Kabat-Zinn

Jon Kabat-Zinn, a leader in the field of mind/body medicine and mindfulness meditation, wrote *Everyday Blessings* with his wife Myla Kabat-Zinn, a childbirth educator and environmental activist. The book reflects the insights the couple has gained from working hard to be fully present to each other and their children during their marriage.

Parenting Is the Full Catastrophe

When we become parents, whether intentionally or by happenstance, our whole life is immediately different, although it may take some time to realize just how much. Being a parent compounds stress by orders of magnitude. It makes us vulnerable in ways we weren't before. It calls us to be responsible in ways we weren't before. It challenges us as never before, and takes our time and attention away from other things, including ourselves, as never before. It creates chaos and disorder, feelings of inadequacy, occasions for arguments, struggles, irritation, noise, seemingly never-ending obligations and errands, and plenty of opportunities for getting stuck, angry, resentful, hurt, and for feeling overwhelmed, old, and unimportant. And this can go on not only when the children are little, but even when they are full grown and on their own. Having children is asking for trouble.

So why do it? Maybe Pete Seeger said it best: "We do it for the high wages . . . kisses." Children give us the opportunity to share in the vibrancy of life itself in ways we would not touch were they not part of our lives. Especially when children are young, our job as a parent is to be there for them and, as best we can, nurture them and protect them so that they are free to experience the innocence and genius of childhood, gently providing what guidance we can out of our own paths.

Children embody what is best in life. They live in the present moment. They are part of its exquisite bloom. They are pure potentiality, embodying vitality, emergence, renewal, and hope. They are purely what they are. And they share that vital nature with us and call it out of us as well, if we can listen carefully to the calling.

Once we have children, we are in touch with the rest of the universe in an entirely different way. Our consciousness changes, rotates from one way of seeing to another. We may find ourselves feeling connected to the hopefulness and the pain in others in ways that we might not have felt before. Our sphere of compassion tends to broaden. Concern for our children and their well-being may give us a different perspective on poverty, the environment, war, and the future.

As for trouble, Zorba, the crusty old character in Kazantzakis's novel *Zorba the Greek,* who, when asked whether he had ever been married, replied, "Am I not a man? Of course I've been married.

Wife, house, kids, the full catastrophe," also said: "Trouble? Life is trouble. Only death is no trouble."

Ultimately, we make our own choices, mindfully or not, and we live with their consequences. Even so, we never know what is coming next. Immanent uncertainty is a big part of the full catastrophe. The question is, can we learn to use all of life's circumstances, even the most trying and stressful ones, to grow in strength and wisdom and openheartedness, much as a sailor makes skillful use of all kinds of wind conditions to propel a sailboat toward a particular destination? For our own ongoing growth is an absolute necessity if we are to serve as effective parents of our children over the long haul, so that they may be sheltered and grow well in their own ways and in their own time.

Live-in Zen Masters

We were married in a Zen ceremony in which our wedding vows were to help each other "attain 'big mind' for the sake of all beings." The Zen tradition has had a deep appeal to me (jkz) from my first contacts with it some thirty years ago. Zen training is arduous and demanding, intense and unpredictable, wild and crazy, and very loving and funny. It's also very simple, and not so simple. It's all about mindfulness and nonattachment, knowing who we are at the deepest of levels, and knowing what we are doing, which paradoxically includes both not knowing and non-doing.

For me, the wild ride of Zen training seemed like it had a lot in common with parenting. They both appeared to be about waking up to life itself, with no holds barred. So it was not such a big jump to think that I could see our babies, who, like all babies, really do look like little Buddhas, with their round bellies, big heads, and mysterious smiles, as live-in Zen Masters. Zen Masters don't explain themselves. They just embody presence. They don't get hung up in thinking, or lost in theoretical musings about this or that. They are not attached to things being a certain way. They are not always consistent. One day does not necessarily have to be like the next. Their presence and their teachings can help us break through to a direct experiencing of our own true nature, and encourage us to find our own way, now, in this moment. They do this, not by telling us how, but by giving us endless challenges that cannot be resolved through thinking, by mirroring life back to us in its fullness, by pointing to wholeness. More than anything, Zen Masters embody wakefulness and call it out of us.

Children are similar in many ways, especially when they are babies. The older they get, the harder it may be for us to see it. But their true nature is always present, and always mirroring our own, if we are willing to look, and to see.

Children have what might be called "original mind"—open, pure, unencumbered. They are undeniably and totally present. They are constantly learning, developing, changing, and requiring new responses from us. As they grow, they seem to challenge every place that we might be holding an expectation, a fixed opinion, a cherished belief, a desire for things to be a certain way. As babies, they so fill our lives and require so much attention to their physical and emotional needs that they continually challenge us to be present totally, to be sensitive, to inquire into what is actually happening, to risk trying something, and to learn from their responses to our attempts. They teach us how to be attuned to them, and to find joy and harmony in our connectedness with them. There is little time for theory, and it doesn't seem to help much anyway unless it is connected to practice.

Of course, children are not really Zen Masters. Children are children and Zen Masters are Zen Masters. But if we are able to look at our children with openness and receptivity, and see the purity of life expressing itself through them, at any age, it can wake us up at any moment to their true nature and to our own.

Nothing anyone ever tells us prepares us for what it is actually like to be a parent. We learn on the job, in the doing, charting our own paths, relying on our inner resources, including the ones we never knew we had, taking our cues from our children and from every new situation that presents itself. We have to live inside of parenthood to know what it is. It is a deep and abiding inner work, a spiritual training all its own, if we choose to let it speak to us in that way, literally moment to moment.

We can ignore entirely, or resist as inconvenient or unimportant, or too messy or difficult, the continual stream of teachings from our children and from the circumstances we find ourselves in; or we can look deeply into them, letting them serve as indicators of where we need to pay attention and discern what is happening and what needs doing in any moment. It is entirely our choice. If we resist, we may occasion a great deal of unnecessary struggle and pain, for to ignore or struggle against the life force of children exploring and learning and growing, to not recognize and honor their sovereignty, denies a reality that is fundamental and will make itself known and felt one way or another.

For example, to forget momentarily that a two-year-old is a child and to rigidly and unfeelingly impose our own expectations about how she should be behaving, is to forget that what she is doing is what two-year-olds do. If we want it to be different from what is happening in that moment, and we resist or contract in our mind and try to force what we want on the situation, we will be creating a lot of trouble all around. We have all undoubtedly experienced the consequences of such a situation at one point or another as parents.

On the other hand, if we can let go of our idea in such a moment of how things "should be," and embrace how they actually are with this child; in other words, if we can remember that we are the adult and that we can look inside ourselves at that very moment and find a way to act with some degree of wisdom and compassion, and in the best interest of our child—then our emotional state and our choices of what to do will be very different, as will be the unfolding and resolution of that moment into the next. If we choose this path, she will have taught us something very important. She will have shown us how attached we can be to having things happen a certain way, that our mind wavers when we are challenged, and that we have various choices available to us. One of those choices would be to allow ourselves to be carried away by our own reactivity and ignorance, forgetting that two-year-olds do two-year-old kinds of things; another might be to affirm that we are capable of seeing our own reactivity and choose to go a different route, one in which we work both with our reaction and with what is actually happening with our child. We may have "known" all this, theoretically speaking, the moment before, or in another circumstance, but perhaps not in a way that prevented us from reacting automatically, from *embodying* our understanding. So our two-year-old showed us, through her being, Zen Master-like, that we can easily lose ourselves in emotional reacting, and that we don't have to. An important teaching, applicable in many different areas of our life. After all, our mind goes everywhere we do, and it usually reacts in a similar way when it doesn't feel in control or like what is happening.

If we can bring attention and intentionality to our own growing edges—in parenting and elsewhere in our lives—painful and frightening as that can be, that very orientation, that tenacious willingness to be present and to look at *anything,* can bring us into greater harmony with the way things actually are. But for that to happen, we must learn to listen carefully to what the world offers us, to look deeply into our experience as it is unfolding.

The funny thing is that if we bring awareness to what is in front of us in every moment, without insisting on it being a certain way, then the discipline of doing just that gives rise to a stability of mind and an openness and clarity of heart that are unattainable by struggling to achieve them through forcing a particular resolution or outcome. For such harmony underlies everything. It is here now, in us, and in our children, if we can but make room, over and over again, for it to emerge.

• • •

First we braid grasses and play tug of war,

then we take turns singing and keeping a kick-ball in the air.

I kick the ball and they sing, they kick and I sing.

Time is forgotten, the hours fly.

People passing by point at me and laugh:

"Why are you acting like such a fool?"

I nod my head and don't answer.

I could say something, but why?

Do you want to know what's in my heart?

From the beginning of time: just this! just this!

RYOKAN, EIGHTEENTH-CENTURY JAPANESE ZEN MASTER,

HERMIT, CALLIGRAPHER, POET

An Eighteen-Year Retreat

Just as it might be useful to look at our children as little Buddhas or Zen Masters in order to help us to parent them better and to continue to grow ourselves, I (jkz) have often felt that parenting could be looked at as an extended meditation retreat—an opportunity to do a certain kind of deep and concentrated inner work of potentially profound and continuing benefit to children and parents alike within a family.

Usually, meditation retreats last for days, weeks, or months; but in this case, the "parenting retreat" would last on the order of at least eighteen years per child. Of course, the demands of parenting from day to day are very different from those of a secluded and intensive meditation retreat, but seeing them as related ways of doing sustained inner work has energized and sustained me at times in bringing a tenacious and overarching perspective to the inner calling of parenting, and to the years of constant and ultimately selfless attention, caring, and wisdom that it asks of us.

What, then, is a meditation retreat? What is its purpose? And how might seeing parenting as a kind of retreat help us understand and deepen what is being asked of us when we engage in mindful parenting, even for those of us who don't meditate regularly or who have no personal experience of such retreats? And how might looking at parenting in this way contribute to our own growth and development?

A meditation retreat is an opportunity to do a certain kind of inner work on ourselves that is extremely difficult to do outside of the retreat setting because of all the competing obligations, distractions, and enticements of everyday life. On retreat, because we are off in a special place for an extended period of time, away from the demands of family and work, we have a rare and precious chance to simplify our lives and give enormous care and attention to the domain of being.

Meditation retreats are often guided by one or more skilled teachers, who serve to encourage, inspire, guide, instruct, and listen to the experiences of the retreatants. The basic practice consists mostly of periods of sitting and walking, all in silence, typically from early morning to late at night. Just sitting. Just walking.

Usually there is a period of work as well, also silent, so that the same mind that we cultivate in sitting and walking can be brought to cleaning the bathroom, or washing pots, or weeding the garden. What the task is is not so important . . . the mind that we bring to it is exquisitely important.

Attention is directed primarily inwardly, toward a few basic aspects of life experience that are ordinarily taken completely for granted, such as the breath flowing in and out, and what there is to be perceived moment by moment in your own body and in your own mind. Other than that, you eat, also in silence, and you sleep. Usually there is no reading, no writing, and no telephone calls, so you are really on your own, except for occasional interviews with the teacher. Such retreats can be extremely arduous and challenging—and deeply healing.

Over time, the mind gradually settles into the retreat. It can become deeply concentrated and one-pointed, remaining focused and relatively balanced and still over extended periods of time. Through the disciplined cultivation of attention, coupled with recognition and acceptance of what you are observing, you can come to know the landscape of your own mind and your own heart in radically new ways. A highly penetrative awareness develops, which can provide a deep look into the very nature of your being, underneath surface appearances, attachments, and personal history. Intensive and sustained attention of this kind can sometimes catalyze profound insights—awakenings that are truly enlightening—and can reveal you to yourself in ways you never knew or thought possible.

Intensive meditation practice is both a mirror and purification process. We may come to a larger and more accurate way of seeing, which can give rise to deep learning about ourselves, and an equally deep letting go, perhaps most importantly, a letting go of whatever we find we identify in absolute and rigid ways . . . our attachments to things, ways of seeing, ideas.

In paying sustained attention to your own mind, you can discover that the mind actually behaves in fairly structured ways, in patterns that are recognizable, if sometimes excruciatingly repetitive and unrelenting. You might come to see, just by sitting and walking in silence, how ceaselessly the stream of thinking flows, how chaotic the thought process is (order within it is sometimes difficult to discern), and how unreliable and inaccurate most of our thoughts are. You might come to see how reactive the mind is, and how powerful its emotional storms.

You might see that the mind spends enormous amounts of time in the past, reminiscing, resenting, or blaming, and in the future, worrying, planning, hoping, dreaming. You might see that the mind tends constantly to judge itself and everything else, depending on whether an experience is felt to be pleasant, unpleasant, or neutral at any particular moment. You might see how strong the mind's attachments are, its incessant identification with things and opinions, and how so much of the time it is driven by wishful thinking and the desire to be somewhere else, to have things and relationships be different from how they actually are.

You might see how hard it is for the mind to settle into the present moment as it is, but also that, over time, the mind can actually calm down enough to see much of this ceaseless activity that it is engaged in, and come to an inner stillness and calmness and balance that is less easily disturbed by its own activity.

If you are motivated enough to stick with the practice through the hard times, if you can stay with the pain in your body that may come from long periods of sitting still, if you can stay with the yearning in the mind for talk, or for entertainment and distraction and novelty, if you can stay with the boredom, resistance, the grief, terror, and confusion that can and do arise on occasion, and if, all the while, you ruthlessly and with utter kindness and gentleness, without expectations, persist in simply observing whatever comes up in the field of your awareness, moment by moment, you may come to encounter, at certain points in your practice, great oceanlike depths of silence, well-being, and wisdom within your own mind.

For, in many ways, the mind does resemble a body of water, a veritable ocean. On the surface, depending on the season, the weather, and the winds, the surface can be anything from completely calm and flat to hugely tumultuous and turbulent, with forty-foot waves or higher. But even at its most stormy, if one goes down deep enough, the water will be very still.

Persisting in the practice, we might come to see on such a retreat that our own mind is much the same—that calmness and deep stillness are intrinsic to its nature, that they are always present, and that even when we are caught up in huge storms of emotional turmoil, for whatever reasons, the calmness and the stillness and the capacity to be aware are still here, underneath, embedded in and an integral part of our being. They can be called upon, and used, not to extinguish the surface turbulence of the mind (just as we don't try to flatten the waves on the ocean), but to understand it and to provide a larger container for it, a context in which the very turbulence itself can be held, seen, and even used to deepen our understanding.

We may come to see that our thoughts and emotions do not have to carry us away or blind us in one way or another, as so frequently happens in life. Nor do we have to make any effort to suppress them to be free from much of the suffering they contain or engender.

Working in this way with the activity of our own mind, we might also come to see that it is a fiction that we are isolated, separate, and alone. We might see that "I," "me," and "mine" are themselves thoughts, powerful, deeply rooted and tenacious habits of mind, but thoughts all the same. Beneath the sense of ourselves as being separate and preoccupied so much of the time with concerns about our individual self and our own personal gains and losses, we might see that we are part of a flowing movement of wholeness that is larger than we are and to which we belong.

We might see that there is a deep mystery in our individual life emerging from the union of our parents and, before them, from their parents, and so on back into time; that we are an intermediary between our parents and our children, between all those who have come before, whom we will never know, and all those who will come after our children's children's children, whom we will also never know.

We may come to see that the deepest nature of the universe is that it is one, a seamless whole, and that everything that is is an aspect of everything else. We may come to see that everything is embedded in and reflected in everything else, that everything and every being is whole *and* part of a larger wholeness, and that interconnectedness and interdependence are the root relationships out of which meaning and the particulars of our fleeting and constantly changing individual lives arise.

And you may come to see with fresh eyes and a new understanding and appreciation that, together with the ways in which the unfolding of life is impersonal, it is all the same very personal. You may realize directly, as the veils of thinking and strong attachment thin, that right now and right here, you are who you are; that the being that is you is unique, with your own face and character and desires, with a particular history that is the legacy of having the parents that you had and growing up the way you did, and with your own unique and mysterious path or calling that can infuse your life with vision and passion. You work where you work, you live where you live, your responsibilities are your responsibilities, your children are your children, your hopes are your hopes, your fears your fears.

We might come to see that "separate" and "not separate" are themselves just thoughts, attempts to describe a deeper reality that is us. We might see the possibility of living more gracefully, knowing that the things that happen to us are happening to us, yet also knowing that it is not wise to take them entirely personally, because everything is also impersonal, and it is problematic— Buddhists would say, impossible—to point to a solid, permanent "you" who is here to take them personally. You are certainly who you are, and you are responsible for many things; but you are certainly not who you think you are because thinking itself is limited, and your true nature is limitless.

On retreat, we might also come to know that we are not our body, not our thoughts, not our emotions, not our ideas and opinions, not our fears and our insecurities and our woundedness, even though they are an intimate part of our experience and can influence our lives enormously, much as the weather influences the surface of the ocean. Their influence is particularly strong if we form strong and unconscious attachments to them, to which we cling for dear life, and through which we see everything as through dark, or light, or colored, or kaleidoscopic glasses.

We are not our ideas and opinions. If we could live our lives knowing this, and take off the glasses through which we filter our experience, what a difference it might make in the way we see, in our choices, and in the way we conduct our lives from day to day. This insight alone might cause us to see ourselves very differently, to see our parenting very differently, and indeed, to live differently.

We may also see that, like everybody else, we are only here very briefly, but that brief moment we call a lifetime is also infinitely long if we can bring awareness to our moments, since there are infinite moments in any lifetime. In living in the present, we step out of clock time into a timeless present. Such experiences may show us that we are not by nature entirely bound by time.

We might, thus, also begin to taste impermanence in a new way, since nothing we focus our attention on endures for long. Each breath comes and goes, sensations in the body come and go, thoughts come and go, emotions come and go, ideas and opinions come and go, moments come and go, days and nights come and go. We may see that, similarly, seasons and years come and go, youth comes and goes, jobs and people come and go. Even mountains and rivers and species come and go. Nothing is fixed. Nothing is permanent, although things may appear that way to us. Everything is always moving, changing, becoming, dissolving, emerging, evolving, in a complex dance, the outer dance of the world not so different from the inner dance of our own mind. We might see that our children are also part of this dance . . . that, like us, they too are only brief visitors to this beautiful and strange world, and our time with them even briefer, its duration unknown.

Might not this realization strike us deeply and teach us something of great value? Might it not suggest how precious the time we do share together with our children is, and how to hold our essentially fleeting moments with them in awareness? Might it not influence how we hug and kiss our children, and say good-night to them, and watch them sleep, and wake them in the morning? Might such understanding not influence how hard a time we give them when, in seeking to find their own ways, they scrape up against our ideas and opinions, the limits of our patience, and our ego investments in being right and all-knowing, forgetting in those moments what we actually know that is far larger and more life-affirming?

Perhaps taking on parenting as a kind of meditation retreat, and doing the inner work of mindful parenting day by day and moment by moment in the same spirit of concentrated and sustained effort of attention and presence as on a retreat, might help us to realize the enormous power in seeing and remembering the larger context of wholeness, so that we are not lost in the surface waves of our own minds and our sometimes narrowly conceived and clung to lives. Perhaps we would hold our moments differently. Perhaps they would not slip by so unnoticed, so unused, so filled up by us with busyness or diversions. Perhaps we would appreciate more what is given to us, from our own body and life, to our relationships, to our children and our parents, and our children's children, to the world in which we get to live and which we pass on to those who will follow.

Perhaps we would care more, and care differently, and attend more, and attend differently, if we held in our own minds and hearts what we already deeply know, but usually forget, or haven't developed to the point where it can serve us as a way of being, a way of seeing, a way of truly living wakefully. Perhaps we would know how to stand in our own life, on our own feet, and feel the earth beneath us and the wind in our face and around our body, and know the place as here, and the time as now, and honor the mysterious wisdom that resides within all beings and within our children.

These glimpses are some of what one might see and realize through intensive practice on an extended mindfulness meditation retreat. Retreats are of great and abiding value when we can arrange our lives to go off from time to time to practice in this way. But there are also many times when it may be neither possible nor advisable to go off someplace else for an extended period, especially when juggling the responsibilities of parenting, family life, and work.

This is where the metaphor of seeing the whole experience of parenting as an extended meditation retreat may be useful. It is not that parenting is a retreat from the world, although to some extent a healthy family can buffer the stress of the outer world and create feelings of inner security and peace. It is, rather, that we are using the very circumstances of the world and of parenting, as best we can, and usually under difficult conditions, to help us cultivate mindfulness, look deeply into our lives, and let our doing come out of our being—not just from time to time, but concertedly, as a way of life.

The daily schedule of family life, of course, is much more complex and chaotic than on retreat, dictated as it frequently is to a large extent by the head teachers, who are our children. It will change as they change and grow, sometimes from day to day, sometimes moment by moment. But the practice is always the same: To be fully present, looking deeply, as best we can, and without judging or condemning events or our experience of them. Just presence, and appropriate action, moment by moment. It can be anchored by a daily period of formal practice at a convenient time, but the major commitment will of necessity be the cultivation of mindfulness in everyday life, responding to the call of parenting, allowing each day and each moment to provide the arena for a deepening of awareness.

In this way, waking up in the morning is waking-up meditation. Brushing your teeth is brushing-your-teeth meditation. Not getting to brush your teeth because the baby is crying is not-getting-to-brush-your-teeth-and-taking-care-of-the-baby-first meditation. And so on. Getting the children dressed, getting food on the table, getting them off to school, going to work, diapering, shopping, making arrangements, cleaning up, cooking, everything becomes part of our practice of mindfulness. Everything.

sacrifice

The Gift of the Magi
by O. Henry (W. S. Porter)

William Sydney Porter (1862-1910) was an alcoholic with no formal education who served five years in an Ohio prison for embezzlement and died penniless at the age of 47. But he spent the last decade of his life writing stories (under the pen name O. Henry) that made him one of America's most beloved writers. "The Gift of the Magi" is one of his classics.

One dollar and eighty-seven cents. That was all. And sixty cents of it was in pennies. Pennies saved one and two at a time by bulldozing the grocer and the vegetable man and the butcher until one's cheeks burned with the silent imputation of parsimony that such close dealing implied. Three times Della counted it. One dollar and eighty-seven cents. And the next day would be Christmas.

There was clearly nothing to do but flop down on the shabby little couch and howl. So Della did it. Which instigates the moral reflection that life is made up of sobs, sniffles, and smiles, with sniffles predominating.

While the mistress of the home is gradually subsiding from the first stage to the second, take a look at the home. A furnished flat at $8 per week. It did not exactly beggar description, but it certainly had that word on the lookout for the mendicancy squad.

In the vestibule below was a letter-box into which no letter would go, and an electric button from which no mortal finger could coax a ring. Also appertaining thereunto was a card bearing the name 'Mr James Dillingham Young'.

The 'Dillingham' had been flung to the breeze during a former period of prosperity when its possessor was being paid $30 per week. Now, when the income was shrunk to $20, though, they were thinking seriously of contracting to a modest and unassuming D. But whenever Mr James Dillingham Young came home and reached his flat above he was called 'Jim' and greatly hugged by Mrs James Dillingham Young, already introduced to you as Della. Which is all very good.

Della finished her cry and attended to her cheeks with the powder rag. She stood by the window and looked out dully at a gray cat walking a gray fence in a gray backyard. Tomorrow would be Christmas Day, and she had only $1.87 with which to buy Jim a present. She had been saving every penny she could for months, with this result. Twenty dollars a week doesn't go far. Expenses had been greater than she had calculated. They always are. Only $1.87 to buy a present for Jim. Her Jim. Many a happy hour she had spent planning for something nice for him. Something fine and rare and sterling—something just a little bit near to being worthy of the honor of being owned by Jim.

There was a pierglass between the windows of the room. Perhaps you have seen a pierglass in an $8 flat. A very thin and very agile person may, by observing his reflection in a rapid sequence of longitudinal strips, obtain a fairly accurate conception of his looks. Della, being slender, had mastered the art.

Suddenly she whirled from the window and stood before the glass. Her eyes were shining brilliantly, but her face had lost its color within twenty seconds. Rapidly she pulled down her hair and let it fall to its full length.

Now, there were two possessions of the James Dillingham Youngs in which they both took a mighty pride. One was Jim's gold watch that had been his father's and his grandfather's. The other was Della's hair. Had the queen of Sheba lived in the flat across the airshaft, Della would have let her hair hang out the window some day to dry just to depreciate Her Majesty's jewels and gifts. Had King Solomon been the janitor, with all his treasures piled up in the basement, Jim would have pulled out his watch every time he passed, just to see him pluck at his beard from envy.

So now Della's beautiful hair fell about her rippling and shining like a cascade of brown waters. It reached below her knee and made itself almost a garment for her. And then she did it up again nervously and quickly. Once she faltered for a minute and stood still while a tear or two splashed on the worn red carpet.

On went her old brown jacket; on went her old brown hat. With a whirl of skirts and with the brilliant sparkle still in her eyes, she fluttered out the door and down the stairs to the street.

Where she stopped the sign read: "Mme Sofronie. Hair Goods of All Kinds." One flight up Della ran, and collected herself, panting. Madame, large, too white, chilly, hardly looked the 'Sofronie'.

"Will you buy my hair?" asked Della.

"I buy hair," said Madame. "Take yer hat off and let's have a sight at the looks of it."

Down rippled the brown cascade.

"Twenty dollars," said Madame, lifting the mass with a practised hand.

"Give it to me quick," said Della.

Oh, and the next two hours tripped by on rosy wings. Forget the hashed metaphor. She was ransacking the stores for Jim's present.

She found it at last. It surely had been made for Jim and no one else. There was no other like it in any of the stores, and she had turned all of them inside out. It was a platinum fob chain simple and chaste in design, properly proclaiming its value by substance alone and not by meretricious ornamentation—as all good things should do. It was even worthy of The Watch. As soon as she saw it she knew that it must be Jim's. It was like him. Quietness and value—the description applied to both. Twenty-one dollars they took from her for it, and she hurried home with the 87 cents. With that chain on his watch Jim might be properly anxious about the time in any company. Grand as the watch was, he sometimes looked at it on the sly on account of the old leather strap that he used in place of a chain.

When Della reached home her intoxication gave way a little to prudence and reason. She got out her curling irons and lighted the gas and went to work repairing the ravages made by generosity added to love. Which is always a tremendous task, dear friends— a mammoth task.

Within forty minutes her head was covered with tiny, close-lying curls that made her look wonderfully like a truant schoolboy. She looked at her reflection in the mirror long, carefully, and critically.

"If Jim doesn't kill me," she said to herself, "before he takes a second look at me, he'll say I look like a Coney Island chorus girl. But what could I do—oh! What could I do with a dollar and eighty-seven cents?"

At 7 o'clock the coffee was made and the flying-pan was on the back of the stove hot and ready to cook the chops.

Jim was never late. Della doubled the fob chain in her hand and sat on the corner of the table near the door that he always entered. Then she heard his step on the stair away down on the first flight, and she turned white for just a moment. She had a habit for saying little silent prayers about the simplest everyday things, and now she whispered: "Please God, make him think I am still pretty."

The door opened and Jim stepped in and closed it. He looked thin and very serious. Poor fellow, he was only twenty-two—and to be burdened with a family! He needed a new overcoat and he was without gloves.

Jim stopped inside the door, as immovable as a setter at the scent of quail. His eyes were fixed upon Della, and there was an expression in them that she could not read, and it terrified her. It was not anger, nor surprise, nor disapproval, nor horror, nor any of the sentiments that she had been prepared for. He simply stared at her fixedly with that peculiar expression on his face.

Della wriggled off the table and went for him.

"Jim, darling," she cried, "don't look at me that way. I had my hair cut off and sold because I couldn't have lived through

Christmas without giving you a present. It'll grow out again—you won't mind, will you? I just had to do it. My hair grows awfully fast. Say 'Merry Christmas!' Jim, and let's be happy. You don't know what a nice—what a beautiful, nice gift I've got for you."

"You've cut off your hair?" asked Jim, laboriously, as if he had not arrived at that patent fact yet even after the hardest mental labor.

"Cut it off and sold it," said Della. "Don't you like me just as well, anyhow? I'm me without my hair, ain't I?"

Jim looked about the room curiously.

"You say your hair is gone?" he said, with an air almost of idiocy.

"You needn't look for it," said Della. "It's sold, I tell you—sold and gone, too. It's Christmas Eve, boy. Be good to me, for it went for you. Maybe the hairs of my head were numbered," she went on with sudden serious sweetness, "but nobody could ever count my love for you. Shall I put the chops on, Jim?"

Out of his trance Jim seemed quickly to wake. He enfolded his Della. For ten seconds let us regard with discreet scrutiny some inconsequential object in the other direction. Eight dollars a week or a million a year—what is the difference? A mathematician or a wit would give you the wrong answer. The magi brought valuable gifts, but that was not among them. This dark assertion will be illuminated later on.

Jim drew a package from his overcoat pocket and threw it upon the table.

"Don't make any mistake, Dell," he said, "about me. I don't think there's anything in the way of a haircut or a shave or a shampoo that could make me like my girl any less. But if you'll unwrap that package you may see why you had me going a while at first."

White fingers and nimble tore at the string and paper. And then an ecstatic scream of joy; and then, alas! a quick feminine change to hysterical tears and wails, necessitating the immediate employment of all the comforting powers of the lord of the flat.

For there lay The Combs—the set of combs, side and back, that Della had worshipped long in a Broadway window. Beautiful combs, pure tortoise shell, with jewelled rims—just the shade to wear in the beautiful vanished hair. They were expensive combs, she knew, and her heart had simply craved and yearned over them without the least hope of possession. And now, they were hers, but the tresses that should have adorned the coveted adornments were gone.

But she hugged them to her bosom, and at length she was able to look up with dim eyes and a smile and say: "My hair grows so fast, Jim!"

And them Della leaped up like a little singed cat and cried, "Oh, oh!"

Jim had not yet seen his beautiful present. She held it out to him eagerly upon her open palm. The dull precious metal seemed to flash with a reflection of her bright and ardent spirit.

"Isn't it a dandy, Jim? I hunted all over town to find it. You'll have to look at the time a hundred times a day now. Give me your watch. I want to see how it looks on it."

Instead of obeying, Jim tumbled down on the couch and put his hands under the back of his head and smiled.

"Dell," said he, "let's put our Christmas presents away and keep 'em awhile. They're too nice to use just at present. I sold the watch to get the money to buy your combs. And now suppose you put the chops on."

The magi, as you know, were wise men—wonderfully wise men—who brought gifts to the Babe in the manger. They invented the art of giving Christmas presents. Being wise, their gifts were no doubt wise ones, possibly bearing the privilege of exchange in case of duplication. And here I have lamely related to you the uneventful chronicle of two foolish children in a flat who most unwisely sacrificed for each other the greatest treasures of their house. But in a last word to the wise of these days let it be said that of all who give gifts these two were the wisest. O all who give and receive gifts, such as they are wisest. Everywhere they are wisest. They are the magi.

sexual desire

from

Passionate Marriage
by David Schnarch, Ph.D.

David Schnarch is an innovator in the fields of sex therapy, marriage therapy and family therapy. He believes that the middle and later years in a marriage can be the most promising time for a couple to build intimacy and experience sexual fulfillment.

F or most of Western civilization low sexual desire has been considered a goal rather than a problem. Since the early days of Christianity people's self-worth was measured by their ability to destroy their sexual desire with their mind. (Sex was not a sin if done without desire.) This attitude continued undiluted through the turn of this century, when the temperance movement held power and George Comstock, U.S. Postmaster General, declared war on sex. In fact, Kellogg's Corn Flakes and Graham Crackers were originally marketed as a cure for carnal striving and masturbation. Honest!

Society's view of sexual desire has reversed in the last three decades, but whether we've become more enlightened is debatable. Today's notion that "sex is a natural function" is a step forward from the moral degeneracy theory that previously prevailed. But we've gone beyond making it okay to want sex. Now, you're *supposed* to want it (unless you're excused for a medical or mental condition). Low sexual desire is almost always considered a problem. (I've found it often reflects good judgment: healthy people don't want sex when it's not worth wanting.)

When I was trained as a sex therapist, I was taught that low desire was a personal characteristic of people who were poor candidates for treatment. Two decades letter therapists see low desire as a treatable disorder—and a lucrative industry. But in their rush to be helpful, therapists have espoused views of sexual desire that create unrecognized problems.

Once it was socially sanctioned, the belief that sex is a natural function reinforced another widely held but erroneous idea that sex therapists dispute: that good sex just happens. Many couples assume good sex should happen naturally, especially if they love each other. It's true that sexual response is biologically programmed for all species but that doesn't mean human partners will necessarily enjoy the experience.

In my years as a sex therapist, I have found that the "naturalized" view of sex is not so liberating because it pressures people to have sexual desire and sexual response, and makes worrying about sexual performance seem inappropriate.

In the late 1970s the fact that some people had orgasms just fine but had little desire for sex upset the entire field of sex therapy. Problems in sexual desire violated basic assumptions about the "natural" way sex worked. But rather than change directions, sex therapists made sexual desire "natural" too, comparing it to the desire for food. Low sexual desire was thought of as "sexual anorexia," a kind of illness.

• • •

Viewing sexual desire as a "natural" hunger masks its complexity
and encourages people to see themselves as defective. One couple
I worked with is a good case in point. Carol and Warren were an
attractive couple in their mid-forties. They looked like the ideal
couple everyone else thought them to be. Their presenting
problem was Carol's lack of sexual desire: they had had no sex in
the last six months of their ten-year marriage. Before that, it had
been infrequent.

This was Carol's second marriage. She had two children with
Warren and she didn't want a divorce. In fact, I was the third therapist they had seen in their quest for a solution. "Sensate focus" sex
therapy and marital therapy had already failed.

Trying to joke about her fears of being too emotionally damaged to sustain a sexual relationship, Carol referred to herself as
"romantically challenged." Prior relationships with men had
broken up because she lost interest in sex once the relationship
developed. A similar pattern unfolded in each sexual encounter:
she would become aroused during foreplay and initially during
intercourse. But her desire would "vanish" during the middle of
sex. From that point on, she didn't want to be touched at all. She
would become passive and "tune out" and eventually Warren
would explode in anger.

"I know you may not be able to help me, Doc," Carol said in a
quavering voice. "I'm pretty twisted. First I want sex and then I
don't. I'm driving Warren crazy. It just makes no sense."

"I've never worked with someone whose sexual desire didn't

make perfect sense. Why do you think you have the pattern you describe?"

"My prior therapist thought it might have come from a bad childhood experience. I was close to my grandparents and often stayed with them when my parents were on the road. My father was a nationally prominent lawyer and my mom often traveled with him. Once when I was five, Grandpa took off his pajama bottoms and encouraged me to touch his penis when we were alone. I started to cry and Grandpa put his pants back on. Nothing really happened."

"Do *you* think that accounts for your lack of desire?"

"No, I don't. But my therapist said I was 'in denial.'"

"I'm more interested in what *you* think."

"When I was twenty I got married the first time. My husband was selfish, arrogant, and crude. He had a violent temper. He pushed and shook me. Maybe that's it."

"Did you have this pattern of 'start-stop' desire before these experiences with your first husband?"

"Yup."

Carol seemed alert and perceptive, yet her words lacked emotional charge. She rarely made eye contact with me; it seemed to make her uncomfortable. It would have been easy to label Carol a sexual abuse victim. But I sensed that Carol would accept *any* label I put on her. I didn't rule out sexual abuse as a contributing factor, but I've learned to look for more complex answers.

"Couldn't Carol's reactions be caused by abuse?" Warren sounded as though he'd be relieved if I were to say yes. Then

Carol's difficulty wouldn't have anything to do with *him*. He held dear the fact that she'd had this difficulty with other partners.

"It could, but that doesn't make it so. Many other things could be involved." Warren said he understood, but I sensed he wasn't thrilled. Except for making brief comments, he was happy to let Carol be the focus, with him as her support. He wanted her "to get as much out of the session as she could." But he also seemed afraid I might ask him more about himself. He was content for Carol to carry the feelings of inadequacy for both of them, which she was quite ready to do.

"What else should I know?"

"Well . . . I've never had an orgasm. Maybe that's why I don't want sex?" Carol sounded apologetic. Warren shifted uncomfortably in his chair. "I've never had an orgasm with anyone—even when I've tried by myself."

"When you're masturbating, how do you know when it's time to stop?" I asked.

Carol's brow wrinkled. She had never thought about it.

"When it's past the time something should happen. . . . When most people would reach orgasm."

"How many people have you watched masturbate to orgasm?"

Carol blushed and laughed. "No one! I just think I should have come by a certain point so I stop."

"How long do you give yourself?"

"Oh, about five minutes." The speed of Carol's response suggested her last attempt wasn't years ago. Warren seemed surprised.

"It sounds like you test yourself to see if you can 'measure up.'"

"Yup."

"Is that the way you generally live your life?"

"Why . . . yes! I never saw the similarity!" Carol was surprised—and not just by the way her sex mirrored her life. Her sexual pattern suggested that she *felt* inadequate. She had thought it meant she *was* inadequate.

"Tell me how this pattern fits who you've been."

Carol teared up. "Daddy" was hot-tempered, emotionally distant, and often critical of her. He belittled her efforts to win his praise while bragging about Carol's older sister. Carol's role in the family was "the stupid, cute one." Carol's mother was a chronically unhappy housewife with a country-club lifestyle. Like many children, Carol interpreted not receiving her parents' approval as a sign of her own unworthiness.

Carol craved acceptance. She had grown up trying to please people in order to feel lovable and worthwhile. In her own words, she was raised "to serve others." She often overspent her credit cards, buying presents for friends and relatives. Her lack of desire interfered with playing out this pattern with Warren: she couldn't ingratiate herself sexually.

"So what's wrong with me, Doc? Why don't I want sex?"

"What makes you think something's wrong with you?"

"I must be defective. Everyone wants sex."

"What makes you think *you* should want sex?"

"It's a natural thing. You're supposed to want it.

"Do you want sex more when you feel inadequate or defective?"

"No. It makes me want to avoid it. I don't want sex when I feel defective—but I wouldn't feel defective if I wanted it."

"From what you've told me, I doubt that. If *you* wanted sex, you'd probably think you were a horny, defective person. You're using your lack of sexual desire to prove what you already believe about yourself."

Warren nodded. He thought that was right on. But where Carol might have felt belittled she was now rather bemused. We were talking about her feelings of inadequacy, but she was feeling less inadequate.

"Do you want to have sex because you and Warren feel horny?"

"I get horny—but it doesn't last! . . . Wait! Now I'm confused! I thought the problem was that my horniness didn't last. But I want making love to *mean* something. I don't want it to be just horniness. Maybe I don't know what I want."

"That may be true. But it also makes perfect sense to me that you don't want sex. I haven't heard anything in your personal experience that would make you want it. I suspect if we put someone else into similar experiences, they might not want sex either."

"They wouldn't?"

Carol seemed amazed and relieved. Warren looked a little afraid, as though he thought I was giving her permission to never have sex again. He had thought that if Carol accepted the "fact" that there was really something wrong with her—that her past was causing her problem—she'd "work on herself" and resolve it. He never considered that therapy might help her accept herself as she was.

"Are you telling us Carol is so damaged by her past we should forget this?" For a moment I couldn't tell which answer Warren wanted.

"Not at all. I'm saying Carol's pattern makes sense—I'm just not certain about what sense it makes. One part already seems clear: Carol's assumption that she should want sex might not be warranted scientifically, but it's a true picture of who she is."

Warren seemed satisfied for the moment. I turned to Carol.

"You start with the common assumption you should want sex and conclude there's something wrong with you if you don't. You use that to pressure yourself, which partly kills your desire. But it's not true you don't want sex at all. You wanted it at the start of this relationship—and other relationships—and at the start of many encounters."

"That's right!"

"Then you might want to phrase your question differently. The question isn't 'Why doesn't Carol want sex?' It's 'Why does Carol want sex initially and then lose that wanting?' The problem is less global than you say it is. I guess you say it the way it seems."

"It seems pretty overwhelming! But why do I stop wanting sex?"

"We don't know *yet*. But I know it will make sense—*good* sense—when we figure this out. I've never seen a single person where it didn't. And that doesn't have to mean we'll discover you're screwed up!"

What Is Human Sexual Desire?

Human sexual desire is the most complex form of sexual motivation among all living things. It's a combination of genetic programming and variables of life experience, producing the utmost sophisticated nuance and variety of sex on the face of the planet.

After several sessions Carol began to appreciate how she, like most people, focused on only three characteristics of sexual desire:

- **Biological programming to reproduce our species.** All aspects of sexual desire have some bio-evolutionary basis. Even while our understanding of how hormones, smells ("pheromones"), and mating displays affect our brain chemistry remains incomplete, we assign this biological basis great importance; in fact, we overestimate the influence of biology on sexual desire. Biological factors act primarily on the primitive parts of our brain we share in common with other mammals and reptiles.
- **Relieving tensions.** This is commonly referred to as "horniness," "blue balls," or a "sexual itch."
- **Craving for sexual gratification.** This is like Sigmund Freud's notion that we are driven by an instinctual sexual energy (*libido* or sex drive) and organized around a "pleasure principle"—we seek pleasure and avoid pain.

If you believe sexual desire is only the result of a "natural" biological drive, you may expect to want sex all the time. Such beliefs shape our picture of sexual desire per se. For instance, consider how we ask each other, "Do you want sex?" The question is about wanting a particular type of *behavior* and *willingness to get started.* It has nothing to do with desire *for your partner* or desire that lasts throughout the encounter. The real question is, "Do you want *during* sex?" or, "Do you want *me*?" The whole notion of desire during sex isn't clear in many minds because it isn't something you think about if you assume sexual desire is primarily biological. Some people expect that you're not supposed to want *during* sex, you're suppose to be *satisfied* (if your partner is any good). And yet, particularly if you're dependent on a reflected sense of self, don't you want your partner craving and panting for you while you're together? Others see desire during sex as a tension buildup that's finally satisfied by climaxing. But, as pointed out above, this is one of the basest ways people understand sexual desire. We're just not used to thinking of sexual desire as something inherently interpersonal and deeply affected by what happens while couples have sex. The ways we approach sexual desire steer us away from the very thing we miss and seek.

Humorists James Thurber and E. B. White observed, "Understanding the principles of passion is like knowing how to drive a car; once mastered, all is smoothed out; no more does one experience the feelings of perilous adventure, the misgivings, the diverting little hesitancies, the wrong turns, the false starts, the glorious insecurity. All is smoothed out, and all, so to speak, is lost." Desire during sex restores the adventure and the passion. But as Thurber and White point out, it's not as simple as shifting gears—as our biological view of sexual desire makes us think, unfortunately.

Here are six often overlooked aspects of sexual desire that have everything to do with sexual potential and the waning of desire:

- **Sexual desire is part of our interpersonal communication system.** Since prehistoric times, when men and women first lived communally, humans have evolved the ability to sense each other. In modern parlance, this is known as "sexual vibes" or chemistry. Not only can we sense each other's sexual interest, but under some conditions we enjoy that feeling.

- **Sexual desire partly reflects our longing for pair-bonding.** Our need for "togetherness" surfaces in our hunger for the touch, warmth, smell, and taste of physical contact.

- **Sexual desire expresses an eagerness to exchange meanings with another person through sex.** Just as our ancestors developed language as one type of communication, sexual "languaging" has also evolved over time; it's how we know the message in a one-night stand is very different from exchanges between long-term monogamous partners. Sexual desire expresses our capacity for intimacy. We enjoy playing with I-thou experiences during courting and sex.

- **Sexual desire includes the intensity and depth of our involvement in sex while we're having it.** Our capacity for passion—healthy lust, sexual aggression, carnality, ardor, and enthusiasm—is part and parcel of our sexual desire. Many complaints about low desire actually refer to our (or our partner's) lack of passion. Passion goes beyond biologically-driven "urges." It comes in delicious flavors of craving, longing, fire, and fury reflecting emotional desire for your partner—affection, ardor, amorousness . . . love.

- **Sexual desire is eroticism in action.** Eroticism involves the *ways* we want to engage our partner—our preferred sexual behaviors and styles. It reveals the way sex is encoded in our mental world. Family and life experiences all leave their mark.

- **Sexual desire—like satisfaction—is partly determined by our culture.** Society shapes what arouses us and how we experience our own desire. Women's bare breasts are "sexy" in Western culture but merely pragmatic in African tribes. In past centuries, Japanese men found women's powdered necks and petite bound (crippled) feet alluring. On an island off the coast of Ireland, people rarely have sex, and when they do, they almost never remove their clothes. Imagine an Irish islander marrying a Polynesian islander whose native culture celebrates sex. Every society defines sexual satisfaction—and it becomes part of our normal neurosis.

Human sexual desire is complex. Although the most fundamental aspects of our sexuality are rooted in biology, hormones don't run our desire as much as we think. In fact, modern research suggests that some "bonding" hormones *follow* rather than precede sexual behavior. With such complexity, it is not surprising that the delicate dynamics of desire are easily disrupted.

Marcel Proust said there's nothing like sexual desire to keep your words from having anything to do with your thoughts. Or, in our cruder times, "A hard-on has no brains; a wet crotch has no conscience." But just because many people live that way doesn't make it true. The physiological connection exists; using it is optional.

Getting the thinking part of our brain (our neocortex) in charge of our sexual desire is a spectacular (and uniquely human) achievement.

Feelings and thoughts contribute to one's total level of stimulation. Desire is an important case in point: our *brain* is our largest sex organ. We've noted three ways in which the neocortex affects sexuality (and desire):

- The neocortex's ability to modulate sexual impulses means that understanding human sexual desire requires more than a purely "biological drive" model.
- Our ability to attribute a variety of meanings to sex increases our susceptibility to sexual dysfunctions and low sexual desire.
- Our mental world is a large part of our sexual potential, and the nature and nuance of our sexual desire play a big role.

Now let's consider other parts of the brain in relation to sexual desire so you can see the big picture. Basically the brain comprises three parts that have increasing evolutionary sophistication: the *reptilian* brain, the *mammalian* brain, and the *neocortex*. We share the most primitive part, the *reptilian brain,* with reptiles by virtue of our common evolutionary path (it's the back of the brain, which sits on top of your spinal column and controls basic functions such as breathing, digestion, and excretion). As humans evolved, the brain's large mid-section (*mammalian brain* or *cortex*) emerged. In later evolutionary steps the forehead enlarged to make space for the *neocortex,* the latest (and most "human") part of our brain. This three-part structure of the brain is why intimacy and sexual desire in humans are a breathtakingly complicated matter.

Human sexual desire has roots in all three parts of the brain. The part of the brain that is engaged determines the character of our desire. Realistically, we experience a mixture of all three levels, but it's still useful to distinguish between "neocortical," "mammalian," and "reptilian" desire. It's the difference between choosing your partner versus rutting or going into heat; creative sex versus preordained mating/breeding; and loving union versus natural selection. It's all a question of emphasis.

Hormones and horniness primarily involve mammalian and reptilian parts of your brain. We can see society's emphasis on mammalian/reptilian sexual desire in how the legal system views eroticism as something that is contagious. Legislators argue that society must restrict sexually explicit material to shield those who might become "inflamed" and lose control—human reptiles running amok. While some restrictions are necessary, the emphasis is misguided. Sometimes we *wish* the legal view were true. Wouldn't you love to be inflamed by your partner's passion? Don't you wish you could ignite him/her? It's just *not* that easy—that's what usually burns us up.

Differentiation determines how much (and what kinds of) intimacy we can handle—how much we can risk in love. Differentiation also permits the kind of desire most of us think we want: *"front-brain" neocortical desire.* It's what makes sex personal. We want to be *wanted* (chosen). Only a neocortex can do that. Your neocortex determines *whom* you have sex with (or don't), *how* you do it (or won't), *why* you're doing it (or not), and *what this means* to you—that is, if the neocortex is the part of your brain that's running the show. Unfortunately, that's often not the case.

Under most circumstances, you want your neocortex determining your behavior because it possesses the greatest adaptive sophistication and variability. When prehistoric mammals' lives were at stake, fast primitive responses served best. Unfortunately, threats to our identity and emotional security often trigger similar responses. When interpersonal pressure is high enough and we get anxious, survival reactions "hard-wired" into the reptilian and mammalian parts of your brain take control from your neocortex. Your anxiety increases your impulse to fight, submit, or run away. The more anxiety and pressure to adapt, the more this tends to occur. When this happens frequently we label it being "poorly adjusted."

Roughly speaking, the part of your brain that predominates determines the characteristics you display. When you're severely anxious, as though your life is at stake, you behave like a reptile. Reptiles and badly frightened people have two characteristics: they have no sense of humor, and they eat their young. Relationships aren't peaceful or stable. Although you're responsible for what you do at such times, the notion of "choosing" is erroneous because the part of your brain that chooses (your neocortex) is no longer in control. Lessons in "fighting fair" are usually forgotten because reptiles don't fight fair.

When you have your anxiety under better control, you stop

going for your partner's jugular vein. You act like mammals do: you're capable of mother-infant nurturance and pair-bonding (like geese who "imprint" on their partner)—but not intimacy or *choosing* someone and being *chosen*. Human sexual desire is only possible when your neocortex is running the show. The mammalian and reptilian parts of your brain follow the 1960s free-love anthem, "If you can't be with the one you love, love the one you're with!"

Differentiation is your ability to soothe your own anxieties and emotional immunity to infection from others' anxiety. This reduces the likelihood of anxiety-triggered regression in functioning, which limits your capacity for intimacy or wanting your partner. Differences in sexual desire in an emotionally committed relationship are a prime example of "pressure to conform" that generates anxiety. That's why spouses commonly act like reptiles when arguing about sex.

It takes lots of years to develop the necessary differentiation to keep your neocortex in charge. That's one reason why humans have the longest (and most sophisticated) postpubertal sexual development in the animal kingdom. Another reason: *neocortical sexual desire has to be developed.* Having your neocortex run your desires doesn't just mean controlling them. It also involves *creating* them: fantasizing and thinking up new things to do. So-called mindless submersion in eroticism actually takes thought and creativity—it is a "thinking person's sex."

You probably don't want lizard-level sex (or mammalian sex either). On the other hand, sometimes you might wish that your partner could be a "real animal" in bed. Having sex with a "sexual predator" can be fun if the "predator" is well-modulated; subtlety and variability go a long way. That's where differentiation and your neocortex come in.

For Carol, understanding the neocortical basis of desire had practical effects. She stopped expecting herself to want sex and became curious about her pattern of desire. Rather than seeing abuse as a compelling force from the past that explained everything, she began looking for other factors that could be involved. She no longer focused on the sexual feelings that were present at the beginning and then vanished. Instead she began watching for other feelings that showed up during sex that possibly interfered. She even went a step further: maybe the "interfering" feelings were really present all along? Maybe they were strong in the beginning but she was too turned on at first to notice?

All of these were possible. Each one might reflect a different emotional possibility. Carol didn't have a clear map, but at least she knew there were places to look. Before, her desire—or lack thereof—was just an immutable given. Now Carol and I could look for nuances together, though neither one of us was sure what we were looking for. I contributed my expertise on sex and marriage; Carol contributed her hunches and reactions, especially her reactions in bed. We started discussing what she and Warren did in great detail: who did what to whom and how each felt about it. Warren was uncomfortable with our "freeze-frame analysis," but it paid off.

In a general sense there was no surprise. Carol's problem boiled down to the inevitable truth: she approached sex the same way she lived her life. But how this pattern played out in bed had an elegance most scriptwriters would die for. Like at the end of a good murder mystery, you want to slap your forehead and say, "Of course!" What if a particular pattern of response emerged as Carol's relationships—and sexual encounters—evolved? What if the same pattern, developed over months or years, replicated itself in microcosm in any given sexual interaction?

Carol's issue wasn't learning to like sex. She already did. Carol entered sex with Warren—and relationships in general—with the thought, *"Who would really want me?"* That's when she was "interested in sex." Actually, her sense of inferiority mobilized her to start having sex—but it really wasn't a desire for sex: it was a desire for a reflected sense of self. That's why she initially "desired" sex at the beginning of each sexual encounter (and each relationship). Her partner's sexual desire for her relieved her anxiety and made her feel worthwhile and secure, temporarily banishing the nagging thoughts.

However, once solidly engaged in sex—or a relationship— Carol's fears of rejection quieted down, and so did her motivation to have sex. Her focus shifted to another core issue waiting in the wings: *feeling like she had to serve others in order to be loved.* In Carol's case—and many others I've seen—her quest for a reflected sense of self played havoc with her sexual desire. It got her into sex, and once satisfied, it also pulled her out. (This is, in part, why I said earlier that dependence on acceptance and validation from your partner has tremendous negative impact on sexual desire.) It illustrates how anxiety can "facilitate" sexual motivation in some circumstances, but it has nothing to do with desire for your partner, or for sex, either.

In the midst of this melange of factors affecting Carol during sex, the struggle of differentiation was occurring: Carol was developing a solid sense of herself. Anxiety initially propelled her into sex, and then her resentment and attempt not to sell out to her fears took over. Carol's mysterious but consistent loss of desire was her way of daring to say "No!" to her partner (in this case, Warren)—no to giving in order to get, no to exploitation and isolation, no to past abuse. What Carol thought of as her "problem" was really the healthy part of herself attempting to stand up and hold onto herself.

Carol didn't realize that her "problem" was really a developmental task everybody faces. She saw it only as damage from her past that needed to be repaired. She never suspected she was in the process of "resolving the past in the present." If this seems extremely complex, it is—that's what I've been trying to show you about sexual desire!

I asked Carol what she felt when she wanted someone to touch her. She couldn't have answered more clearly. She changed the topic to "Why would someone want to touch *me*?" She had difficulty hearing, let alone heeding, her own voice because she lived her life according to how she thought other people saw her. Warren, in contrast, acted as if he were the center of the entire world, demanding that Carol cater to his every whim. Carol was jealous and resentful of his selfishness.

"When Warren has an orgasm, he seems to go off into his own world!" she complained.

"Maybe that's an inner world you can't validate for yourself," I suggested. "If you are cut off from your memories and emotions and devalue your perceptions, where do you have inside *yourself* to go? You tune out from yourself. It's not someplace you want to be . . . yet."

Carol's issue was basic: developing an *internal* sense of self she could value, maintain, and live by. In the end, this developmental task proved to be her pathway to a lot more than just "good sex." But even the complex process just described didn't fully explain Carol's pattern of desire. Other issues were involved—and not all of them were hers.

Desire Always Has a Context

Sexual desire within marriage isn't reducible to two sets of the various aspects of sexual desire outlined earlier (one for each partner), or two sets of reptilian-mammalian-neocortex brain systems, or both partners' unresolved individual differentiation issues. There's more involved than each partner's thoughts, feelings, past histories, anticipations, replays of parental dynamics, or unconscious processes. That any single issue seems to "fit" isn't the point—it may indeed be involved. The point is that sexual desire in marriage involves all of these but is more than any of these parts.

Growing social consciousness highlights forces and factors surrounding and shaping marriages that transcend individual characteristics (for example, intergenerational family loyalties, gender roles, economics, sexism). But we have to expand our view further: we must consider individual and social factors *and* recognize the unique forces within the interaction itself. Try keeping neocortical desire alive while your partner is in full reptilian mode and you'll see what I mean. Think back to Carol's pattern of shifting desire: notice that *elapsed time* in her relationships and sexual encounters was a significant factor. *Duration* is a property of an interaction, not a personal characteristic. Sex in marriage forms a *system* that is more than the sum of its parts.

Marriage is a system the same way families, government, and corporations are self-adjusting, self-perpetuating systems. Some aspects of sexual desire are properties of "the system" of marriage. Couples allude to this reality when they speak of their relationship as if it were an independently existing entity (for example, "I think our relationship is in trouble").

Carol and Warren each had their own differentiation issues, some of which reflected their particular histories. Their childhoods had shaped who they became, which partner they selected, their patterns of sexual desire, and what surfaced when they hit gridlock. Like most of us, they tried to handle their marital problems in accordance with widely held beliefs. But this perspective doesn't consider the process of marriage itself: any move Carol made to differentiate had an immediate impact on Warren and "the relationship," which reverberated back through these component processes. (The fact that childhood issues heat up in the boiler room of marital conflict doesn't mean they "cause" the sexual difficulty.)

Think of marriage as similar to ecology. Every little part (species extinction, shrinking rain forests, oil spills, etc.) affects the operation of the earth as a whole, which in turn affects every little part. You and your spouse are complex entities made up of physiological subsystems (for example, endocrine, respiratory, excretory), as well as emotional/psychological ones (for example, unconscious processes, family of origin issues, and anxiety regulation and brain functioning as discussed above); in loving and living together you create a new and larger entity (marriage), which itself is part of larger entities (extended families, communities, societies), giving rise to still larger entities (nations, human evolution). Each higher level contains parts not found in the lower one; each higher level is more than the sum of its parts or the operation of its components.

Here's the point for sexual desire: the common tendency to reduce sexual/marital problems to any single underlying process (or a simple collection of processes) overlooks the complexity of marriage and human sexuality. Reviving sexual desire is not as simple as "resolving past hurts." Some aspects of sexual desire problems are inherent to the system of marriage and can't be fixed, rebuilt, or resolved; they are part of marriage's people-growing machine. In the latter half of this chapter I'll show you why low sexual desire is a normal developmental stage in the evolution of an emotionally fused couple.

In marriage, we create a new process beyond ourselves—and become an interacting part of that process. The ebb and flow of sexual desire within marriage is the end result. You have to deal with marriage on its real-life level of complexity. Can anyone track

all levels of human operation at the same time? No, but that's not
the problem. The problem is that we erroneously view each individual piece in ways that are actually contradictory to or isolated
from the others. We don't have to figure out how to put all the
levels together because they already *are*. Our task is to remain open
to seeing how the levels interact and shape the whole system.

The Person with the Least Desire
for Sex Always Controls It

If sex is supposed to be satisfying and anxiety-free once we are safely
ensconced in marriage, how come that's when many of us stop
wanting it? Part of the answer involves the *system* of sex in marriage.

Some processes are simple but powerful. Consider that it takes
only one partner's preoccupation with an actual or anticipated
sexual dysfunction to desynchronize both partners during sex.
Men with rapid ejaculation often take this a step further. They
condition their partner to be sexually inert and unenthusiastic.
It's done by verbal request or it's the wife's automatic response to
her husband's "shooting off" when she gets aroused. This is the
sexual version of the systemic reality that it takes two people to
make a marriage but either one can unilaterally create divorce.

There is a still bigger sexual conundrum that affects all relationships. It holds true in every bedroom (unless physical force is
involved): *the person with the least desire for sex always controls the
frequency of sexual contact between spouses.*

For example, early in their marriage Warren wanted sex more
often than Carol did. Although he made most of the initiations,

Carol actually determined when sex happened: she chose which offers she accepted. Warren acted as if *he* made sex happen (and didn't like the burden), but Carol was the one in control, whether she liked it or not. In fact, Carol controlled the content and style of their sexual contact as well: Warren felt he had to accept sex on her terms—since she might not want it at all. When Carol lost her desire during intercourse, for example, Warren felt he had to "hurry up" and reach orgasm.

When they came for treatment Carol was "the identified patient"—the one with "the problem" of low desire. But long before they visited me, Carol's identity in their relationship had been established as "the one with the sexual problem." Warren's role was "the sexually normal one"—and the resident sex expert. Together these rigidly assigned roles created several powerful processes:

1. Carol had actually been more sexually active and erotically inclined than Warren before they met. So while Warren was flaunting his superior sexual status, Carol had a different view of things, and her husband's inflated view didn't exactly inflame her with desire.

2. Warren tried to make Carol want sex. Warren needed Carol to respond to his advances because it gave him indirect validation and a positive reflected sense of self. As a bachelor he measured his desirability by how many women wanted him and how aroused they became. So Warren repeatedly tried to "cure" Carol to prove his desirability. When he was unsuccessful, he blamed her and told her she was inadequate instead of facing his own feelings of sexual failure. Warren's reaction is an excellent example of social programming (culture as a system). In response to the cultural belief that "a good

lover satisfies his partner," men try to establish their sexual adequacy by pleasing their partner the same way a boy (supposedly) becomes a man by "scoring." Unfortunately, women aren't pleased or interested when their partner is more eager to demonstrate prowess than to be with them. The men are then unable to explain their partner's sexual disinterest—until they think it's her gender training that's in the way—which blinds them to the truth about themselves.

3. Warren's attempts to make Carol want sex made her want it (and him) even less. Carol had less "status" than Warren regarding sexual ability, desire, and initiative. Furthermore, she couldn't "gain" status by increasing her desire because any success would accrue to Warren's competency. It would also validate that Warren had been right all along.

4. With little to gain and little to lose, Carol was relatively unmotivated to improve their sex. After all, she had already forfeited her sense of sexual competency. Warren was the one still afraid of looking inadequate, which fueled his desperate attempts to keep her interested in sex. When Warren berated her she became more passive—and resentful. Carol had greater control over their sex life by doing nothing and looking helpless.

5. Warren escalated by alternately becoming more indifferent to Carol or more insistent. His goal was to keep Carol from having an impact on him or their sex, but he just struggled and suffered more. (Differentiation gives you the option of *letting* people affect you.)

6. Warren's dependence on a reflected sense of self indirectly put

Carol in control of whether or not he felt adequate. As a consequence, she had the paradoxical experience of feeling simultaneously inadequate and powerful. When she was angry, she could "jerk his chain" by simply not responding. Even when she wasn't angry she found his "little boy" neediness unappealing. On the surface Carol accepted her position of inadequacy but secretly smoldered underneath.

Carol's behavior didn't always reflect withholding from Warren; it was often a matter of holding onto her *self.* However, that's not the way it felt to either of them. At his reptilian worst, Warren attacked Carol's adequacy with greater frequency, which made their marriage worse. We dealt with this in our sessions:

"You must think Carol is a masochist," I said to Warren.

"Why? Because she's married to me?"

All three of us burst into laughter at Warren's unexpected honesty.

"No. Because you act as if hurting Carol's feelings makes her more likely to have sex with you."

My comment wasn't lost on either of them.

"You two have created an elegant sexual gridlock: Warren, *your* efforts to increase Carol's sexual desire make you powerless. Your frequent invitations allow her to remain passive. She can have all the sex she wants, when she wants it—without ever initiating. Blaming Carol and disowning any responsibility don't help because you make her angry and give her total control. If her low sexual desire is totally of her own making, then you are totally dependent on what she does. Every so often, you can pressure Carol into having sex more frequently or staying in it longer, but you can never pressure her into *wanting* you. In fact, the more you demand sex the less she wants sex—or you."

Warren started to realize why he was so frustrated. The fact that it was partly his own making and partly the system of marriage at work frustrated him more. The fact that the person with the least desire (in this case, Carol) controls sex is part of marital systems. Having that person also control your sense of adequacy is optional. Warren digested this for a minute and nodded in begrudging agreement. I turned to Carol.

"At the same time, *you're* conditioning Warren to badger you. Aside from 'rewarding' him when he whines and cajoles, you're teaching him what really motivates you: you don't have sex with Warren simply out of desire. You do it when he gets you to feel sufficiently guilty or frustrated—or when you start to feel afraid he might not want you. You're training Warren in the chicken-pellet model: the chicken that gets a pellet of food when it pecks at a lever in its cage—not every time, but after a large number of pecks. Like any smart chicken Warren thinks he'd starve if he waited to peck (initiate) when he was hungry (horny/needy). Now he's just like that chicken pecking away while he still has food in his mouth. You've trained him to initiate more frequently than he wants to. He knows he has to get enough pecks (initiations) in before you feel guilty, frustrated, or insecure enough to have sex with him."

Warren didn't know if he should be offended by the analogy. Carol started to laugh uproariously. It was clear she was laughing at both of them. Warren chortled in spite of himself—it did describe the way he often felt. He took some pleasure in seeing that Carol was as trapped in her own way as he was in his. We laughed for several moments. Discussing such prickly issues as *withholding* and *controlling* could have gone a *lot* worse.

"Some of what's happening isn't personal or intentional, although it feels that way. You're both up against the realities of sex in marriage. That's why some aspects of this pattern don't change. For example, even when your relationship is wonderful, the partner with the least desire will still control sexual contact, although it will probably feel quite different to both of you. Some couples try to approach this dilemma by fighting over who's going to want sex—or the other person—the least. *Wanting* your partner more than he or she wants you means giving up a pivotal position of choice, unless you become more differentiated."

Carol chuckled at the thought of fighting over who wanted sex the least. It hit home differently for Warren. For the moment, he focused less on what he thought Carol was doing to him and more on how he was going to deal with his situation.

"What are you telling us to do?" Carol asked.

"Yeah," said Warren, "are you telling us we're doing something wrong?"

"I'm not telling you to do—or not do—anything. I'm just pointing out conundrums of sex in monogamous relationships. What you do with it is up to you. I think the solution usually involves holding onto yourself. You both seem to think the solution is getting your partner to accommodate. What you've got is sexual gridlock. Neither of you can take the pressure off yourself without taking on some issue you haven't resolved or giving your *self* up altogether."

Carol and Warren Move Forward

There was a lot more going on in this relationship than the possible aftermath of Carol's childhood abuse. At best, her traumatic experience was a piece in a much larger puzzle. In any case, it was easy for me to couch our discussions in ways relevant to someone who'd been abused, because resolving their current issues and Carol's past abuse involved similar trials of differentiation. It simply meant we had to approach this so that past and present issues "lined up" in overlapping ways. This isn't hard to do—that's how dynamics in marriage usually occur. We used their presenting problem: Carol had already begun the process of "resolving the past in the present" when she "lost" her desire in the middle of sex.

Carol needed to establish a stronger relationship with herself, to learn how to *not* give herself up to *anyone.* Once she approached sex (and therapy) with that goal in mind, she moved forward relatively quickly. From the outset she had shown interest in sex: some initial interest in their encounters was genuine. She was experimenting with masturbation. And she seemed eager to have her "disappearing" sexual desire stick around.

Carol, Warren, and I continued to meet for therapy and to

watch and discuss the process of their sexual relationship. Carol and I started focusing on masturbation as a useful tool. Warren was delighted because his exposure was minimal—he declined my offer to discuss masturbation in the same way. Little did he realize what was to come next.

We chose masturbation because it was something Carol was already doing. It was also a picture of her relationship with herself: what she did sexually was totally up to her. We *didn't* focus on masturbation because she was most likely to reach orgasm that way (although this is also true). In fact, we confronted *pushing* herself to orgasm as self-abuse and selling out to her fears—not good practices if Carol wanted to have "a good place to go inside her." If Carol believed she wasn't inadequate, there was no need to *try* to reach orgasm (not that she should avoid it if it happened). The point wasn't to go looking for an orgasm or focus on her sensations—it was to watch how she dealt with *herself.*

Masturbation became the place where Carol answered the question, "What do you think you're worth?" She struggled with herself in real time. Telling herself "You deserve it!" wasn't enough. She had to live it—giving to herself and receiving like she meant it. Was she worth enough not to cut her time short? Was she deserving enough to touch herself any way she wanted—and ways she'd never done? Was she a slave to her perceptions of other people's standards? Was she just rubbing her crotch and trying to measure up?

The sex and the impact on her development were electric. Carol started having orgasms—and a lot more. She felt better about herself. She felt less defective and enjoyed her sense of mastery. But it wasn't from having orgasms as much as how she got them. She took on self-worth issues *before* she had her orgasm.

It wasn't too surprising that Carol became more interested in sex with Warren. She was excited by her development. She was starting to come alive. She started staying present throughout their sexual encounters. That's when the entire system of their marriage started changing.

Did you take Warren's sexual desire for granted, as if only Carol's required explanation? That's the mistake therapists and couples make when they assume sexual desire is a given—a "natural function." Carol and Warren were surprised by what happened next, but I've seen it many times: Warren stopped wanting sex.

To understand this you have to keep in mind the multiple aspects of sex in marriage we discussed above. Warren was shifting strategies in response to a shift in their marriage, instigated by the changes in Carol. Now he tried the strategy of trying to be the partner who wanted sex the least. The rule "the partner with the least desire for sex controls it" always applies, even when spouses switch roles. We approached Warren's about-face in treatment on many levels. I'll point out two of them, one *systemic* and one *individual* (realizing the distinction is somewhat artificial).

Borrowed functioning—the systemic process that occurs through emotional fusion—can help us understand Warren's puzzling disinterest in Carol's rejuvenated sexuality. I had helped Carol move forward sexually by changing the meaning of her sexual progress. It now had to do with differentiation (her relationship with herself) rather than her relationship with Warren. Carol's progress didn't validate Warren's contention that she was defective—in fact, quite the opposite.

Carol wanted sex now, but not because she loved Warren more or because she realized he was a great lover: it was because she liked *herself* more than she ever had in the past. Her new attitude didn't do much to enhance Warren's reflected sense of self. (Warren and I discussed how it takes strength to watch your partner grow, but it didn't help. That wasn't really what he wanted.) Carol had done more than increase her sexual functioning. She had changed the world inside her head. In the process she took a big step in changing her marriage: borrowed functioning was coming to an end.

Borrowed functioning artificially inflates one partner's performance beyond the level he or she can maintain in the face of adversity. The inflated partner looks more differentiated than he or she really is. (This is *pseudo* differentiation versus *solid* differentiation.) The other partner's functioning is correspondingly reduced. This decrease in functioning is the basic difference between borrowed functioning and mutuality. Mutuality involves one partner sacrificing his or her own goals to facilitate those of the partner—but the sacrifice *enhances* both people's functioning.

Borrowed functioning is like an emotional transfusion that "fills up" the receiver but drains the donor. Its vampire quality may not be readily apparent because the donor is quite willing to donate—

at first. (Often he or she reports very pleasurable sex, security, and romance for a while.) But when the partners hit gridlock, the erotic aspect ends and both sides struggle for emotional survival. Often the donor feels sucked dry and his or her emotional functioning declines. This can go on for so long that it's mistaken for the donor's real level of ability.

When gridlock intensifies, the donor's functioning can plummet precipitously, especially if the partners decide to divorce. This is commonly described as "going through a rough time around the breakup of a relationship." During this time, the donor takes the breakup as a negative reflection upon him/her. The receiver takes the donor's difficulty functioning as vindication of personal culpability in the marital problems and "proof" of deserving somebody "better." The receiver's reflected sense of self is inflated by the donor faltering, and the donor's functioning is further diminished by the receiver's apparent lack of distress. The donor looks terrible and the receiver "does great"—unless differentiation takes place. Once the emotional fusion is lessened, both partners return to their unilateral level of functioning (solid differentiation). The donor improves, the receiver "gets worse"—unless he or she finds another relationship on which to "feed."

Without borrowed functioning, Warren "fell apart" as Carol "got on her feet." Without Carol "underneath" him to lean on, Warren started to go downhill. "Helping" Carol from his one-up position had helped Warren sustain a comfortable self-image. When Carol started helping herself, Warren lost his equilibrium in the relationship, and in his head. He didn't like Carol controlling his sense of adequacy, but he liked having responsibility for it even less. His anxiety was going up and his ability to reduce it through his marriage was going down. His neocortex was losing out to the parts of his brain programmed to take over in life-threatening situations. Warren was becoming a frightened reptile.

As Carol became more interested in sex, Warren said he didn't want her at all. Partly he was poking her where she had previously been vulnerable. But there was something to what he said: Warren didn't *want* to want her. This wasn't just about not wanting what he could have or being intimidated by Carol's sexuality. Let me explain by looking at his background. As you read about Warren, keep in mind the two basic "rules" about differentiation mentioned earlier:

- We come out of our family of origin at about the highest level of differentiation our parents achieved.
- We pick partners at the same level of differentiation as ourselves.

As a young boy Warren grew up with his erratic alcoholic mother after his father died. Warren ran the house as soon as he was able—and tried to keep Mom sober. She could be a fun drunk but got spitting rageful in an instant. She was frequently depressed for days. Warren was embarrassed to be seen with her in public—and afraid to leave her at home. In fact, Warren was nervous, insecure, and "all alone" most of his life—at the same time he was emotionally fused to his mother. There was never enough stability at home to start differentiating from her.

Warren tried to stop wanting his mother to change. *If I don't care, I can't be disappointed* became his childhood mental litany. Warren tried to suppress the part of him that *wanted*—wanted her to stop drinking, wanted to feel secure with her, and wanted to respect her. He never succeeded. Warren suffered every time his mother stumbled or her speech slurred, and it affected how he treated Carol from the outset.

Warren found little "faults" in Carol. He insisted that she didn't do enough to please him. Actually Carol was *too good* for Warren's comfort. Warren thought he'd feel safe with Carol, but the opposite occurred: he felt endangered by his very love for her. His fears of losing her grew the more he enjoyed being with her. He feared she would manipulate him with his desire for her . . . or withhold herself from him . . . or worse—she'd die.

Warren didn't *want* to want Carol because it made him vulnerable in a way he had never learned to tolerate. Finding "flaws" was Warren's attempt to "reassure" himself that Carol *didn't* love him and prove she wasn't so special and could be replaced. Warren probed for things Carol wouldn't do, which immediately became the subject of his next diatribe. His outbursts led Carol to back away from him and intimidated her to a level he could deal with. He felt destructive and selfish, but he wasn't about to let her get close.

Sometimes Warren encouraged Carol to talk him *out* of his fears of wanting her. He wouldn't let her alone until she tried—and things really went crazy when she did:

"I don't trust you."

"Why don't you trust me?"

"I don't know. I just don't."

"What can I do to make you trust me?"

"Nothing."

"Well, then, what's the use of my even trying?"

"See, you don't really care! I knew I couldn't trust you!!"

Warren was trying to reject her so he would have nothing to lose. And at the same time, he was trying to engulf her so she couldn't control him and he couldn't lose her.

Carol tried harder to please Warren, but the more she tried the worse things got. The more she pleased him, the more he wanted her. The more he wanted her, the more vulnerable he felt. The more vulnerable he felt, the more he had to find fault with her. The more he complained, the harder Carol tried (at least for a while). They were caught on the merry-go-round of marital paradox. To understand the power driving this kind of pattern, you have to keep in mind the complex interplay of two people's unresolved issues as well as the larger context of their relationship system. I'm describing a systemic conundrum, a mind-boggler arising from the essence of human relationships—not simply individual craziness.

Throughout their relationship it looked like Warren wanted more sex than Carol. What he really wanted was a "transfusion" of borrowed functioning. That changed when we reached a particular point in treatment: when Carol no longer occupied a one-down position in the marriage, Warren became "disinterested." He could have sex, but not with the same borrowed functioning and reflected sense of self. And without the benefits of borrowed functioning Warren was "overextended." He was exposed to his lurking fears of *wanting* in ways he couldn't soothe on his own. He had to pull back.

The Politics of Sexual Desire

Lots of things are set into motion when partners start to differentiate, including their unresolved childhood issues. Specifics are as diverse as people's experiences growing up. However, many adults adopt a strategy every child knows: *not wanting to want* is an attempt to protect against the pain of wanting, longing, caring, and depending—and not getting. Parents like Warren's mother control their family with the threat of self-abuse. It was as if she put a gun to her head and said to Warren, "Give me what I want or I'll kill myself!" (You don't have to be a "horrible" parent to do something like this. People who refuse to have medical checkups and those with serious illness who are "negligent" taking medication are using the same strategy.)

Once you appreciate what that's like as a child, fighting with your partner makes more sense. It's easier than wanting him or her. Besides, fighting *makes* it easier not to want your partner. Like Warren, we'd often rather fight than *want*. The politics of *wanting* are truly powerful—and volatile. Low differentiation requires a rather tricky balance: it's only safe to want your partner as much as your partner wants you. On the other hand, it's only safe to *not* want your partner when your partner wants you. If your partner stops wanting you while you don't want him or her, you might end up divorced.

We can't delay *wanting* until we know our wants will be fulfilled. Marriage and life offer no such guarantees. Wanting, as an adult, takes strength. The "too much" in "wanting/loving/caring too much" is code for "more than I can self-soothe and maintain my sense of self." Differentiation (your ability to calm your anxiety and soothe your own heart) makes *wanting* tolerable, though still not safe.

People who don't *want to want* are unable to tolerate the vulnerability involved in choosing their partner. One fateful session I asked Warren and Carol the question that usually brings this issue to light: *"Who chose whom when you were deciding to get together?"*

Carol realized that it was she who had chosen Warren. And Warren married her because he never had to choose. Realizing she had never been chosen—not by Warren, her first husband, or her parents—profoundly affected her. Carol was back in her crucible once again.

Spouses' interlocking crucibles are an inherent part of the *system* that is marriage. Carol wanted Warren to want her—to choose her deep down in his soul. But this meant Carol had to face the possibility that he might not pick her now if he had a choice. If she couldn't live through that gamble, she would never be wanted the way she desired.

There was another level of gridlock: the only way Warren had a choice was if he *didn't* need Carol. But that challenged Carol's bottom line: she wanted to be wanted *but she needed to be needed.* Warren needed her as long as he couldn't take care of himself—at those low times he had no choice. Carol had the impulse to "help" Warren with his unresolved issues—to make herself indispensable as she had in the past. (This is the role Carol had assumed in their prior days of borrowed functioning.) But then she would never be certain Warren *wanted* her. As long as she pandered to her need to be needed, she would never know if she was wanted for herself.

Carol's crucible fit snugly with Warren's struggles. (Remember, that's the essence of gridlock.) He had much the same issues of wanting to be wanted but needing to be needed. And there was the twist that the only way Carol could be wanted was if he exposed himself to the vulnerability of wanting and choosing. They both benefited when Carol let Warren struggle with himself. In the process Carol had to struggle with herself, too. If Warren went through his crucible and came out wanting her, *then* she would know he had truly chosen her.

The Strength to Want

Sexual desire shares three commonalities with intimacy in marriage: *borrowed functioning* often masquerades as either one; dependence on *other-validation* causes problems with both; and we mistakenly think *indifference* is the culprit when sex or conversation stops. *Not wanting to want* contradicts the "indifference hypothesis" because it expresses *importance,* not indifference. Paradoxically, emotional fusion is the foundation of *not wanting to want.*

One property of marital systems is the *vulnerability of increasing importance of one's partner:* your partner's increasing importance over time naturally increases your vulnerability, which in turn fosters sexual boredom and low desire. Two fears bring this about:

- **Fear of losing your partner's acceptance.** No one wants to be rejected by a valued and needed partner. When your partner's acceptance means more to you than your own integrity, you only reveal your eroticism in ways that will receive acceptance. Your spouse becomes "too important" for sexual experimentation. You can't create sexual novelty or expand your repertoire for fear of disapproval. The resulting boredom contributes to low desire.

  It's a lot easier to introduce sexual novelty and undisclosed aspects of your eroticism in a one-night stand or an affair than in your marriage. It's a greater challenge to your sense of self when you're with your spouse. That's why sexual boredom (and affairs) are so prevalent. We demand stability in marriage—and when we get it, we complain that things are always the same. This is not quite the benefit we anticipate when we yearn for being important to each other.

- **Fear of losing your partner altogether.** The longer and better your relationship with your partner, the more you stand to lose if you want something important your partner doesn't want—or if he or she dies. When your partner's importance exceeds your differentiation (your ability to self-soothe), your partner becomes too important to *want*. The end result is *not wanting to want*. It's a matter of time and personal development. Warren and Carol are a poignant example. The problem wasn't that they became dependent on each other. It's that poorly differentiated people can neither tolerate nor maintain true *inter*dependence. The realistic dependencies, contingencies, and vulnerabilities of long-term emotionally committed relationships frightened both of them.

I've seen lots of people try to dodge this issue of *wanting*. There are those who say, "I'm dying to really want somebody again! I just keep picking the wrong partner!" But they pick the wrong partner because they don't want to want a *person*. Wanting someone gives that individual unique importance and leverage in your life. Wanting a *person* involves spending time with him or her, which diminishes the credibility of repeated "bad picks." This complaint about picking the wrong person reflects the cravings of an unresolved emotional fusion.

Others have no illusions about wanting their partner: they simply make sure they don't. It never gets to the level of *not wanting to want*. They don't *want*—period. They don't have much capacity for wanting, and they like it fine that way. Their partner is always replaceable. But don't confuse lack of significance with lack of connection. There's still lots of emotional fusion in these couples as well. Borrowed functioning is central to their relationships; it's just harder to see.

Are you among those who might dare to *want* your partner? Then you have additional reason to remember what we discussed about intimacy, because it applies to desire, too: *if you want to keep desire (and intimacy) alive in your marriage, your continued differentiation must keep pace with your partner's increasing importance. When your partner becomes more important to you than your relationship with yourself, you have four choices:*

- Withdraw emotionally.
- Engulf your partner.
- Allow your partner to engulf you.
- Raise your level of differentiation.

The first three options attempt to avoid wanting your partner or to reduce the vulnerability of wanting rather than increase your capacity for it. Differentiation makes the difference between love deepening and saying, "I love you but I'm not *in love* with you anymore." In this code, "being in love" involves *wanting,* "loving" simply means caring for and good wishes.

Give it some thought and you'll see society holds paradoxical expectations of marriage: we think it creates passion *and* sexual boredom. The irony is, it actually works that way! Some sexual boredom in marriage is inevitable (given the way differentiation moves forward). *Long-term* sexual boredom, however, is not. Resolving sexual boredom depends on your willingness to tolerate pain for growth (another facet of differentiation).

Sex often improves on vacation for more reasons than reduced interruptions and pressures. When removed from things that define one's persona, the sense of being unknown in one's environment significantly disinhibits displays of eroticism. You *can* capitalize on novelty of the situation to compensate for inability to innovate in your sexual relationship. But you'll have horrendous hotel bills—or only have hot sex when you travel. The inability to "really get it on" at home reflects a need for greater differentiation rather than a change of scenery.

Low sexual desire can't be cured with provocative lingerie or sex toys (if such items increase your interest, that's fine). Low sexual desire is no fun, but it does have a purpose. It's part of marriage's intricate people-growing machine: it invites you to stretch yourself and your relationship. Whether you accept the invitation to change from within—or just "dress up"—is your choice.

friendship

Love
by Grace Paley

Grace Paley is best known for her short stories, which often depict the complex lives of city dwellers. In this story, an older husband and wife discover a context that helps define their love's meaning.

F irst I wrote this poem:

Walking up the slate path of the college park
under the nearly full moon the brown oak leaves
*   are red as maples*
and I have been looking at the young people
they speak and embrace one another
because of them I thought I would descend
into remembering love so I let myself down
*   hand over hand*
until my feet touched the earth of the gardens
of Vesey Street

I told my husband, I've just written a poem about love.

What a good idea, he said.

Then he told me about Sally Johnson on Lake Winnipesaukee, who was twelve and a half when he was fourteen. Then he told me about Rosemarie Johanson on Lake Sunapee. Then he told me about Jane Marston in Concord High, and then he told me about Mary Smythe of Radcliffe when he was a poet at Harvard. Then he told me about two famous poets, one fair and one dark, both now dead, when he was a secret poet working at an acceptable trade in an office without windows. When at last he came to my time—that is, the past fifteen years or so—he told me about Dotty Wasserman.

Hold on, I said. What do you mean, Dotty Wasserman? She's a character in a book. She's not even a person.

O.K., he said. Then why Vesey Street? What's that?

Well, it's nothing special. I used to be in love with a guy who was a shrub buyer. Vesey Street was the downtown garden center of the city when the city still had wonderful centers of commerce. I used to walk the kids there when they were little carriage babies half asleep, maybe take the ferry to Hoboken. Years later I'd bike down there Sundays, ride round and round. I even saw him about three times.

No kidding, said my husband. How come I don't know the guy?

Ugh, the stupidity of the beloved. It's you, I said. Anyway, what's this baloney about you and Dotty Wasserman?

Nothing much. She was this crazy kid who hung around the bars. But she didn't drink. Really it was for the men, you know. Neither did I—drink too much, I mean. I was just hoping to get laid once in a while or maybe meet someone and fall madly in love.

He is that romantic. Sometimes I wonder if loving me in this homey life in middle age with two sets of bedroom slippers, one a skin of sandal for summer and the other pair lined with cozy sheepskin—it must be a disappointing experience for him.

He made a polite bridge over my conjectures. He said, She was also this funny mother in the park, years later, when we were all doing that municipal politics and I was married to Josephine. Dotty and I were both delegates to that famous Kansas City National Meeting of Town Meetings. NMTM. Remember? Some woman.

No, I said, that's not true. She was made up, just plain invented in the late fifties.

Oh, he said, then it was after that. I must have met her afterward.

He is stubborn, so I dropped the subject and went to get the groceries. Our shrinking family requires more coffee, more eggs, more cheese, less butter, less meat, less orange juice, more grapefruit.

Walking along the street, encountering no neighbor, I hummed a little up-and-down tune and continued jostling time with the help of my nice reconnoitering brain. Here I was, experiencing the old earth of Vesey Street, breathing in and out with more attention to the process than is usual in the late morning—all because of love, probably. How interesting the way it glides to solid invented figures from true remembered wraiths. By God, I thought, the lover is real. The heart of the lover continues; it has been propagandized from birth.

I passed our local bookstore, which was doing well, with *The*

Joy of All Sex underpinning its prosperity. The owner gave me, a dependable customer of poorly advertised books, an affectionate smile. He was a great success. (He didn't know that three years later his rent would be tripled, he would become a sad failure, and the landlord, feeling himself brilliant, an outwitting entrepreneur, a star in the microeconomic heavens, would be the famous success.)

From half a block away I could see the kale in the grocer's bin, crumbles of ice shining the dark leaves. In interior counterview I imagined my husband's north-country fields, the late-autumn frost in the curly green. I began to mumble a new poem:

> *In the grocer's bin, the green kale shines*
> *in the north country it stands*
> > *sweet with frost*
> *dark and curly in a garden of tan hay*
> *and light white snow . . .*

Light white . . . I said that a couple of questioning times. Suddenly my outside eyes saw a fine-looking woman named Margaret, who hadn't spoken to me in two years. We'd had many years of political agreement before some matters relating to the Soviet Union separated us. In the angry months during which we were both right in many ways, she took away with her to her political position and daily friendship my own best friend, Louise—my lifelong park, P.T.A., and antiwar-movement sister, Louise.

In a hazy litter of love and leafy green vegetables I saw Margaret's good face, and before I remembered our serious difference, I smiled.

At the same moment, she knew me and smiled. So foolish is the true lover when responded to that I took her hand as we passed, bent to it, pressed it to my cheek, and touched it with my lips.

I described all this to my husband at suppertime. Well of course, he said. Don't you know? The smile was for Margaret but really you do miss Louise a lot and the kiss was for Louise. We both said, Ah! Then we talked over the way the SALT treaty looked more like a floor than a ceiling, read a poem written by one of his daughters, looked at a TV show telling the destruction of the European textile industry, and then made love.

In the morning he said, You're some lover, you know. He said, You really are. You remind me a lot of Dotty Wasserman.

infidelity

from

Sexual Detours
by Dr. Holly Hein

Psychotherapist Holly Hein suggests that infidelity is more a betrayal of ourself than of our partner. Here she writes about the aftermath of an affair, suggesting that such times can create opportunities for new beginnings.

The aftermath of an affair begins with the discovery of betrayal. And while the affair and the marriage may continue for a good deal of time, discovery of an infidelity is the beginning of the end. I have witnessed the lives of many of my patients over the arc of their entire dramas. Life in the wake of an affair brings pain, anguish, and heartbreak, but it punctuates the end of illusion. As tumultuous as it is for both partners, the aftermath is the start of a new beginning. Whether it heralds the end of the affair, the end of the marriage, or the end of both, it can usher in an age of enlightenment, restoration, and rebirth.

The Discovery of an Affair

Whether it takes weeks, months, or years, eventually an affair will be exposed. Some affairs get exposed inadvertently in unusual ways. We read about them, we are told about them, we get diseases from them, we even walk in on them. The most common method of discovery is confession, with confrontation close behind. After the truth is revealed, the laborious job of rebuilding, either with the partner in marriage, the partner in the affair, or alone, needs to be undertaken. In the wake of an affair, we have the opportunity to uncover our personal cover stories and learn to communicate our inner truths. I'm not saying this is easy. There is no painless exit on the route of a sexual detour.

What happens in the wake of an affair basically reflects a desire to preserve the marriage or dissolve it. The beauty of the aftermath is that there are simple answers to complicated situations. One of the two paths available before the affair started is open to both partners again, only this time much more obviously. There is a fork in the road. The third alternative, which was presented by the introduction of a secret lover, is no longer an option. The marriage is now back where it started when it had only two alternatives:

improve the marriage

or

end the marriage

If an affair is not revealed consciously, it will be detected unconsciously. An affair, like a cough, cannot be kept hidden. What keeps us from knowing the truth, no matter how fail-safe the secret, is our own denial. What makes us unconsciously reveal betrayal, no matter how cunning the deceit, is this same denial. Unknowingly, no matter how cleverly we think our tracks have been covered, we leave traces. We may believe that the truth about an affair is buried in cement, but this is simply our own denial, which is an illusion lighter than air that can float away to reveal an affair with one breath of reality.

In whatever method the affair is exposed, the discovery of betrayal is experienced as a catastrophe. An affair sits us down on an emotional roller coaster where we rocket from denial to obsession, rage to sorrow, self-pity to blame. Worst nightmares come true. Long-held assumptions are in doubt. Trust is shattered, and the age of innocence is formally declared dead. The last shred of romantic love is drowned by the flood of knowledge about an affair. We often think of love as a safe harbor, but in truth we are as vulnerable as if in a storm. If we have been betrayed and love has proved to be an unsafe passage, surviving the journey may be the greatest challenge of our lives. *Regardless of which side of an affair we find ourselves on, in the aftermath, we are faced with nothing less than restoration of the self.*

The burden of truth does not rest lightly upon the shoulders of any marriage. The marital union, if not shattered by the disclosure of an affair, undergoes severe stress. For both partners, there is an abundance of fear, terror, and emotional (sometimes even physical) trauma. Inner worlds collide upon the discovery of an affair because problems we sought to deny are brought out into the open. Feelings long buried and forced underground come boiling up. Emotions not only surface, but come armed in defense.

In the aftermath, we face each other with problems not just magnified, but multiplied. Each partner in the marital union experiences disclosure of an affair differently. A woman well out of the marriage, and a man devastated by loss, have distinctly different experiences about the same event. The resolution of two individual sets of emotions (and perhaps two separate goals) is what we deal with in the aftermath. The likelihood is that whether the truth fountains out in a confession or is squeezed like blood out of a turnip, the effect is devastating.

For those of us on the other end of betrayal, discovery uncovers more than just infidelity. There are painful insights and hard choices. Nancy tearfully recognized the quandary she was in. I had helped her to see Ned for who he was. But who Ned was meant he could continue to have affairs. For the moment, at least until I helped her regain some strength and clearer emotional vision, she desperately wanted to remain married but knew that staying married to the same person who had been sexually unfaithful meant she would be betrayed again. As it turned out, because trust was dead, it was impossible to continue the marriage. Her feelings of hopelessness were eased by her recognition of the part she played in the affair. And while I helped her to see that a marital relationship is something for which two people are responsible and that nothing happens in a vacuum, especially not an affair, it also revealed how incapable her partner was of change. It gave her strength to feel she had control over the future.

The Role of Jealousy in Discovery

Jealousy plays a major role in the discovery of an affair. It is an archaic emotion and represents a fear of loss. It has its roots in the separation anxiety of infancy. Like a passionate lover, a baby's attachment to his mother is a possessive one. A baby acts as if his mother's body belongs to him. This is so complete and natural that the baby never wants his mother to leave. In fact, in anticipation of this dreaded eventuality, the baby develops an eagle eye. If the mother so much as thinks of leaving, the baby becomes piteously inconsolable. There is no better picture of misery and despair than a baby's face. Unless, of course, it is the face of the bereft, betrayed adult lover.

Many romantics mistakenly define jealousy as proof of love. Jealousy, like territorial response, is a protective instinct and has more to do with that primal fear than with love. The fear of loss is felt as if there cannot be any replacement. The loss of a love object is a threatening feeling fraught with abandonment and rejection. The fear of loss, nourished by low self-esteem, can be easily provoked. Jealousy may inflate a suspected relationship out of proportion. Or not. Good self-esteem guards against jealous overreactions.

Jealousy is like the smoke alarm of the unconscious and usually indicates the presence of something lurking below the surface. If nothing else, jealousy suggests that there is some distance in the marriage. Usually, where there is smoke, there is fire. Smoke may come from ourselves or from the reality of an affair. A suspicious partner may feel pangs of jealousy because he or she has good reason. Usually, most husbands or wives allay reasonable fears. Unreasonable jealousy is something even a faithful marriage partner cannot cure. Conversely, a guilty partner can rarely set at ease an astute partner's suspicion. Guilt often provokes defensiveness and, in turn, increases suspicion.

The Role of Denial

Suspicions about an affair are sometimes hidden under a blanket of denial. Often, even when reality points a finger, we don't want to see. Our senses, however, continue to operate in defiance of our denial. Pieces of evidence are filed away in the unconscious until further notice. Discrepancies, which in retrospect may pop out like a bumper crop of freckles, go unrecognized. Later, we put together pieces of this unconscious puzzle and are surprised we didn't know all along. But, of course, we did.

Our senses are never fooled. Blatant evidence may stare us in the face and we still refuse to notice. Later, we discover what we knew already. We may overhear bits of conversation where the same name comes up one too many times for comfort. Our mate may have a drastic new look. Weight alters dramatically. Workouts at the gym increase. New hairstyles. Sexier new clothes. Even the scent of lotion or perfume may linger. We may sense an emotional difference. Distance and tension stalk a sexual detour like shadows. In these ways, we know without asking, all along.

Gerty had been married for more than twenty years when she came to see me. She painted a portrait of a marriage pockmarked by obvious deceit. The excuses her husband had given her for one kind of behavior or another had as many holes as Swiss cheese. Gerty didn't see that. Instead she saw a curtain that had been drawn over a truth too painful to bear. She hoped, as many of us do, that whatever it was would blow over. Of course, it never does. Most of us are afraid to directly confront the question of a spouse having an affair. Suspicions are hard to live with, but they often are easier to tolerate than the truth. To ask or not to ask. To tell or not to tell haunts sexual detours.

The Opportunity to Take Action

The discovery of an affair ushers in real action. It removes us from the comfortable place of ennui where we don't have to do anything. Discovery of an affair makes something happen. Suddenly, we can no longer deny the truth. An emotional imperative exists to take stock of ourselves for a marriage to redefine itself, or for an affair to become part of a new reality. Uncovering a secret betrayal forces both marriage partners to consider the options, to take a stand, to make a decision. Issues are forced. Change has broken free from the entangling web of an affair and is once again on the march.

What I tell patients who have suffered betrayal, especially the ones on the brink of despair, is that the real hope of resolution lies in the aftermath. I remind them that the only way out of the pain is through resolution. Either with or without the partner, hope lies ahead. With honesty, the future becomes real. The illusory world we have constructed about ourselves or our marriage evaporates like white-hot steam when the lid is lifted off an affair, but the truth is not easy to bear. For ourselves, for our marriage, even for an affair, honesty can feel like a terrible curse. We know too much. Sometimes we may feel unable to bear the burden. There is too much to process, too much to alter. The mountain of truth may seem insurmountable, simply too hard a climb.

Even more daunting than the burden of truth is the reward that honesty holds forth: intimacy. For those of us who have fled in fear from this threat, it is difficult to suddenly embrace it. Both partners in a marriage where infidelity has occurred have colluded to some degree in legitimizing distance. For Jennifer, the aftermath of betrayal forced her to accept some truths about herself that she would rather have avoided. Her husband, Bob, had taken to staying at work later and later, until some nights he didn't come home at all. Jennifer had accepted his explanations more easily than even Bob would have liked. The truth was that Jennifer didn't mind being alone. She enjoyed the perks of Bob's dedication to his career. She found interaction more difficult than being alone. When Bob was home, more often than not Jennifer was involved in a solitary pursuit. She needed emotional distance more than Bob. It was by no means easy for Jennifer, this business of honesty, of facing inner truths. We are all so adept at running away.

How to Avoid Transference and Regain Intimacy

Under the influence of transference, we run away from the role we have cast upon our partner. The person from whom we run and hide may not be our wife but the grandfather of responsibility wagging his finger at us. We frequently try to outrun the demands of our own adulthood by fleeing from what the partner in our marriage represents. We have no clear picture of who a husband or wife indeed really is unless we penetrate the veil of transference by developing intimacy with our inner selves.

With the discovery of an affair, we can no longer hide from our marriage partner. We are free to leave, but we can no longer hide. When secrets are no longer present, distance disappears. After disclosure of an affair, feelings perilously close to intimacy can exist. Strange as it may seem, *in the aftermath of an affair, marital partners often have a more intimate relationship than they did before.*

An affair suffers from its own baptism by fire once the secret is revealed. Once the cocoon has been punctured and some air is let in, metamorphosis must occur. Something has to change. Change is necessary in order for an affair to transform into a real relationship. An affair must develop the ability to live in truth, breathe reality, and fulfill needs. For a relationship steeped in fantasy and overt lies, the demands of truth can be overwhelming. Marriage, on the other hand, must improve to survive.

Two Methods of Revealing the Truth

When we are suspicious and want to know the truth, instead of creating a forum for discussion, we often set traps and seek to ensnare the enemy. We do this, of course, not because we really want the truth but because, above all, we want to be right. I chide my patients about this universal condition. When we are suspicious, in order to prove our suspicions correct, instead of asking, we assault. This is not the best way to go about dealing with the question of an affair. This question, whether coming from the side of confrontation or confession, should be approached with as much preparation as possible.

Confrontation

The thought of confrontation usually makes our blood run cold. Questions about an affair are ones we are afraid to ask out loud because we dread the answer. This fear buys us exactly what we need: time. Time to think. If we are going to ask, it is imperative that we think first. Confrontation about an affair needs to be carefully thought out. Any negotiation demands rehearsal and preparation in order to achieve emotional control and our emotional comfort zone. We must sift through inner chaos to find a uniquely personal goal for our marriage. This is not to say that we need time to scamper back to hide in some fantasy or wishful thinking, but time to discern a reasonable outcome and path for the future of our marriage.

I tell my patients who want to confront husbands or wives about their suspicions to take enough time to prepare themselves for all the possibilities of what the truth may reveal. Before blurting out questions and levying accusations, they need time to envision all the possible scenarios. They need to go through it in their heads, and with me, before it comes out of their mouths. They need time to figure out what is realistic for them. To figure out what is unacceptable or acceptable. To know how to go about negotiating the future. Then, and only then, after enough soul searching, do I tell them to go ahead. Ask.

Asking for the truth about an affair can be like pouring kerosene on a fire. Often, the one suspected of being on a sexual detour resorts to a defensive, indignant, angry offense. The truth may be denied to the bitter end. The besieged partner may act as if heinous and outrageous accusations have been made.

In another scenario, when confrontation is met by the admission that the accusation is true, the same detonation can occur. In the ensuing explosion, sane human beings are wiped out and only furious animals remain. Like mad dogs we go at each other, shredding what is already torn asunder. Pain, rage, and fear exist in both marital partners, for different reasons and in varying degrees. What seems most important is to gnash each other to bits.

Ask me no questions and I'll tell you no lies. We shouldn't ask if we can't accept the answer. When we ask about infidelity, we must be prepared to deal with infidelity. There is a crucial difference between being able and willing to handle what the truth reveals and simply fishing for an answer to allay the anxiety and dread knotted in the belly of the question. Revelations will be shocking. Hurtful. Painful. Maybe even shameful and humiliating. Problems that have been put on hold will be brought out into the open. Answers will demand action, whether it includes forgiveness and restoration or acceptance and separation. Bear in mind that asking will not bring an affair to an end. It will reveal the problems that need to be dealt with.

Confrontation can be an excuse to shift the blame onto an affair. Affairs can get blamed when, in reality, the marriage is over for another reason. Lorraine badgered her husband, Dennis, who was my patient, with her accusations. She was angry, critical, and suspicious. She went from one accusation to the next, obsessed with her rights. After a particularly heavy round of artillery fire, where she demanded to know whether he was having an affair, Dennis told her the truth. He felt confused and anxious about their marriage. He had sought out his old girlfriend, seeking solace. He couldn't remember if they had sex once or twice. Lorraine went berserk. She was not prepared to understand or offer second chances. She jumped at the chance to righteously end the marriage. The truth is that the affair provided Lorraine with an excuse to end the marriage. Dennis had sought my help precisely because he feared she was going to leave him. And she did.

Rita and Derek presented a totally different picture. They came to me because Rita suspected that something was going on and she wanted to give their marriage the best chance to survive. Rita felt sympathetic to Derek's distress. He seemed miserable, and his angst was a physical presence that seemed to eat away at him. Sex was tense, the distance between them palpable. Something was going on. Rita was very clear about what she wanted. She wanted to know what was wrong, and no matter what was going on, she wanted to hold onto her marriage. When she confronted Derek, it was in my presence in an empathic manner and with a calm and organized plan she had forged out of an exhaustive inner struggle with her own emotions. Derek confessed to an affair, but Rita was prepared to ask him to stay in marital therapy with her. As it turned out, he did, and in doing so they gave their marriage the best chance to survive. With or without professional help, this is possible. Forgiveness and empathy are not unique to a therapist's office and are found within ourselves.

In the wake of an affair, the storm of emotions makes it difficult to hold onto what we really want. Many marriages are thrown away simply because we don't know how to overcome the challenges presented by infidelity. More marriages are destroyed by the response to betrayal than by the affair itself. Trust can be rebuilt. Wounds do heal. We cannot undo the reality of a sexual detour, but we can shape our future. When faced with the reality of confronting an affair, what we strive for should be grounded in the bedrock of an inner truth as well as an external reality.

How to Confront

Plan when to confront the issue of an affair. Choose the time and place carefully. Asking the question nonchalantly on the way out the door, or just as our mate is dozing off to sleep, is guaranteed not to bring about an answer, but a catastrophe.

Ask calmly.

Listen empathetically, thoughtfully, patiently.

Be prepared to experience disbelief, shock, humiliation, rage, self-pity, and blame.

Allow yourself to feel pain, sadness, and loss, as well as grief.

Rehearse. Practice the scenario as if it were a drama. It will be.

Do not expect anything to be resolved as yet.

Do not use alcohol or drugs.

Do not use threats.

Do not employ punitive, angry, or damaging words or deeds.

Do not be a judge or a jury.

Do not wield the sword of righteousness.

Do not take any negative action.

Do not act on your feelings of anger.

Confession

Truth is a strange beast. As slippery as an eel for many. A chimera
to some. Often, especially to those of us who choose a sexual detour,
truth can be elusive. Truth with the trappings of illusion and the
firmament of denial attached may feel more acceptable. Before we
unload a confession upon a partner, it is incumbent upon us first
and foremost to discover an unadorned inner truth about ourselves. Unless we are able to see ourselves and accept responsibility
for our actions, confession will only complicate our lives.

Confession is by far the most common way for the truth about
an affair to surface. With confession, secrecy is brought to a close.
Bear in mind that telling may not bring about an easy end to
entanglements, especially if an affair is still in progress. Confession
will not cure the problems that helped pave the road to a sexual
detour. What confession will do is provide an opportunity to
wrestle with real issues and deal with problems in ourselves and in
our marriage. Revealing an affair, especially one over and done
with, will change the nature of the marriage relationship. However
lightly an indiscretion is undertaken, it will be felt more heavily by
the betrayed marital partner. Ideally, a confession will reflect a
desire to save the marriage and be made in order to bring about
that specific goal.

Diana came to me as the result of her husband Harvey's confession about his affair. Harvey had finally decided to tell Diana the

truth. Harvey had spent most of their married life involved in affairs, and Diana had spent it hiding from the truth. He was still involved in the affair when Diana came to see me. I was pessimistic about the marriage because she couldn't convince Harvey to come with her. Harvey didn't know if he wanted a divorce or not. He wasn't particularly interested in therapy. He was tired of subterfuge and was really feeling quite sorry for himself. When he told Diana of his affair, he exploded at her reaction. He was resentful of Diana's pain, unwilling to face the consequence of his actions, and reluctant to undertake the hard work of rebuilding a marriage.

I helped Diana understand that he wanted her to fix it. His confession was a bid for Diana to do the work of the marriage for him. Make life easier for him. He wanted someone to alleviate his doubts, fill his emptiness. In short, to be the self he was unable to become.

It didn't take long for me to help Diana face the question she had been avoiding most of her married life. Diana thanked him for sharing and left the marriage. She couldn't make his life work for him. Luckily for Diana, childless, it was easy to leave. For others with more complications and unable to leave, living with Harvey would have been like being slowly sawed in half.

Christy was lucky to have come for help before it was too late. She had allowed herself to be abused not only physically but emotionally as well. When her husband, Kevin, decided to tell her about his affair, what he called a confession turned into an accusation. Kevin couldn't begin to fathom that he had cast Christy into a complicated mother role. Moreover, a mother toward whom he felt great resentment. Like a child, he had run from Christy's (his mother's) control, yet blamed Christy (his mother) for everything in his discontented life. He threw out a hundred and fifty excuses for his behavior. Most of them landed on Christy's broad shoulders, until excuse one hundred fifty-one. That was when Kevin made the unfortunate mistake of using the "you drove me to it" ploy. His assaultive stance dropped the nickel for Christy. Kevin's issues were siphoning off her self-esteem, blame by blame. The answer was clear to me and, fortunately, to Christy as well. Her decision to leave restored a sense of the self that had been eroded.

After nearly twenty years of marriage, Henry and Justine came to see me. For some inexplicable reason, Henry told Justine about an affair that had ended five years earlier. He confessed to an affair that occurred during a turbulent period in their lives. He and a coworker had been lovers. He had been in a midlife crisis, his future at work was clouded, and the affair served as a crutch. The affair ended when his crisis resolved. Henry even went so far as to describe the details to Justine.

It was at this point that Justine and Henry came to see me. Justine was distraught and confused. The confession had no point. Justine couldn't get over it, couldn't get under it. There was nothing that would assuage her hurt, restore her belief system, or put Humpty-Dumpty back together again. Justine confided that she rues the day she asked, recognizing that she was asking for reassurance, not truth. Henry curses himself. Not for the affair. For telling. For wanting absolution. This couple did not need my help beyond a few sessions of commiseration and helpful hints. Time and their own long-established empathic union would do the rest.

Goal of Confession

We need to search for truth before we confess, both in the interest of preserving a marriage or ending one. Endings need to be undertaken with as clear a view as beginnings. In order to do this, we must turn our attention, sometimes uncomfortably so, to an inner self we have long avoided and see what truths are reflected in the cover story of an affair. What were we *really* looking for? What truths have we discovered? What truth is being reflected by a wish to confess? In the final analysis, what we confess to should reflect what we want, for we certainly will get more of it than we bargained for.

There is no reason to believe that denial, which has played such a prominent role in the architecture of the sexual detour, will dissipate with the wish to confess. When a decision to tell the truth is reached, we must assume that denial continues to grease our psychological operations. It is imperative to take a second look at where denial may camouflage the real reasons for wishing to disclose an affair. A wish to confess an affair may be due to guilt, or a need to seek forgiveness and gain approval, or a need to end subterfuge—or it may simply be a way of getting rid of a burden. But to what end? We must assess the practicality and purpose of confession. Sometimes the most positive action we can take in the wake of an affair is to shoulder what is past alone.

Confession works best when an affair is over. It's plain and simple. The most constructive reason for confessing is to reinvest in the marriage in a committed, restorative way. When we confess to an affair, the burden is upon us to make an effort toward emotional repair of the damage that betrayal has inflicted. The degree of this effort should not depend on how much we want to continue the marriage. This burden falls upon the marital escape artist, and it is not always successfully undertaken. The perilous job of dealing with the fallout is shouldered by the one least able to do so. It's hazardous to assume that revealing an affair is not going to require attending to our partner's needs, no matter what course we want the marriage to take.

Confessing to a sexual detour should include compassion, because presumably a person about whom we care or cared in the past has been hurt. It is our responsibility to display sensitivity and tenderness. To be kind. Being kind does not mean we capitulate to demands or suffer abuse. It simply means being a friend. Being kind does not mean we have to pay with our lives or be responsible for another person's life. We do not have to give up ourselves in order to care for another's pain. Very simply, we should take responsibility for our actions, without displacing it onto blame, or causing unnecessary wounds. Do not make a confession without displaying empathy or offering some solace.

For those coming off the path of a sexual detour, confession may be a relief. Often a sexual detour is experienced as if the affair were a hole we tripped into and needed a hand out of. *Embroiled* is a word often used. The truth is that sometimes sex still just happens. And sometimes one thing does lead to another. And before we know it, we're in deeper than we want to be or intended to be. When this is the case, and when the marital partner is forgiving, confession can be a light in the window, leading the way home.

How to Confess

It is imperative to have a specific goal. We should not confess in order to relieve tension, or because we expect our mate to offer a solution. We should not confess in order to displace the responsibility of having to make a decision and force our spouse to make one for us.

If the goal is to save the marriage, that objective must be stated first, foremost, and repeatedly. The marital partner needs to be aware of our love and intentions. Problems can be addressed later. Not while confessing.

If our goal is to end the marriage, or we are not sure where the marriage is headed, we must be kind and patient. Confession in this instance can be used as a springboard for a recovery. Over time, the future of the marital relationship can be addressed as we decide our priorities.

Keep the truth simple. Speak calmly. After saying what needs to be said, be available to empathetically hear a response. Empathy means stepping outside of ourselves and walking in someone else's shoes. Above all, recognize that:

> Confessing to an affair is not blaming the other person.
> Confessing to an affair is not telling the other person
>   what is wrong with him or her.

Plan when to confess an affair after you've come up with a good reason why you should confess. Choose an appropriate place, where you will be able to speak uninterruptedly, without pressure of time or hindrance of emotional availability.

Recognize the legitimacy of your spouse's injured feelings.

Empathize with your spouse's pain, fear, and sorrow.

Display tolerance of his or her reaction.

Listen patiently.

Help your spouse understand what happened.

Behave like a friend.

Accept responsibility for your actions and choices.

Ask for forgiveness for the pain inflicted.

Do not use alcohol or drugs.

Do not talk about your lover.

Do not under any conditions become defensive or accusatory.

Do not reveal sexual details.

Do not criticize your spouse.

Do not blame your spouse.

Do not lie.

Do not frighten or threaten your spouse.

Do not defend or justify your actions.

After you have revealed your affair, remain focused on your spouse's feelings and reactions. This is no longer about you but about his or her reaction to what you have said. Remember, it was your affair, your spouse's betrayal.

In the aftermath of a confession or confrontation, we can be certain of one thing: *Something will happen.* The end of secrecy brings options to the table. It may mean that the affair will end and the marriage will survive. It may reveal the end of the marriage, or it is entirely possible that both the marriage and the affair will end. Whatever the result, in the aftermath we have the opportunity to become familiar with the key players in our lives. We can finally come face to face with not only the marital partner from whom we desire to escape, but ourselves. Finally and irrevocably, it's about who we really are, what we really want, and why.

forgiveness

The Anniversary
by Louis Auchincloss

Novelist Louis Auchincloss, author of more than fifty books, is among our most astute observers of contemporary American life—in particular, the mores and manners of the upper middle class. This story is about infidelity.

To me the county of Westchester is the most beautiful of all the counties of the state of New York. I know how many voices would be raised in protest at such a view, playing up the dramatic wilderness of the Catskills and the Adirondacks, or the lovely green stretches of Lake Erie's coastline, but I prefer the more civilized, the delicately ordered and bordered, residential estates of Westchester, with its rolling acres of modestly wooded hills and pleasant verdant valleys. Of course, I realize that much of the countryside has been preserved from the multitudes of the great metropolis to our south by rigid zoning, and perhaps it ill becomes a man of the cloth to over-relish his immunity from a too promiscuous herding of the human flock, but if I start to count my immunities in this globe of starvation and terror, where will I end?

How many Episcopalian clergymen, for example, in all our nation, enjoy the comfort of so large and luxurious a rectory as mine—a near mansion, almost—or the aesthetic delight of the most beautiful of Ralph Adams Cram's Gothic churches, or the social amenities of so welcoming and hospitable an affluent parish? I can say in my defense that I have served my Lord in much humbler surroundings, and that my call to the South Bedford Church came in no way from my instigation, and that, as my wife points out, the rich have souls as well as the poor. But it is still true that I am enjoying the material advantages of my present post rather more fully than a minister should. Oh, yes, I must face that. And I must also face the more insidious danger of a smug satisfaction at my own courage in facing it. Let this journal be my conscience!

All of which is the start of the weekly entry dated September 10, 1961. Does it give me, as is the great purpose of the journal, an idea for tomorrow's sermon? I think not. My considerable (could I call it great?) reputation as a preacher would not long survive a tendency to wax too personal. Episcopalians stem, after all, from the Church of England, and we Anglo-Saxons distrust—with good reason, I impenitently think—the sloppiness of personal revelation. I never need worry too much about sermon topics. I can always use an old one—I am a magpie at keeping things—and there are even those who think my earliest ones were my best. Ah, why is that, why is that? So I can pause here and look out the window over my green lawn and the still leafy woods and the tops of the distant blue hills just visible in an opening I had cut, and enjoy being alive at fifty-six and in the best of health and knowing that tomorrow I shall face a full church and an approving congregation. And that some of the latter may even have forsaken the golf course to bring their worldly houseguests to hear the golden words of the renowned Canon Truesdale!

There, dear Lord, have I sufficiently exposed my vanity?

But He *knows* all that. Just as He knows that I am not really thinking of my sermon. He knows, as He must always know, my innermost fears and doubts. Even when I doubt *Him!* For I have those moments, yes, alas, more and more of them! Didn't He himself? Didn't He voice despair on the cross? My mind is seething with the problem of how to deal with the dinner party that the parish is giving for me and Lally next Saturday night to celebrate our twenty-fifth wedding anniversary.

We shall be toasted by many of the leaders of the community, and I will be expected to respond. How could it be otherwise? And every man and woman in that chamber will be thinking, if I have the presumption to speak of two and a half decades of marital bliss, how I account to myself, in the deep recesses of my tumbled thoughts, for the gap in my orated number of five dark years— from our ninth anniversary to our fourteenth—when Lally was not with me. Not with me! When Lally had eloped, *bolted, run off with,* Eustace Brokaw, abandoning me and our small son and daughter for a life of flesh and sin!

I look at the words I have written and feel the tingling glow of resentment and wrath as if the intervening years had evaporated, and I had never forgiven or forgot. Good God, is it all still there, inside me? Is there no way to wash out the wickedness of abiding hate? Even when I love the wonderful woman who has made my life so good a thing for the last eleven years?

And does it make it worse if I have never shown, by so much as a chewed lip or darkened brow, that the ashes of my old humiliation are still smoldering? That I have convinced my family, friends, parishioners, and even my too sympathizing and vengeful old mother, that I harbor no grudge, that the past has been washed clean off my doorstep where, indeed, the welcome mat was never removed? Was there a subtle hypocrisy in my not having taken a single legal step to establish a separation, let alone a divorce? Or did people say that if I so easily took back the prodigal wife when she so unexpectedly and unrepentantly reappeared to resume quietly her old duties as a spouse and mother, that I couldn't have been *that* much stricken by her desertion? That, after all, I must be a pretty cold fish? Or, worse, that I took her back because I sorely needed her strong support as a minister's consort, which the subsequent dramatic rise of my fortunes as a preacher and clergyman has demonstrated?

And I suppose I must face another aspect of this whole sorry business of my continued agitation and dismay. Has the amount of control that I must have had to exert over my nature in the past eleven years to maintain my attitude of serene beatitude actually nurtured my stifled anger and outrage? I was recently much struck in rereading my favorite of James's novels, *The Golden Bowl,* by the passage where Maggie, the wronged wife, pictures her repressed rage of jealousy as "a wild eastern caravan, looming into view with crude colours in the sun, fierce pipes in the air, high spears against the sky, all a thrill, a natural joy to mingle with, but turning off short before it reached her and plunging into other defiles."

The sudden exultation that James's metaphor excited in me may well be evidence of the violence I have done to myself.

Which may give me at last an idea for my sermon: the importance of one who has suffered a wrong not only to forgive it, but to forgive it articulately, rather than simply behaving as if no wrong had been inflicted. "Father, forgive them; they know not what they do." But supposing they know very well what they do? Should this not be stated, made clear? And should they not—ah, here's the rub; I knew it *had* to be coming—at the same time be given the opportunity to defend, or at least to explain, what they had done and why they had done it? Did I not play a role in the swerve of Lally's heart—or even soul—from myself to Eustace Brokaw? Face it, Titus! If you dare to call yourself a minister of the gospel!

Very well. I'll write it out.

When we were married I was thirty and Lally only twenty-one. After four years in a Boston church, I accepted a call from a small parish on Mount Desert Island in Maine, not in a fashionable quarter of that very fashionable resort, but in a village in the south-western area, whose church, however, was amply attended in the warm months by members of the summer colony of nearby North-east and Seal Harbors who preferred our devout and simple service to the dressier ceremonies of the larger Episcopalian temples.

I had been attracted to the position because of the opportunity it offered me to do some serious writing. In the long dark winters when my work was light, when the summer crowd and their multitudinous suppliers and hangers-on had disappeared and the shops had closed, I could take long walks on the rocky shoreline and gaze at the gray sea and the screeching gulls and contemplate the chapter in process of my exegesis of the Gospel of Saint Luke and the Acts of the Apostles, both the work of one hand and that of the man I liked to think of as the first great novelist of the Western world. An historical novelist, I hastily add; a clergyman can hardly imply that he made anything up. Lally was busy, I assumed, with our housework and the total care of two small children. It was bliss—for me. I actually believed that in those five Maine years I had attained the perfect fusion of my churchly duties, my domestic obligations and my worldly ambitions. For I had worldly ambitions—oh, yes, I did. I had no idea of remaining forever in that obscure northern clime. My writing and my talent as a preacher were to bring me to the notice of the great world. Ambition was to be forgiven if it was dedicated to God.

Unhappily, as events were to bring out, our life did not offer the same outlets or satisfactions to Lally. She found the winters cold and lonely, and the occasional company of the "natives," as the summer people called the permanent residents of the isle, dull and gossipy. She was always gracious to them, however, and she never complained to me about the strictures of her life, but I should have taken note that her silences—she had always been on the quiet side—were increasing. And that when I sometimes talked to her about my book in the evenings she wasn't always listening.

And then came the summer when Mrs. Brokaw, a stylish matron from Northeast Harbor, took to attending my Sunday service, and on one fatal occasion brought her son Eustace, not a young man religiously inclined but who could occasionally, particularly when in financial straits, be brought to heel by his despotic mama. Mrs. Brokaw always waited for me on the steps of the church after a service to comment, in her rather florid sincerity, on my sermon, and on this particular day, when my discourse had been on the parable of the laborers in the vineyard, and why they had received the same wage for differing hours of work, God's love being indivisible, our discussion had lasted for some little time. I never cared to interrupt her, even when others were waiting, as I hoped to induce her to contribute substantially, if not in whole, to a much needed new roof on our little church. It was during this discussion, while Mrs. Brokaw was protesting the unfairness to the longer employed laborers, that her handsome and worthless son, glorious in white flannels and a red blazer, was carrying on a flirty chat with my wife. I had thought Lally was despising him. Evidently she was not.

From then on Eustace attended his mother regularly on her Sunday-morning appearances at our church. Lally and I were invited twice to dinner parties at the Brokaws' great shingle mansion in Northeast Harbor, invitations that I accepted eagerly in anticipation of our hostess's future beneficence. I was too much concerned with cultivating Mrs. Brokaw to more than casually note my wife's silent but still noticeable acceptance of her son's vulgar amiability. I even tried to turn the matter into a joke, likening, on our way home from the Brokaws one evening, the three of us to the trio in *Tess of the D'Urbervilles*: Eustace as Alec, Lally as Tess, and myself as Angel Clare.

"Angel Clare," repeated Lally, who so far had not said a word. "It sounds like a dessert." And she offered no further comment.

Came the day when she went off with him. Without a word or a note to me or a parting kiss for the children. Without even most of her clothes or any of her few little jewels.

Brokaw had taken her to Italy, where they lived for a year in Sicily before he abandoned her. She then went to Rome, where she worked in a travel agency, never once communicating with me, for four inexplicable years. Do I understand her, even to this day? Mama Brokaw, in an awesome fit of apology, virtually rebuilt my little church, and used her considerable influence in ecclesiastical circles to get me reappointed to a modest parish in Long Island, far from the scene of my shameful treatment by her son. There I toiled to rebuild my shattered career with some degree of success. My book was published and enjoyed a gratifying sale and even more gratifying reviews; my preaching brought me invitations to speak at other parishes, but, as our bishop once confided in me, my peculiar matrimonial status was a distinct bar to the advancement that I might otherwise have expected.

Which I must admit was one reason that I gave careful consideration to the offer made in a letter from Lally that arrived out of the blue one morning. She had returned to New York for her father's funeral and was ready, she wrote, to stay, if I was willing to take her back. Her explanation of the past was of the briefest.

"You have always taken comfort in literary comparisons, so I offer you this one. Hamlet feared the devil might be preying on his weakness and his melancholy, 'as he is very potent with such spirits.'

All I can say is that summer in Maine I was both weak and melancholy. I was attracted to a worthless man whom I knew to be worthless, and I went off with him in a kind of suicide. Four years of a chaste life have convinced me that nothing like that will happen to me again. But I shall quite understand if you cannot believe that."

I answered her letter, committing myself only to an interview, and a day later she appeared in my study in the parish house.

She had certainly not been punished physically by her sin. My anguished heart took in the bitter fact that she was even lovelier. There were some streaks of premature gray in her blond hair, but they conveyed a sense of greater depth of character, a sense confirmed by the sad serenity of her opaline eyes and a couple of extra lines below her cheekbones. She had said I was prone to literary comparisons, and I half-irritably asked myself if she was going to put *me* in the wrong, as the returning and unapologizing Helen of Troy does to Menelaus in John Erskine's famous tale. How else could his novel have been written? How else could mine?

She seated herself before my desk, apparently at her ease. She even placed her handbag on it and then settled back in her chair.

"Well, Titus, you have read my proposition. I am ready to resume my place as a minister's wife and a mother. I should not expect any exuberant welcome. Our relationship could be as formal or informal as you wish to make it. But I would promise to honor and obey you. Love, where both you and the children are concerned, would have to be earned by all of us. I understand that the situation would not be an easy one. All I can say is that I would do my best to make it work."

If it were going to be a game between us, a contest, that is, of apparent magnanimities, I still held a high trump. "You would be resuming a place I never felt you had vacated," I pointed out. "When I pledged you my troth, it was for my lifetime."

She seemed to be seeking for something behind this. And wasn't there? If what I said was true, why hadn't I accepted her offer the moment it was made? "Was that why you took no steps to divorce me?"

"I do not believe in divorce."

"Then it's agreed? I'm to come back?"

Had I wanted it to be quite this quick? But there I was. What else could I say? "Everything will be as before."

"You mean we will share a bedroom?"

"If you wish."

She paused. "Perhaps not quite at the beginning."

I just repressed a smile. No, the big scene was not going to be entirely hers. "That will be up to you. At home, in the house, I shall treat you just as before. Of course, I can speak only for myself. The children you may find more difficult. But I daresay you'll manage it."

"I can only try."

I said nothing to this, and she glanced about the room as if seeking a clue as to what next to discuss. "Is that all, then? When shall I come?"

"Today, if you wish."

She rose. "Let's say Monday. I think we both need a little preparation. I had not expected that we should come so rapidly to terms. But I guess it's better this way. We may as well get right on with it." She turned to the door and then back to me. "Have you *no* other comment, Titus?"

"What would you have me say?"

"Oh, that you're glad to have me back. Or sorry. That you still have a rag of affection left for me. Or that you don't. That you hate my guts! Anything! Something for me to go on."

"I have nothing to add, Lally."

She smiled, as if to tell me that now she had all she needed. "I see that the children aren't going to be the hardest part!"

Nor were they. Harry was duck soup with her. He and his sister, thirteen and twelve, had promised me that they would be polite to a returning mother whose absence their unforgiving paternal grandmother, despite my injunctions, had secretly coached them to resent, but I suspected—quite rightly, as it turned out—that behind my back they had formed a pact to confine themselves to frigid good manners. However, that had to be Lally's problem. Her behavior, I soon saw, was perfect. When they met she made no attempt to kiss or embrace them. She faced them with a small friendly smile and addressed them clearly and calmly.

"Your father has allowed me to come back on a kind of trial. You will both have the chance to look me over and decide what you think of me before I exercise any kind of parental authority. That I shan't do until we all three agree that the time has come. Until then it will be your father who is entirely in charge. I will simply hope that you treat me with the same courtesy that you would a houseguest, say, a visiting aunt."

If Harry and Hattie were surprised at her mildness and reasonableness—and I think they were—they did not show it. At meals, in those first weeks of our reunion, Lally and I conversed, in rather stilted tones, about the weather, current events and plans for the day. The children addressed their few remarks to me.

Then, one Saturday morning, when I was at the parish house and the children at home, Lally went to the garage to take our car to the village to shop and found one of the tires flat. She returned to the house to ask Harry if he would change it for her. Without a word he promptly and efficiently did so. In thanking him she apparently simply said this:

"I don't suppose there's any job I can do for you as well as you've done this one. But if there is, just call on me."

The following night, when Lally and I were reading in the parlor, Harry came down from his room to consult me, as he often did, on his homework for school. He was desperately looking for a subject for his weekly theme. I had been watching Lally's quiet tactics with the children, and I saw my chance now to give her a hand and alleviate the tenseness of the home atmosphere which was beginning to get on my nerves.

"Why don't you ask your mother? She used in the old days to give me some good tips for my sermons."

Harry hesitated but at last went to her, and they left the room together for a private conference. A week later he got an A for a composition about a boy on an African safari who had changed the tire on his jeep just in time before the dangerous rogue elephant he had been seeking to kill found *him*.

"I didn't write a word of it," Lally assured me when I protested. "I got it all out of him by asking questions."

"Leading questions, no doubt."

"Well, we weren't in a court of law."

When Harry wanted to thank her, she said: "Just give me a peck of a kiss on the forehead." She lowered her head, and he hugged her. Harry was won.

Hattie, of course, belonging to the stronger sex, was harder. One night at family supper she related to me the story of a girl in her class at school whose mother had left her father for another man. She spoke in a high censorious tone, never once glancing in her mother's direction.

"Of course, her mother's a bad, bad woman," she concluded.

I told her sharply that I didn't want to hear another word about it, and Hattie remained sullenly silent for the rest of our uneasy meal. Afterwards I retired to my study, and it was only through Harry that I learned what ensued.

Lally had addressed herself gravely but not reproachfully to her daughter.

"I want you to know, Hattie, that the reason I did not wince when you described your friend's mother as a bad woman was not because I was not hurt. I knew that jab was meant for me, and you can be sure it found its mark. I was very much hurt. But I know how it pains your father if I wince—he is very sensitive— and I have had to control my reactions. You are not the only person who has thrown my past at me. One learns to bear such things. But please try, Hattie, to spare your father in the future.

When you and I are alone together you can call me anything you want."

When at the end of two months Lally announced at breakfast that she was giving up the struggle with Hattie and would be leaving us, it was Hattie who, in a flood of tears, flung her arms around her and begged her, successfully, to stay.

After the first year of our reunion, when the church fathers had been convinced that it was working, I received my call from the South Bedford parish, and my career ever since has been one of continual success. Lally has been beyond praise; beloved by our parishioners, indefatigable in her committee work, her neighborhood calls, her hospital visits and in organizing the social events at the rectory. She has been a gracious hostess to visiting clerics and, most importantly of all, a devoted mother and a sympathetic spouse. For ten of the last eleven years we have, as in the first five of our marriage, shared a bedroom. As one of the elders of our church only half-jokingly told me the other day: "If you become Bishop Truesdale, Titus, as we all expect, you'll owe half of it to Lally."

The only thing that has bothered me in our relationship, at least until the doubt that has assailed me today, has been that Lally never loses her temper at me, never shows the natural impatience that any spouse—and mine in particular—is bound on some occasion to feel. That has to be deliberate, doesn't it?

It is obvious that I am getting nowhere with my sermon. I shall certainly be constrained to use an old one tomorrow.

And I still have not decided whether I can state at the anniversary party: "Bless you, my dear, for a quarter century of happiness!"

• • •

September 17, 1961. Well, it's over. The party has been and gone. And I certainly provided something of a shock to all those present, including our two children, who came home from their medical and law schools to attend. Lally's reaction, as might have been expected, was the most unexpected. She jumped to her feet when I had finished my little speech and cried out: "Thank you, dear Titus!"

I had not known just how I should end that little speech until I actually ended it. My opening remarks had been benign and banal, the kind expected on such an occasion when a too florid oratory or a too witty cleverness may be deemed a bit to impugn the deep and supposedly unchallengeable sincerity of the speaker. Yet as I spoke—as I heard my own voice, hollow and far away, not at all as I did when I delivered a sermon—I had the distinct impression that everyone in that large chamber was reducing in his or her mind the twenty-five years of our marriage by the five of Lally's absence from our hearth and wondering if I would dare to refer to that gap, and, if I did, how I would still manage to preserve the congenial feeling of the occasion.

And then, in ending, I turned to Lally and raised my glass of champagne. "I want to thank you, my dear, from the bottom of my heart, for eleven years of perfect bliss!"

What a disciplined crowd it was! Hardly an eyebrow was raised. Lally's enthusiastic response was received with smiles and exclamations of pleasure. Further toasts were offered, and in the bidding of good nights at our host's doorway an hour later not a soul indicated by so much as a twinkle or a frown that any exception had been taken to my perhaps too meticulous calculation of the period of my marital bliss. Nor did Harry or Harriet, even when we had all returned to the rectory and dispersed to our respective rooms. The only unusual thing that happened was that Lally lingered behind when I went upstairs and reappeared in our chamber a few minutes later with a small tray, a bottle of bourbon, two tumblers and some ice.

"Really, my dear," I remonstrated, "haven't we had enough to drink?"

"Just one apiece." She poured me a stiff one and another for herself. "For the road, as they say. The new road we've taken tonight. At long last!"

"Lally, I hurt you! I'm so sorry. I don't know what came over me. Can you ever forgive me?"

"There's nothing to forgive, Titus. Don't be absurd. You've wanted for years to let people know just how rottenly I treated you when I ran off with Brokaw. You've watched me worming my way back into everyone's affection and respect. You saw that people were beginning to forget that you had ever been wronged at all. That they were giving you no credit for your generosity in taking me back. That they might even be saying you were lucky to have me! Well, thank God you got it out! Or some of it, anyway. For I'm sure there's more. But the point is that now you and I can work on it together!"

I sat down suddenly on the side of the bed, weak with relief. What had I ever done to deserve a wife of this calibre?

"What can I do to start?" I gasped. "What can I do to show you I'll be a new man?"

"Go and get the children in here before they go to sleep. Get two more glasses. And then tell them what we've just said to each other! We'll all drink to it!"

"Oh, not that!" I groaned in dismay.

But I did exactly what she suggested. And I knew that I was going to continue to do so.

the sacred

from

Soul Mates

by Thomas Moore

Best-selling author Thomas Moore holds degrees in theology, musicology and philosophy; lived for twelve years in a Catholic monastic order; and has worked as a psychotherapist. He argues in *Soul Mates* that marriage is a mystery, a sacrament and a vessel for the expression of the soul.

M arriage is not only the expression of love between two people, it is also a profound evocation of one of life's greatest mysteries, the weaving together of many different strands of soul. Because marriage touches upon issues charged with emotion and connected to absolute meaning, it is filled with paradoxical feelings, far-flung fantasies, profound despair, blissful epiphanies, and bitter struggle—all signs of the active presence of soul.

Many people turn to marriage hoping to find ultimate happiness and grace for their lives. Some find a pot of gold, others face disillusionment and regret. Even "successful" marriages that offer many levels of fulfillment can sometimes be trying, and teeter on the edge of dissolution. Most disturbing of all, some people fall in love, create a family, and then turn violent toward each other.

In the midst of all these contradictions, it's easy to be cynical about marriage, or to come up with yet another plan for making marriages "work." It's more difficult to look at marriage as we actually experience it, taking note of its deep fantasies, its hidden emotions, and its place in the life of the soul; not looking for perfection, but asking what the soul is doing when it entices us toward such a demanding form of relationship.

The distance between our intentions and expectations of marriage on the one hand, and the reality it presents on the other, indicates how far removed from consciousness and reason marriage can be. Marriage has less to do with conscious intention and will than with deeper levels of soul. In order to gain insight into marriage and its problems, we have to dig deeper than the familiar therapeutic investigation into parental influences, childhood traumas, and the illusions of romantic love. The soul *always* reaches deeper than we expect, especially in marriage, which lies far beneath matters of communication and even interpersonal relationship, touching areas of absolute importance to a meaningful and soulful life. We approach its soul when we understand that marriage is a mystery, a sacrament, as some religions say—a sacred symbolic act.

In order to grasp this sacred symbolic level, we need to set aside the modern penchant for scientific social analysis and instead look to sacred stories for instruction. Scientific analysis and therapeutic theories leave out the sacred dimension, and therefore they always come up wanting in their portrayals of marriage. But stories that evoke a mythic imagination, however simple they may be, offer us an opportunity to look at the soul's role in what is sometimes treated merely as an interpersonal structure.

The Native American Cochiti people of New Mexico tell a strange story about marriage, a story that can lead our thoughts in a fresh direction. According to the story, a young girl living with her poor parents taught herself to make many fine items of clothing on a simple loom. Her weavings caught the attention of the young men of her village, many of whom wanted to marry her, but she kept her eyes focused on her work and showed no interest in the men, even though they offered her beautiful things. Then Coyote, that mischievous figure of the mythology of the American West, decided he wanted to marry her. "I shall offer her none of these things, but she will belong to me," he said proudly. Then he went off to the mountains to fetch some black currants.

He came to her village and ritually donned a human costume. Stamping four times with his foot, he drew on a pair of white buckskin moccasins. Looking down at his feet, he said, "Do I look pretty? Yes, I look pretty." Using the same magic, he dressed himself in all his finery. Then, after taking the black currants in his left hand, he went to the village center and danced.

The girl watched him dance and was charmed. She saw the currants in his left hand and asked him for them. Then she took him home, made love with him, and in no time had little coyote children. One day he took her away from her parents to a hole in the ground. "How can you go in?" she asked. "It's so small." But he crawled in effortlessly, followed by all the little coyotes. She looked into the hole and beheld a house not unlike that of her parents, filled with the kind of clothes she had been making. So she, too, went in and lived there forever after.

This story "marries" two entirely different modes of experience—the mundane and the magical. Notice that the woman is not interested in an ordinary human marriage. When such opportunities arise, she keeps her mind on her weaving. In many traditions weaving is one of the preferred images for the imagination. It's an important image of a people making a culture—weaving together families, communities, and nations, as well as all kinds of work and creative endeavors. Among the Greeks, Athena was the great weaver, the goddess who brought all the artisans and families together as a city and a nation. A person, too, is woven from many influences, many fateful events, and many raw thematic materials.

As I have mentioned, the soul is *complicated,* a word whose literal meaning is "woven together." Our young woman is an excellent example of a person giving all of her effort to the work of soul-making. In some ways, she is like the Virgin Mary as she appears in paintings of the Annunciation: when the angel appears with his announcement, Mary is reading a book, preparing herself for her supernatural fate by becoming acquainted with the sacred stories and prayers of her people. The young Cochiti girl is also preparing herself for a remarkable marriage by waiting for the magical enticement of the black currants and by devoting herself wholly to making culture and to bringing her creative talents into the world.

We may learn from her that we can't enter marriage soulfully without first preparing ourselves, by being in the world creatively and by weaving the tapestry of our own talents and destiny. Marriage is

not separate from other aspects of life; on the contrary, our capacity
to knit all the many parts of life into a persona, our own way of being
in the world, represented here by the clothes the young woman
makes, culminates in marriage. Marriage itself is a kind of weaving,
not only of two individuals, but of every aspect of personal, social,
and even cosmic life.

This, then, is one lesson we can take from the story. An essential part of becoming marriageable is to be a maker, a person who
cultivates a life of beauty, rich texture, and creative work. If we
understand marriage only as the commitment of two individuals
to each other, then we overlook its soul, but if we see that it also
has to do with family, neighborhood, and the greater community,
and with our own work and personal cultivation, then we begin
to glimpse the *mystery* that is marriage. A person prepares for marriage by becoming a cultured person, not in the superficial sense
of refinement in the higher forms of art and the sophisticated life,
but as someone who has achieved an identity through cultural initiations and has found a unique way of being creative in the
world. This creativity doesn't have to be grand. It may be no more
than the discovery of how to make a simple yet individual contri-
bution to the community, like the Cochiti bride making clothes
on her loom.

The mate to this work of cultivation is a Panlike, devilish
dancer who is fertile, interior, and magical—Coyote. Marriage is
accomplished not only by human design and will, but also by
grace and magic. Coyote is a magician who knows esoterically how
to dress himself, how to clothe his magical, mythical being in

human form. All intimate relationships require some degree of magic, because magic, not reason and will, accomplishes what the soul needs.

Every marriage has both an external life and an interior dimension. The externals may be dealt with by reasonable means, but the interior requires myth and magic. The Cochiti girl married an enchanting figure from the world of animal dream who was able to make by magic what she was used to making by her own industry and talent. His home was an interior version of her earthly home, a microcosm within the earth. In this kind of home she could live out the rest of her days, because he was a worthy mate, his home an appropriate fulfillment, a deep interior vision, of the mundane home she knew so well.

Our expectations of marriage, those profound and far-reaching fantasies we have of life in the perfect married state, hint at the depths of marriage itself. When we marry, we are not only linking our lives to another individual, we are also entering a myth that reaches far into the most meaning-giving areas of the heart. The "happiness" we hope for in marriage is a catchall word that embraces many spoken and unspoken wishes for fulfillment. In a sense, the person we marry offers us an opportunity to enter, explore, and fulfill essential notions of who we are and who we can be. In this sense marriage is not fundamentally the relationship between two persons, but rather an entry into destiny, an opening to the potential life that lies hidden from view until evoked by the particular thoughts and feelings of marriage.

The all-important mystery the Cochiti story teaches is not the kind of lesson one reads in modern books on marriage. Textbooks teach us how to get along in life, while myth shows us what the soul experiences in those same life events. Marriage seems to be about relationship with another person, but this mythical story reveals that marriage is also more mysterious, that it is a strange but fulfilling union with the world of dream and fantasy. Genuine marriage takes place in a realm that is not identical with outward life; our soul partner is always of another species—an angel, animal, or phantom. The familiar Beauty and the Beast theme hints at the way love and marriage bring us into communion with a realm far removed from human life. Perhaps the ultimate object of all desire is bestial, demanding from us a broadening of understanding and feeling beyond mere human sympathies.

In the ancient tale of Eros and Psyche, a story much prized by psychologists in recent years, Psyche, the young girl, falls in love with Eros, who is Love himself. She visits him nightly in his beautiful home at the bottom of a cliff. One of her sisters, jealous of Psyche's lover and the opulent life he gives her, tells her that he is really a beast. She convinces Psyche that she should light a lamp one night—breaking a promise she had made never to shed light on her lover—and see for herself. Psyche gives in to her sister's scheme, lights a lamp, and beholds a beautiful winged Eros in her bed. A drop of hot oil from the lamp spills onto Eros, waking him. When he sees that he has been betrayed, he gets up and rushes away. The rest of the story tells of Psyche's desperate attempts, through a series of trials, to recover her life with Eros.

It's tempting to see the sister's ploy as simply that, a ruse to spoil

Psyche's good fortune, but the sister's observation is at least partly true. Eros *is* a beast, a dragon, and sometimes a coyote. Every marriage brings the soul in its innocence into union with an erotic sprite who may have some mischief in mind. Perhaps if we were to recognize that deep in the scheme of things the lure toward marriage is always mischievous, we wouldn't be so shocked and disillusioned when the animal appears. We think it's a human institution, when at least in part it has a mysterious dimension that not only transcends but may contradict our human intentions, a dimension that is as devilish as it is angelic.

The Cochiti girl is clever. Before Coyote makes an appearance, she will not be satisfied with an ordinary human marriage, even when it is dressed up with fine gifts and extraordinary human talent. She is attracted more powerfully, though less directly, by these seemingly insignificant indications of an underworld fruitfulness—the black currants in Coyote's left hand. These currants are reminiscent of the pomegranate seeds that, in the popular Greek tale of mystical marriage, keep Persephone married to the underworld lord. In that story, too, the ultimate seduction is not accomplished by something obvious; it's achieved by what is dark, sweet, and in seed form rather than fully matured. We are drawn into intimacy by possibilities rather than by realities, by the promise of things to come rather than by proven accomplishments, and perhaps by seductions that are darker than the bright reasons to which we admit.

From the point of view of our story, it is the primary task of the marriage partners not to create a life together, but to evoke the *soul's* lover, to stir up this magical fantasy of marriage and to sustain it, thus serving the particular all-important myth that lies deep in the lover's heart and that supplies a profound need for meaning, fulfillment, and relatedness. It isn't unusual to hear of marriages in which all the reasonable life elements are in order— a good home, fine children, happy days—and yet one or both of the partners is deeply dissatisfied and often charmed by an erotic attraction to someone else, usually someone quite different from the mate. Apparently it isn't enough to make a *human* marriage. In order to fulfill its need for divine coupling, the soul needs something less tangible than a happy home. The moral I take from the Cochiti story is that every soulful marriage requires Coyote's presence. It requires in the people involved a vivid sense of its own mystery and an awareness that purely human efforts to keep it alive and thriving always prove insufficient.

The young men in the story tried to entice the girl to them by giving her their best weavings, things she herself could make better. Coyote, on the other hand, offered her nothing except the deceptively simple currants. In marriage we may not all need a fully functioning home, several children, a hefty bank account—a fantasy that seems strong in our day. These human goals may even stand in the way of the more mysterious needs of the soul for an interior home. Oddly, the attempts of many married people to create an affluent environment might even be the cause of marital failure, because the point in marriage is not to create a material, human world, but rather to evoke a spirit of love that is not of this world.

Once again I'd like to amend, or at least interpret, Rilke's famous advice to couples that one should protect the solitude of the other. One should rather protect and feed the deep fantasies that surround the other's imagination of love and marriage. This is one way to understand the "solitude" of the other. Getting to know our partner's soul, we may discover what charms his or her imagination. We may glimpse deeper hopes our partner has for marriage, even those goals beneath conscious awareness.

As a marriage partner, I could ask myself, "How can I evoke Coyote and make him part of this marriage? What are the black currants my lover enjoys and appreciates? What simple but not necessarily obvious things stir her heart and feed her notions of love? What can I hold in my subtle left hand to charm her, as my right hand goes about the mundane business of making a living and building a home?"

The Cochiti girl wonders if she and her family can live in the small space of Coyote's home. The realm of soul sometimes appears small and even insignificant in comparison to "the big world out there" in which our lives are lived out. Tradition sometimes calls the realm of soul a microcosm. It's tempting to focus on the cosmic element rather than the micro, yet we might recognize that to the soul the most minute things can be crucial. In several places in his writing, Jung discusses the "little people"—gnomes, dactyls, elves, Tom Thumbs—the ones who do the work of soul. The soul of marriage is no exception: it is created by small acts, small words, and small, everyday interactions.

How do we keep Coyote dancing in our marriage? Marriage works best not by keeping the contract up to date and doing all the right things, but by stamping our feet four times on the ground, by doing and saying things that touch the feelings and the imagination, not just the mind. If we lose that power, then we know Coyote has vanished. "The magic has gone out of my marriage," a person says, knowing intuitively and precisely that marriage, like all matters of soul, works by means of magic rather than by effort.

This is not an easy idea for a twentieth-century, enlightened, technologically and scientifically sophisticated person to accept, yet it is crucial. In matters of soul, a well-conceived ritual act, well-chosen words, an inspired gesture, a symbolic gift, even a well-modulated tone of voice can achieve the desired effect. Often a very small gesture or action will have great consequences—this is one of the traditional rules of magic.

I find in therapy that couples often bring a mechanical and structural image of their marriage. They believe that they can examine their behavior the way their mechanic studies the working of their automobile, find what is wrong, and be assured that their expert therapist will know how to fix it. Couples often try also to find some new pattern of behavior that will inject the needed element into their marriage. They reassign household tasks, set times for discussion, and look for balance in spending time with the children or devoting attention to their careers. These structual approaches are sincere, but they depend on mechanical resolutions that usually sustain a new vision for a surprisingly short time.

Over and over again as a therapist I have seen remarkable changes in a marriage take place when, after all the reasons and suggestions have been presented, some more intimate, more raw expression of the heart finds its words. As serious magicians over the centuries have taught, words, and sometimes the mere sounds of words, have a powerful effect. This is certainly true of the magic needed to keep soul in our marriages.

Genuine though they may be, the problems of mundane life are not always identical with the concerns of the soul. The soul of a marriage asks for intuitive insight into its ways and needs. It demands wisdom, the kind of knowledge that lies far deeper than information and understanding. Sometimes the demands of the soul are paradoxical, so that it may ask for something that on the surface may look contrary to a "good" marriage, but soulful marriages are often odd on the surface. People make unusual arrangements, as in the case of one friend of mine who lives in one town while her husband lives in another, or another friend who commutes two thousand miles to his wife's home. As we saw in the first chapter of this book, the soul may need periods of distance, poor communication, doubt, and regret. These need not threaten the marriage as such, but they do show that the soul of marriage is a more mottled weave than the plain, sentimental, structural image of marriage we often try to maintain.

The soul generally does not conform to the familiar patterns of life. Whenever the soul appears strongly—in love, passion, symptom—its mood and behaviors seem odd and are difficult to fit into life. It follows that a particularly soulful marriage may look oddly individual, its forms and structures contrary to accepted patterns. When soulfulness appears in any human institution, it asks of us unusual tolerance and broad imagination.

Mortification in Marriage

We all know some marriages that are living hells and many that are full of difficulties, and yet we enter marriage with the hope that our marriage will be different. We bring a degree of innocence to marriage, hoping that in spite of statistics about divorce we will find in marriage a meaningful and fulfilled life. While innocent hope and expectation are a natural part of getting married, they invite experiences that are wounding, that bring us unwillingly and usually unexpectedly into the crucible of marriage. We need some innocence in order to enter marriage in the first place, and then we discover that marriage is not unadulterated happiness, but is rather another of life's initiations.

Excessive innocence about marriage can breed trouble. We might see the sentimental view of marriage that is often presented in movies and in advertising as a defense against the dark challenges that marriage offers, or at least a compensation: the more we are aware that marriage can be hell, the more frivolous will be our conscious presentations of it.

On the other hand, humor is one of our best ways of acknowledging the shadow aspects of our lives, and so jokes, comic movies, funny greeting cards, and many family stories poke fun at marriage. Through humor we can admit that marriages are not made entirely in heaven, that the devil has a role as well.

When I was in college I paid my way in part by playing music for weddings in churches. I'm sure I played for over one hundred weddings, and one of the interesting things I saw on these occasions was the way the trickster and underworld spirits interfered with the sentimental perfection of the planned wedding. I wondered even then if these unholy visitations were an indication that the marriages themselves would be similarly thwarted in their perfectionistic fantasies.

One time, for instance, at a large and costly wedding, the bride was walking down the aisle behind her dozen or so attendants, her father at her side and slightly behind. At the middle of the church the father got nervous, lost his stately gait, and stepped on his daughter's train. The long train ripped off at the waist, taking with it a good part of the dress. There, in the middle of the church, the ceremonious music playing, the attendants swarmed around the bride, protecting her modesty like the nymphs of Artemis at her bath, while one of them stitched her up before the wedding continued.

At another wedding the bride fainted, not an unusual occurrence. I saw the attendants rush to her aid, while I also glimpsed a flash of the groom running out the side door of the church. This is not the idealistic image of the hero always standing by the side of his beloved, but it may be a good indication that marriage is as much about division as it is union. I also recall a wedding in which the soprano reached an extremely high sustained fortissimo note, and her voice cracked, creating a screech that gave shivers to all present. In sympathy, I suppose, babies began to cry, and the ceremony had to be interrupted until peace was restored.

What is particularly liberating about these incidents is that the wholesome, beautiful, and perfect image of marriage is spoiled at the very outset. A realistically rounded view of marriage might allow us to restore some human dimension to our very idea of what marriage is. Ambrose Bierce's *The Devil's Dictionary* defines marriage as "the state or condition of a community consisting of a master, a mistress and two slaves, making in all, two." Marriage *is* a bondage, and a degree of knowing masochism in approaching it may be in order. Our very idea of what marriage is needs to be broad enough to include much shadow and many difficulties.

According to the Swiss Jungian analyst Adolf Guggenbühl-Craig, marriage is not a route to happiness but rather a form of individuation process. *Individuation* is Jung's term for the lifelong process of becoming an individual, of working at the stuff of one's soul so as to be less identified with collective images and more a unique person. In this view marriage would also be a form of alchemy and the relationship a true crucible.

The value of Guggenbühl-Craig's analysis lies in taking us away from the sentimental image of marriage as instant happiness, reminding us that it is an arena in which the soul matures and ripens. At one level marriage is about relationship, but at another it is the creation of a vessel in which soul-making can be accomplished. At the same time, of course, marriage is much more than an opportunity for each individual to suffer his or her way toward individuality.

Marriage is an Athenic weaving together of families, of two souls with their individual fates and destinies, of time and eternity—everyday life married to the timeless mysteries of the soul. Life and culture get more complicated with every marriage. Not just personalities, but cultures, ideas, politics, emotions, myths are all being woven together by means of marriage, and each marriage in a community affects all of its members.

It's interesting to notice that society loves stories of trouble in marriage. The worm in marriage is the very core of gossip, sensational magazines and newspapers, soap operas, and movies. We hunger for an acknowledgment of the dark powers of marriage: its capacity to disillusion, to inflict severe emotional pain, and to make life miserable. Along with humorous depictions of marriage, these stories save us as well from the burden of sentimentality that surrounds marriage. Sentimentality may at first feel as if it defends us against the weight of life, and yet it eventually becomes an onus, an unbearable lightness.

Marriage in its fullness is a soul institution and as such necessarily carries the weight of life. There can be satisfaction in the grittiness of marriage and dissatisfaction in its being sentimentalized. The Cochiti story reminds us that merely working hard at having a "good" marriage may not be enough to make it work. What the industrious young woman desires is the one who carries black currants—the darker animal world. The story is reminiscent of one of Wallace Stevens's thirteen ways of looking at a blackbird: "A man and a woman are one. A man and a woman and a blackbird are one." The dark animal figure always has an important role to play, for no profoundly affecting human institution is without its challenging mysteries that visit us as from another species.

Jung learned from alchemy an important yet easily avoided truth about the life of the soul: its presence and thriving depend upon mortifying experiences. Our sunny understandings and expectations, our reasonable efforts and methods, and our high values and convictions all are subject to mortification, which means "making dead" and which is pictured in Jung's alchemical sources as the slaying of the king or the sun. Those places from which we exercise control and our bright and healthy visions must submit in the work of soul to processes of dissolution, and the keystone of Jung's insight is realizing that these mortifications are necessary in the making of a soulful life.

Insofar as it serves as an initiatory structure in the service of soul, marriage can be expected to provide all kinds of mortification, and it does. Through intimacy's very difficulties, our personhood deepens, the relationship becomes more solid, and life itself takes on added intensity as our too sunny thoughts and emotions fall victim to the corrupting and eroding processes of marriage. The source of our pain isn't just that our partner is "impossible"—such an attitude would be taking marriage too personally. Marriage itself places us in impossible situations, impossible because they can't be resolved by human ingenuity. If we had Coyote around, of course, he would merely stomp his feet and the dance would recommence. We need his crafty, hole-in-the-ground, mischievous art if we are to meet the mortifications of marriage with the necessary insight and craft.

Marriage requires of us the slaying of our initial ideals and values—about marriage, about our partners, about ourselves. How do we do this without developing a cynical view of marriage or without becoming literal victims of the abusive potential in marriage? What we need first is some way out of oppositional thinking. Perhaps if we widened our image of relationships to include their being occasionally blissful and occasionally mortifying, with a mixture of all possibilities between, we might not be so surprised when challenging difficulties appeared.

Still, it isn't enough to be prepared for trouble. What is required is an appreciation for the profundity of the ghostly beast we conjure up with such apparent innocence in a wedding ceremony. The intimacy we pledge at the wedding is an invitation to open the Pandora's box of soul's graces and perversities. Marriage digs deep into the stuff of the soul. Lifelong, intense, socially potent relationships don't exist without touching the deepest, rawest reservoirs of soul. Few experiences in life reach such remote and uncultivated regions of the heart, unearthing material that is both incredibly fertile and frighteningly primordial.

Marriage may look like an arrangement of persons, but at a deeper level it is a profound stirring of souls. Like all initiations, it marks a fundamental shift in perceptions of oneself and one's world. Just as initiations are often ritualized with blood and pain, so marriage rearranges the emotions and one's view of life itself, often with painful stretching of the heart and the imagination. Often people who expect to find bliss in the arrangement discover bitter confusion in the re-sorting of feelings and thoughts occasioned by the marriage. They may blame each other for being outrageously inappropriate, not realizing that they have evoked a maelstrom in the soul through the "simple" decision to live as a couple rather than as a single person.

In the soulful marriage cynicism and disillusionment are replaced by an appreciation for the impersonal powers at work in what we imprecisely call human relationship. The Native American story reminds us that the "other" in marriage is not only a human being. It is also an animal, and a special animal at that—a tricky, resourceful, earthy, dark, untamable coyote, who brings to a marriage the potential for joy and fun as well as fear and power. In a marriage cognizant of soul, the partners find a brand of intimacy that is deeper than personal trust and mutual understanding. Oddly, it is rooted in mistrust and lack of understanding, in a distance that allows the soul of the other and of the marriage to be unpredictable and inexplicable. Oscar Wilde once said, "Only the shallow know themselves." The same could be said about marriage partners.

Caring for the Soul in Marriage

If we are going to care for the soul of a marriage, we may want to keep in mind a saying of Heraclitus that I have been using as a guide: "The soul is its own source of unfolding." One false temptation is to take the initial intentions of the people getting married as a guide for how the marriage should be lived. For example, people blame each other for not living up to promises made at the time of their wedding or engagement, but this kind of blaming is only a defense against the soul's incessant movement. At the beginning of any form of life the soul is in a raw, undeveloped stage; it makes sense that the marriage will be significantly different a few years into it than it was at the start.

Honoring Fate

We can honor the fateful spirit that brought us together at the beginning. From the viewpoint of soul, nothing happens by accident. The fatefulness that surrounds the beginning of a profound relationship suggests an intentionality far beyond the ken of the people involved. In acknowledging this turn of fate, we may find some peace and grounding, and also some humility as the relationship continues to offer unexpected challenges. Throughout the relationship we could remember its fateful beginnings, and notice further signals that the marriage has an impetus beyond the couple's intentions. It may take unexpected turns, or reveal surprising elements that may be both satisfying and threatening. Naturally, some relationships and marriages turn out to be disasters; but even then we can respect whatever arrangement of stars brought us into this story.

The fatefulness of a relationship may appear not only as extraordinary circumstances or synchronicities, but also as an element in the most ordinary events where it isn't appropriate to take full credit for what has happened. If a person's career goes off in a certain direction, that development may be due in part to decisions and conscious choices, but also in part to a gradual unfolding of soul; unknown forces and the deeper motivations are involved. Couples sometimes spend a great deal of energy and time arguing over choices that have been made, whereas they might be better off examining together, with a degree of humility and receptivity, the mysterious elements that have entered their lives.

Responding to the fateful dimensions of their own experience and of the relationship itself, a couple can lay the foundation for genuine spirituality as an ingredient in their love. By reacting not only to the partner's choices and reasons but also to deep impersonal factors, they reach down into their soul and establish a kind of intimacy that is more profound than the kind mutual analysis can generate. Then the relationship can be founded on ground not fully human, on a bedrock that is much firmer than anything human ingenuity could create.

Our conscious intentions are often colored by neurotic material and may have underlying mechanisms and purposes that serve more to resist than to respect the soul. But when we express ourselves so as to reveal less conscious material, we approach the realm of fate and providence where a spiritual attitude respecting destiny and other transpersonal factors creates a much deeper intimacy. If we are going to tend the soul in a relationship, we have to use means that match the soul's sacred dimensions.

Honoring the Genius of the Marriage

Something deeply mysterious and profound, like an animal lying at the very heart of relationship, far within its marrow, keeps a marriage moving, changing, and shifting. This is what the Romans called the genius, others called the daimon, and still others the angel—an influential yet hidden presence that is impervious to our explanations and rationalizations.

Traditionally the genius served procreation. We can understand *procreation* not only in the physical sense, but in the fuller sense of all kinds of creativity issuing from relationship. Marital creativity involves not only the making of children, but also the making of a new family culture, a home, and an intimate relationship that is vital, changing from season to season, and affecting the married people and their friends and communities.

When we respect the genius of our marriage, we focus as much on its own creativity as on our intentions for the relationship. In getting married, we lay ourselves open to the influence of the genius, not just to hold the marriage together but to make something out of it. Just as the Romans poured libations to this spirit, so we might honor and respect it in our attitude and in listening to its voice as a source of guidance. In this way, we tend the character of the marriage instead of our abstract ideas about what a marriage should be.

I once worked with a very sincere couple widely read in the field of psychology and practiced in the art of studying their relationship. The man told me that the reason their marriage was stagnant was that he had been raised in a home that was cold and unloving. The woman's idea was that she needed freedom in her life, more than her husband did, and so she was feeling tied down. My sense was that both explanations, though subtle and convincing to an extent, were rationalizations, protecting both people from looking more directly at their marriage itself and noticing what it was now asking of them. I didn't know exactly what this demand was, but I had the feeling that the marriage, like any living thing, was animate and now moving in a new direction. What better way to avoid the challenge of that development than to become preoccupied with reasons and explanations that in a very quiet way argued against the validity and value of the felt changes? Instead, I suggested that they read the changes they were sensing as expressions of the marriage's genius, and turn their focus away from pathologizing each other.

A return to an appreciation of genius, while drawing from archaic beliefs and practices, could enrich modern life. Some people might even be comfortable thinking of it as a "postmodern" way of living everyday life—a recovery of old soulful ways that can coexist with modern sophistication. Recognizing that every marriage has its own autonomous spirit could help us with the problems that inevitably appear, and also give marriage its own personality and deeper value.

Techniques for Tending the Marriage Soul

In marriage we need ways to keep the soul in mind. The details of daily life can so take over that we neglect the mysterious genius that holds it all together. Marriage requires many different kinds of reflection and mindfulness, ways of communicating not only to our partner but also to the daimon that gives marriage its character and dynamics. A famous saying of the sixth century B.C.E. Greek philosopher Heraclitus, "One's daimon is one's character," applies to marriage as well as to individuals. The daimonic charge or genius in a marriage reveals something of its unique character.

One simple way to glimpse the genius is to tell each other one's dreams. For this purpose it isn't necessary to interpret the dream as a whole, but merely to notice the various situations one's spouse finds herself in night after night. Without any overt analysis at a symbolic or mythic level, we might still come to appreciate the less predictable aspects of our partner's soul life. One way to understand the complexity and puzzle of a dream is to see it as a revelation of the soul that is far wider in scope than ordinary life. Simple talk about dreams might introduce partners to the idiosyncratic imagery and themes of each other's souls. Talk about dreams also moves conversation away from rational interpretations and solutions toward a more poetic style of reflection, an important move since the soul is motivated more by poetics than by reason.

Societies in which people build shrines to families or to marriages acknowledge the daimonic aspect of marriage and honor the residing spirit who cannot be controlled willfully or trusted naively. We might either actually build a shrine to our marriage—a sculpture, painting, tree, pile of stones, a ring—and thereby maintain an idol of sorts as a way of remembering this important truth, or, less physically, keep in mind the mystery that lies at the core of our partner and at the very base of the marriage.

Not only while discussing dreams, but also in ordinary conversations we could give attention and validity to the indwelling spirit of our partner and of the marriage. Plato describes Socrates as a person who was guided in his relationships by his daimon, always alert to signs as to whether the daimon would allow real conversation and community. In Plato's dialogue "Theatetus," Socrates is talking about students who come to him to learn. "When they return and with strong arguments ask for further conversation, sometimes the daimonic sign that comes to me doesn't allow it. With other persons it may be permitted, and these make progress." This is an example of living in tune with the genius, paying attention to signs that soul, through the daimonic presence, is involved. If it is, then the relationship has deep grounding. Otherwise, in spite of much talk, nothing significant will happen.

We can be alert to the genius in ourselves and in our partner. It may show itself in such simple things as preoccupation, a sense of being driven, strong desire often unsupported by good and convincing reasons, or a tinge of irrationality. Ficino, a follower of Plato's ideas, said that if we don't pay attention to the daimon, our efforts in the most ordinary areas of life will be wasted. We might take seriously our partner's intuitive, unreasoned, but strongly felt desires or inhibitions, giving them even more weight than she does. A life sensitive to the daimonic is overall based more on intuition than reason, allowing ephemeral inspirations a place of prominence, and inviting excursions into the unknown and unpracticed.

This soul-centered image of marriage I am advocating respects the less subjective, less intentional elements in a relationship. The result may be a life in which the individual has room to play out his or her eccentric potentialities. We may honor a marriage's soul by discovering what it wants. Some marriages characteristically ask for distance, others for closeness; some for children, some for the life of a couple. Some apparently want to be brief, some lifelong. Some want frequent changes, some get into a mold and want to stay there. Some accent emotions of bliss, some pain. Some are

flat, others are peaked or gulched. Some marriages prefer sentimentality, others like pragmatism. We can find out these prefer-
ences only by bringing to our own marriage a spirit of openness
and inquiry that will cut through preconceptions and society's
models. Only through many small acts of trial and error will we
learn the flavors of our own, unique marriage.

Precisely because fate is unpredictable and by definition doesn't
reveal a chain of causes or offer explanations, it can throw a couple
into confusion. At this time, the first thing the people can do is to
talk from the heart so as to meet life exactly as it presents itself. We
all have a tendency to defend ourselves first and look for justifica-
tions for our actions. Fate asks for some loyalty from us, so that we
might find a way of talking about it that is suited to its mystery.
Without evading responsibility, we can express our wonder at the
progress of events, speak for what feels unexplainable, and
acknowledge that the life fate is creating in us is something we are
willing to take on and for which we have responsibility.

Sometimes the only way to open a path to soul is the negative
way—by noting ways in which we are unconsciously protecting
ourselves from the sting of life's intentions. We could explore what
is painful and challenging in certain developments, where we feel
most resistant, and ways we have of evading or fleeing the challenge. Without berating ourselves or looking for sympathy, we
could reveal the impact of the soul on us, and in that way show our
partner with unusual candor what is shaping us and influencing
our lives. This kind of objective honesty about oneself may be
more revealing than subjective, personal confession.

Another way to care for the soul in marriage, a way that seems to have been understood better in ancient times than today, is through praise and celebration. This can be done in obvious ways—anniversary dinners and gifts—or through less common ways. We could, as chapter 6 will discuss, find occasions to write letters to our mates, even though we live with them every day. The letter could be a simple, heartfelt expression of feeling; or it could take the form of a poem. Poetry doesn't have to be professional or even "good" in order to do the job of celebrating the marriage. It also offers an element of formality and thoughtfulness that is not at all removed from feeling.

Yet another way is to take opportunities when they present themselves to praise and celebrate our partners, either expressing our feelings directly to them or to others. It's easy to overlook such opportunities and end up speaking only about the problems. There is something in modern culture that distrusts praise; one often hears judgments about being selfish, self-centered, and narcissistic. This concern about narcissism is a modern problem in itself, wrapped up certainly in our equally difficult task of being genuinely humble. It has harmful results, because the heart craves recognition and appreciation; only a neurotically puritanical mind would deny the soul these graces.

Sometimes the soul wants something not quite as strong as praise, but more like interest. What an interesting thing marriage is! We could all take more interest in our marriages, becoming sensitive to what they ask for every day, noticing how each is unique, and day by day discovering what marriage in general is all about. Our standard ideas about marriage may be dull, but the lived relationship subjected to wonder may present an altogether unstandardized view of marriage. The interest itself can also unveil its soul by turning attention away from the persons to the process.

Marriage and the Sacred

Tradition teaches that the soul has an important spiritual dimension, so that living soulfully, even in marriage, entails a spiritual life that emerges directly from the relationship. In many of his writings, Jung talked about the *hieros gamos,* or "sacred marriage," which is a union at a far deeper or higher level than personalities and lives. In a sense, every marriage evokes and participates in the "marriage" of all dualities. Work and play, night and day, feeling and thought—all contraries we can imagine come together in a holy wedding of qualities. At the beginning of his massive work on alchemy, *Mysterium Coniunctionis,* Jung lists some of the pairs that come together in the "soul wedding":

moist / dry
cold / warm
upper / lower
spirit / body
heaven /earth
fire/ water
bright / dark
active / passive

gaseous / solid

precious /cheap

good / evil

open / hidden

East / West

living / dead

masculine / feminine

Sol / Luna

The marriage two individuals enter upon may be seen as a ritual and a common life in which over time these other "mystical" elements are successfully wedded. It might be worthwhile to meditate on these tandems in order to see beneath the surface of marriage to the elements that are in play in it. Working through the relationship is a way of performing an alchemy on these soul qualities, and ultimately this alchemy could prove to be more important for the marriage than working out personality problems.

It is not surprising that in the New Testament the first miracle of Jesus is set at a wedding, in Cana. There Jesus transmutes water into wine, the flat necessity of life into the spirited, Dionysian, active substance of spirit. All marriages take place at Cana, for in all marriages the necessary raw material of life (water) is changed into a sparkling, tingling, inspiriting element of the soul (wine).

It is entirely appropriate that at weddings and at renewals of vows couples celebrate the union of their lives and the qualities of their souls with traditional prayers, poetry, wine, and ritual actions. Marriage is holy not only because it is a precious and revered way of forming human lives, but also because it is a form of religion in itself, a special way in which spirituality pours into life.

There's no need, of course, to think about myth, theology, and alchemy in order to live the miracle of marriage. One need only enter into it fully and tend its soul, of whatever kind and in whatever direction it leads, even into darkness. Marriage is by nature miraculous and magical. We do not understand it and cannot know where it is headed. To care for its soul, it is more important to honor its mystery than to try to outwit its intentions for what we, with our small minds, may think is a better outcome. If you want to ensure the soulfulness of your marriage, it would be infinitely better to build a shrine to it, find its god or goddess, and tend its image than to follow the "manual" and do it all properly and intelligently. For all of us, of whatever religion or nonreligion, a marriage is a sacrament. To care for its soul we need to be priests rather than technicians, and to draw from the wellspring of ordinary piety rather than from theory or formula.

passion

from

100 Love Sonnets
by Pablo Neruda

translated by Stephen Tapscott

Pablo Neruda (1904–1973), born in Parral, Chile, won the 1971 Nobel Prize in Literature. One of Latin America's greatest poets, he also was a diplomat, lawmaker and courageous political activist. He married well-known Chilean singer Matilde Urrutia in 1951. These poems were inspired by their mutual love.

To Matilde Urrutia

My beloved wife, I suffered while I was writing these misnamed "sonnets"; they hurt me and caused me grief, but the happiness I feel in offering them to you is vast as a savanna. When I set this task for myself, I knew very well that down the right sides of sonnets, with elegant discriminating taste, poets of all tunes have arranged rhymes that sound like silver, or crystal, or cannonfire. But—with great humility—I made these sonnets out of wood; I gave them the sound of that opaque pure substance, and that is how they should reach your ears. Walking in forests or on beaches, along hidden lakes, in latitudes sprinkled with ashes, you and I have picked up pieces of pure bark, pieces of wood subject to the comings and goings of water and the weather. Out of such softened relics, then, with hatchet and machete and pocketknife, I built up these lumber piles of love, and with fourteen boards each I built little houses, so that your eyes, which I adore and sing to, might live in them. Now that I have declared the foundations of my love, I surrender this century to you: wooden sonnets that rise only because you gave them life.

October 1959

XVII

I do not love you as if you were salt-rose, or topaz,
or the arrow of carnations the fire shoots off.
I love you as certain dark things are to be loved,
in secret, between the shadow and the soul.

I love you as the plant that never blooms
but carries in itself the light of hidden flowers;
thanks to your love a certain solid fragrance,
risen from the earth, lives darkly in my body.

I love you without knowing how, or when, or from where.
I love you straightforwardly, without complexities or pride;
so I love you because I know no other way

than this: where *I* does not exist, nor *you*,
so close that your hand on my chest is my hand,
so close that your eyes close as I fall asleep.

XLIV

You must know that I do not love *and* that I love you,
because everything alive has its two sides;
a word is one wing of the silence,
fire has its cold half.

I love you in order to begin to love you,
to start infinity again
and never to stop loving you:
that's why I do not love you yet.

I love you, and I do not love you, as if I held
keys in my hand: to a future of joy—
a wretched, muddled fate—

My love has two lives, in order to love you:
that's why I love you when I do not love you,
and also why I love you when I do.

LXIX

Maybe nothingness is to be without your presence,
without you moving, slicing the noon
like a blue flower, without you walking
later through the fog and the cobbles,

without the light you carry in your hand,
golden, which maybe others will not see,
which maybe no one knew was growing
like the red beginnings of a rose.

In short, without your presence: without your coming
suddenly, incitingly, to know my life,
gust of a rosebush, wheat of wind:

since then I am because you are,
since then you are, I am, we are,
and through love I will be, you will be, we'll be.

XCI

Age covers us like drizzle;
time is interminable and sad;
a salt feather touches your face;
a trickle ate through my shirt.

Time does not distinguish between my hands
and a flock of oranges in yours:
with snow and picks life chips away
at your life, which is my life.

My life, which I gave you, fills
with years like a swelling cluster of fruit.
The grapes will return to the earth.

And even down there time
continues, waiting, raining
on the dust, eager to erase even absence.

illness

from

Elegy for Iris
by John Bayley

Novelist John Bayley was born in India and educated at Oxford, where he later became a fellow. He married philosophy professor Iris Murdoch in 1956. She was a prolific writer of poetry, novels, plays and essays, and died in 1999 after a five-year battle with Alzheimer's disease. John's book about their 43-year marriage is in large part an account of those last five years.

April 15, 1997

Moving from stage to stage. How many are there? How many will there be? I used to dread Iris's moment of waking, because the situation seemed to strike her then in full force, at least for a minute or two. Reassuring noises, so far as possible, and then she would go back to sleep, and I would sit beside her, reading or typing. The sound of it seemed to help as reassurance. Iris's greed for sleep had something desperate about it, and yet she slept, and still sleeps, so easily and so long in the morning that it was a great mutual comfort. Lying beside me, she is like an athlete who had passed on the torch to a back-up member of the relay. I couldn't do what she had done, but I was doing something.

Not a good metaphor, though. It would be truer to say that I myself was reassured by her unawareness of anything that I might be doing on my own. It would have been unbearable if she had shown her old friendly interest. Where work was concerned, we had always left each other alone, so that being cut off now about such things was positively welcome. The simpler and more primitive our needs and emotions now, like those of babies for their mothers, the more absolute they feel. The exasperation of being followed about the house now by Iris is as strong and genuine as is my absolute need for it. Were she to avoid me, or "tactfully" leave me alone, I would pursue her as anxiously, if not quite so obsessively, as she now pursues me. I don't feel any particular pleasure or emotion when her whole face lights up at the sight of me when I return to the car after ten minutes of shopping. But I remember it if I wake up in the night, and then I reach out to her. The "lion face" of Alzheimer's used to be transformed in that way when her mother saw daughter Iris. Not that Iris's face has grown as expressionless as her mother's used to be. Sitting waiting for me in the car, she looks quite alert and amiable, and passing strangers smile at her.

But thank goodness that the stage of that old despair on waking seems to be over. Now she makes a soft chuckling sound and looks at me like the Teletubby baby in the blue sky on TV. No anxious queries. We exchange a few of the old nonsense words before she goes to sleep again. As the condition gets worse, it also gets better. It seems to compensate each new impoverishment. Should be more thankful for that.

The agony of travel nowadays. Iris has always loved travelling, and she craves it now more compulsively than ever. I have always detested the business of leaving home, and I was so thankful in the old days to drive her to the station and wave her good-bye. Now I have a fever of travel angst—taxis, tickets, train times. Iris never worried about all that. She used to arrive at the station like a Russian peasant and wait for the first train to arrive.

The worst of both worlds. Although Iris is compulsively eager to be "going"—somewhere, anywhere—she is in as much of a flap in her own way as I am. At the station, she keeps repeating, "Why didn't you tell me we were going?" I had told her many, many times. Now I tell her again sharply, and with her own degree of querulous repetition. People look round at us. I am fumbling in my wallet, checking the tickets. They are hard to separate, and after shuffling them wildly again and again, I can still find only one return ticket. The whole system is absurd; why must they give us four separate tickets when two would do? It's definitely not there. I rush to the ticket office, where a queue is made to unwind in serpentine fashion between rope barriers. The ticket man has drawn his little curtain and gone off. The customer at the other guichet seems to want a round-the-world ticket, and to be in no hurry about getting it. He and the ticket clerk canvass the possibilities in leisurely fashion. Iris clutches me anxiously, urging us to run to a train which has just come in, the wrong train, I hope. At last, the ticket man is free. I produce the receipt and the delinquent tickets. No, he can do nothing—it wasn't his sale. I turn away in despair. Why can't we just go home?

Iris has not understood the problem and keeps urging me towards the wrong train. At that moment, a man comes up to us and holds out a ticket. It is the original ticket man himself, strangely naked and unrecognisable now he's not behind the counter. He doesn't explain what happened, but just gives me a small collusive smile and walks rapidly back to his place of work.

On the train, I keep counting the tickets. The elderly couple opposite look sympathetically at Iris. I am clearly the one who's become a problem.

Utterly exhausted and drenched in sweat. Vague heart sensations, too. And the whole thing so trivial. Alzheimer's obviously has me in its grip, and the ticket man, too. As well as Iris, and probably everyone else.

Does the care-giver involuntarily mimic the Alzheimer's condition? I'm sure I do.

Sitting exhaustedly in the train, I suddenly recall a droll moment at the time when Iris seemed more or less to have decided to marry me. She was going down to her old school—to give the prizes or something—and suggested I should accompany her. After her business there was over, she wanted to call on the retired headmistress, a famous old white-haired lady who lived in a flat on the school premises. In her bleak way, the headmistress had been very kind, regarding schoolgirl Iris as the jewel in her crown. I was introduced, and after a few minutes I managed to slip away, leaving the pair of them together. When Iris came out, she was looking much amused. "Do you want to know what BMB thought about you?" she asked. I expressed a natural curiosity. "Well," said Iris, "she just said, 'He doesn't look very strong.'"

I didn't bother about being strong in those days. Now I have to try, but I'm sure the attempt wouldn't deceive BMB.

Kind friends up our street are giving a Sunday-morning drinks party. I used to enjoy the quiet of Sunday mornings, the Sunday paper, leisurely breakfast, with Iris working upstairs, absence of morning anxiety about what I had to do that day. In those days, I should have made some excuse, Iris acquiescing. She wouldn't have minded going but knew I wouldn't want to. Now it offers a welcome distraction. I say nothing about it until eleven. If I did, she would panic, demand why I hadn't told her sooner. She does not distinguish now between what she wants to do and what is happening.

"Are we going to London?"

"No, just up the street. You'll know them when we get there. They're very nice. You'll like it."

I know this is true, but it produces a "trouser grimace," as I now call it in my mind. Every evening, we have the battle of the trousers. She wants to go to bed in them, and in everything else she is wearing, too. My resistance to this is halfhearted, compared with the determination she shows on the issue. Sometimes I win, more or less dragging them off. Iris gives up the struggle, but she produces a frightful grimace, an expression wholly new and different from anything her face ever did in the past. It always unnerves me, and it is becoming more frequent in other situations.

Not that I care about her trousers. Our habits have never been exactly hygienic; and yet distinguishing day from night now seems vital to our saving routines. Twice in the day, at ten in the morning and five in the evening, panic and emptiness descend, not because there is something we have to do, but because there isn't. Routine has no suggestions to make. All I can do then is to promise the next thing soon: a drink, lunch, or supper.

Iris's fear of other people if I'm not there is so piteous that I cannot bring myself to arrange for caregivers to "keep her company," or to take her to the age therapy unit. All that will have to come. Meanwhile, I am ruthless about getting her ready for the party, confident that she will enjoy it when she gets there, as they used to tell us in childhood.

She does. It is a nice party. I marvel, as I have often done before, at the way in which guests enjoy being guests. Standing opposite someone and keeping going, holding eye contact in the same practised, precarious way that one holds glass and canapé. Like a naval battle in Nelson's times: ship to ship, yardarm to yardarm. Sometimes another ship looms up through the noise of battle. Should I switch targets, or redouble broadsides against the present opponent? There is something remorseless about the concentration required. No one wants to be drifting aimlessly through the battle, guns silent, disengaged. . . .

The extraordinary thing is that Iris can serve her guns and return fire, as it were, just like everybody else. I wouldn't have brought her if I hadn't known it would be so. Her face becomes animated—no trace of trouser grimace; she is playing her part just like the rest of us. Mustn't this be good therapy? I should like to think so, but exercise in that sense would imply improvement, recovery. This happy distraction can be only for the moment. I close cautiously on the stern (still automatically Nelsonian) of the guest who is talking to Iris. He is giving a tremendous impression of being good at his work, and happy at it. Half-listening, while at the same time engaging my own opponent closely, I overhear a lively account of the way things are done in an insurance adjustment office. Smiling, Iris listens closely—her attention must be flattering. Then I hear her say, "What do you do?" From the face opposite her, it is evident that the question has been repeated several times is the last few minutes. Undiscouraged, he begins all over again.

Some people might actually find it more restful at a party to talk to someone more or less with Iris's condition. I think I should myself. Apart from making you feel you are performing a service to the community, it is also in the short run less demanding and taxing than the conventional art of party intercourse.

Coming up to me, the hostess says, "Isn't Iris wonderful?" She sounds surprised, perhaps thankful that there is no squeaking or gibbering going on. I am conscious of a base sense of annoyance, even exasperation. People who see Iris on such occasions assume there must be nothing much to worry about. Suppose I were to say to our hostess, "You should see how things are at home." Thank goodness one cannot or does not say things like that at parties.

When we get home, I try to keep Iris interested in the party, saying how much people had liked seeing her. In retrospect, the party does seem to have been a happy time; I am already looking back on it with nostalgia. But it is not remembered. Iris begins to say anxiously, "When do we go?" I wonder how many times she asked the insurance man what it was that he did.

May 10, 1997

I am continually surprised by the way in which the most unexpected people look a little embarrassed if I make some flippant remark about the caring services, the welfare ethic, even "lone" mothers (previously single mothers). Can it be that nice people don't mock such things, even as a joke? No one needs to be nice about sex anymore, or religion. But the modern feeling about social or state "compassion" is uncannily like the old silence about sex, or the reverence about religious beliefs. It's puritanical, too, blasphemy not now recognised as a part of faith, as it was in the older religions.

"Niceness" is always with us, and a good thing, too, but it shifts its ground, even though still clinging precariously to its ambiguities of meaning. Iris's novel *The Nice and the Good* implied these in a masterly way, with as much humour as precision. Does that novel—her others, too—nonetheless demonstrate in some way the inescapability of innocence, perhaps arising from a secure and happy childhood? Iris was both a nice child and a good one, and her parents were the same. None of the three had religion; all were, in the theological sense, naturally Christian souls. Like many philosophers, Iris is impatient with wickedness, its commonplaceness, its knowing conceit. The bad despise the good, confident, and with some justification, that the hapless good may think they "understand" the bad, but in fact can have no true awareness of them. In the characters of her novels, Iris substitutes the desire for power, which fascinates her, for commonplace, disgusting wickedness, which she is neither fascinated by nor understands. To understand wickedness, you must resemble it, at least possess some of its knowing conceit and its inherent dullness. You must be, as Isaiah Berlin said of Dostoevsky, "not a very nice man."

An argument with Iris once about that—or rather, about the

good man, Alyosha Karamazov. A projection of the author's will, I said, whereas Dostoevsky's Underground Man slides effortlessly and absolutely into existence. Why? Because Dostoevsky was as boringly familiar with his Underground Man as he was with himself, while Alyosha is basically an idea, a good idea, of course. Iris objected that great novelists were explorers as well as natural knowers. Wasn't Dostoevsky going to send Alyosha into the pit of hell in a later volume, make him commit all the sins of man? Not real sins, I objected, because they wouldn't have been dull enough, nor conceited enough. Not *natural*. They would have been sins in the author's will, not in the book's reality.

I said this, as it made a reasonably smart point, but I knew my position was undermined by Iris's quiet good sense, by her niceness, in fact. I was point-scoring, something she never did in her novels, nor in her daily life. At the same time, I think one reason we fell in love, and got on so well, is that both of us have always been naïve and innocent, at some deep healing level. Finding it in each other, but not saying so, or even knowing so. Iris is good. I'm not good inside, but I can get by on being nice. A wit remarked of Cyril Connolly, from whose features amiability did not exactly shine, that he was "not so nice as he looked." Iris is just as nice as she looks; indeed, in her case, the feeble though necessary little word acquires an almost transcendental meaning, a different and higher meaning than any of its common and more or less ambiguous ones.

Knowingness. Have got it in my head today, instead of "learning." Peter Conradi told me that the French word for it is *déniaiserie.* Fear of being naïve?

And that awkward word, which I can hardly believe really exists, reminds me in some Proustian way of a disgustingly knowing boy at school. Haven't thought about him for years, if at all. One Sunday, his eye lit up with malicious glee when the lesson was read in school chapel. I couldn't help being curious, and he was delighted to tell me why. It was the story of the woman who anointed Jesus' feet with a precious ointment. "Jesus was awfully pleased with himself. When they said the ointment should have been sold and the money given to the poor, he said, 'Bugger that for a lark—I'm the one who matters, not the poor.' I'm going to take the piss out of God Clark about that."

"God" Clark was the chaplain. When I enquired how, as I was meant to, he said he'd do it in the Divinity Essay we had to write at half term. He did, too. But he failed to get a rise out of the chaplain. All too knowing about the ways of boys, the chaplain returned the essay without comment, merely congratulating the crestfallen youth on the fact that it was "well written."

"God" Clark, a saintly-looking old fellow with white hair, had a dark-haired young assistant chaplain with saturnine good looks, who was known as "Jesus" Steed.

Now why should I have remembered that? Having done so, I would once have rushed to tell Iris, sure that the story would amuse her. Now it wouldn't, alas. I can see her face if I were to tell her, with its bothered and confused look. We can still have jokes, but only very simple ones. Not anecdotes. Least of all anecdotes about "knowingness."

Iris once told me she had no "stream of consciousness." She did not talk to herself. She did not say to herself (I had said that I did), I am doing this—and then I must do that. Sainsbury's—the clouds—the trees are looking nice.

No trivial play with inner words? Did all once go into the world of creation, which lived inside her?

They say people with a strong sense of identity become the worst Alzheimer's patients. They cannot share with others what they still formulate inside themselves. Does Iris speak, inside herself, of what is happening? How can I know? What is left is the terrible expectancy. "When?" and "I want."

Is she still saying inside herself, like the blind man in Faulkner's *Soldiers' Pay:* "When are they going to let me out?"

Escape. The word hovers, though she never utters it.

Home is the worst place. As if something should happen here for her, which never does. Anxiety pushing behind at every second. Picking up things, as if to ward it off. Holding them in her hands like words. Wild wish to shout in her ear, "It's worse for me. *It's much worse!*"

This after the TV breaks down. It Is I who miss it more obviously than Iris does, but in its absence she becomes increasingly restless. The recommended sedative seems not to help.

When are they going to let *me* out?

June 4, 1997

Nightmare recollection of a day in the hot summer last year, just before or after our only swim in the Thames. What provoked the trouble, apart from the heat and a drink or two I had at lunch (when I normally try not to drink, Iris has her few drops of white wine with orangeade)? I must have been feeling unusually low. Rows like that are unpredictable, blowing up like squalls out of nowhere and subsiding as quickly. Then the sun is out, the water calm. One can even forget it is going to happen again. Quite soon.

The cause, though? The reason? There must be one. I remember being struck once, when reading Tolstoy, by his description of anger and emotion, a description which resembles the one theorised about by William James, the novelist's philosopher brother. According to James, at least as I recall, the anger or fear or pity is itself its own cause. I doubt this means much, but in Tolstoy, the notion becomes extraordinarily graphic: as when the movement of the tiny wrinkled fingers of Anna's baby are imitated involuntarily by Karenin's own fingers and face. His pity, even love, for this child of another man by his unfaithful wife existed purely in physical terms.

Was it for me some memory of the smell of Iris's mother when she was daft and elderly, arising now from Iris herself in the muggy heat, which expressed itself not in love and pity but in repulsion and disgust? Smell, as Proust knew, can certainly coincide with pleasure and relaxation, and become identified with those things. Or with their opposites? Iris is not responsive to subtle smells, but I have a very acute sense of them. Perhaps that divides us. I like almost all smells that one becomes conscious of without having to sniff at them, or recoil from them. All our houses have had their different smells, neither good nor bad in the obvious sense, but characteristic—that of Hartley Road, ironically enough, was especially memorable and attractive.

To me, the smell of Iris's mother's flat, though quite faint, was appalling. I had to nerve myself to enter; but Jack, who for quite a while looked after the old lady, never seemed to notice it; nor did Iris herself. The ghost of that smell certainly comes now from Iris from time to time: a family odour and a haunting of mortality. But it wasn't that which caused the row I made, although if William James was anything near right, physical causes are too wrapped up in their emotional results to be disentangled.

The trouble was, or seemed to be, my rage over the indoor plants. There are several of these along the drawing-room windowsill—cyclamen, spider plant, tiger plant, as we called a spotty one—to which I had become rather attached. I cared for them and watered them at the right intervals. Unfortunately, they had also entered the orbit of Iris's obsession with her small objects, things she has picked up in the street and brought into the house. She began to water them compulsively. I was continually finding her with a jug in her hand, and the windowsill and the floor below it slopping over with stagnant water. I urged her repeatedly not to do it, pointing out—which was certainly true—that the plants, the cyclamen in particular, were beginning to wilt and die under this treatment. She seemed to grasp the point, but I soon found her again with a jug or glass in her hand, pouring her water. Like Danaïds, those sad daughters in Greek mythology, condemned forever to fill their sieves with water, punishment for having killed their bridegrooms on their wedding night.

I was not put out at the time: I was fascinated. I took to coming very quietly through the door to try to surprise Iris in the act, and

I frequently did. Once when her great friend and fellow philosopher Philippa Foot (her mother, born in the White House, daughter of President Grover Cleveland) had come to see her, I found them both leaning thoughtfully over the plants, Iris performing her hopeless destructive ritual, Philippa looking on with her quizzically precise, polite attention, as if assessing what moral or ethical problem might be supposed by this task. I was reminded of their colleague Elizabeth Anscombe, absently bringing up her immense brood of children, and once amusing her audience at some philosophical gathering with a sentence to illustrate some subtle linguistic distinction. "If you break that plate, I shall give you a tin one."

Whether or not the fate of the plants, or the ghost of an odour, had anything to do with it, that day I went suddenly berserk. Astonishing how rage produces another person, who repels one, from whom one turns away in incredulous disgust at the very moment one has become him and is speaking with his voice. The rage was instant and total, seeming to come out of nowhere. "I told you not to! *I told you not to!*" In those moments of savagery, neither of us has the slightest idea to what I am referring. But the person who is speaking soon becomes more coherent. Cold, too, and deadly. "You're mad. You're dotty. You don't know anything, remember anything, care about anything." This is accompanied by furious aggressive gestures. Iris trembles violently. "Well," she says—that banal prelude to an apparently reasoned comment, often heard in that tone on BBC discussions, usually followed by some disingenuous patter that does not answer the question. Iris's "Well" relapses into something about "when he comes," or "must

for other person do it now," or "dropping good to burrow when."
I find myself looking in a mirror at the man who has been
speaking. A horrid face, plum colour.

While I go on doing horrible things, as if kicking a child or a lamb,
I suddenly think of the bursar of St. Catherine's College, a charming
scholarly man, a financial wizard, a Parsee, who was telling me about
his little son Minoo, a year or two old. "He's very tiresome. He's
always breaking things. But it's not possible to be angry with him."

The bursar looked surprised and interested by his own reaction.
I wonder briefly, if we'd had a child, would I have learnt not to be
angry with it? In which case, would I not be angry with Iris now?

November 20, 1997

Anger sometimes seems now to be a way of still refusing to admit
that there is anything wrong. Like a sincere compliment. You are
just the same as ever, bless you (or curse you), and so shall I be. I
wouldn't insult you by pretending otherwise.

A happy stay, with our friend Audi in her little house in the middle
of Lanzarote. Getting there is an ordeal, the chartered flight always
packed to the doors with holiday-makers. I am reminded of the old
joke about Géricault's painting *The Raft of the Medusa*, with stricken
castaways clinging on at all angles in the last stages of exposure and
thirst. Reproduced with a holiday brochure caption: "Getting there
is half the fun." But Peter and Jim come with us and look after us, so
the whole ordeal is almost pleasurable.

Return a fortnight later. I have a heavy cold and feel unnatu-
rally tired, although the journey up to this point could not have

been easier. Peter puts us on the bus for Oxford. I sink back thankfully. Nearly home. The bus cruises steadily on through the dark, seeming to shrug off the rush-hour traffic on either side of it. The few passengers are asleep. But we have no sooner started than Iris is jumping up and down in agitation. "Where are we going? Where is the bus taking us?" She won't sit still, but rushes to the front and looks out anxiously ahead. I manage to get her sitting down. I say, "We're going back to Oxford. Back home." She replies, "No! No home. Why travelling like this? He doesn't know."

Before I can stop her, she is speaking agitatedly to the bus driver. She has caught hold of one of the bags, whose contents begin to spill on the gangway. I pick the things up, then push Iris into a seat opposite a sleeping woman. I apologise to the driver, who remains ominously silent. When I get back, the woman, a nice-looking person, is awake, and distraught, desperately trying to regain the handbag and other possessions which had been on the seat beside her. I take them from Iris and put them back, apologising again in a whisper. Iris says, "So sorry," and gives the woman her beautiful smile. I get Iris into another seat and give her a surreptitious violent punch on the arm by which I am holding her.

Gatwick to Oxford in the late Friday rush hour is a long way, every second of it occupied by tormented squirrel-like movements and mutterings. Iris grips the seat in front and stares ahead. A feeling of general distraction and unease eddies through the calm of the darkened bus. I can make out faces now alert and fixed resentfully. As the bus at last nears Oxford, I try to point out things she might recognise, but the agitation gets worse.

Clumsy escape from the stares of the passengers. Only one ancient taxi left, driven by a villainous-looking Indian with a gentle cultured voice. He starts to go the wrong way half-way up Banbury Road, and I distractedly put him right. He says, "Oh, no, I should know better, really. Very sorry about that." I give him a ten-pound note through the wire grille and get very little change, but I can't be bothered about that. I give some of it back as a tip and he says nothing. Open the door. Get inside the gate. The house feels deathly cold. I find Iris looking at me in a wonderful way, just as she used to do when we returned home together from some trying outing. I ignore her look, rush to the central-heating switch. Then I come back and say in a cold, furious voice, "You behaved disgracefully on the bus. I felt ashamed of you."

She looks surprised but then reassured, as if recalling an old cue. She would just be defending her corner by the kind old method—that is to say, not defending it. Leaving me to work out my nastiness, as if I were a child. "Well," she says. Her equivalent now of what might once have been a soothing "So sorry." I have lost my voice, can't hear, and am drowning in a cold that seems more ominous than an ordinary cold, as the bus driver's silence seemed more ominous than words. My chest hurts when I cough. After a few more ugly words, I say that I've probably got pneumonia. Hasn't she noticed I'm ill? She looks uncomprehending again. The moment of realisation and reassurance has gone with my own fit of cold fury, which brought them on. My appeal for sympathy leaves her lost and bewildered.

What'll she do if I die? If I'm ill and have to go hospital. If I have to stay in bed—what'll she do then? Still exasperated by the bus business, I make these demands with increasing hostility and violence. I am furious to see my words are getting nowhere, and yet relieved, too, by this, so that I can continue to indulge my fury. She knows none of these things can or will happen. While I am still screaming at her, she says, "Let's go. There now. Bed." She says this quite coherently. We squeeze together up the stairs, huddle under the cold duvet, and clutch each other into warmth. In the morning, I feel a lot better.

Iris, I think, has never felt bad. She never caught my cold, as if the Alzheimer's is a charm against mere mundane and quotidian ailments. Jim washed and cut her hair in Lanzarote; Audi gave her a shower and a bath. She said to Audi as they stood together in the shower, "I see an angel. I think it's you." Having caught my cold, poor angel was in fact suffering from asthma and a serious chest infection, for which she had to start taking tetracycline, fortunately available over the counter on the island. How sensible, because Audi has never found a proper doctor there, though she has lived on the island on and off for years. Her temperature went up to nearly 103 degrees, but then came down quickly, much to our relief. I think we were all grateful in some way that Iris knew nothing about it. She reassured us by not knowing of troubles, and the tears of things.

Or rather, troubles touch her heart in invisible and mysterious ways. To Audi's cats, which she was once very fond of, she now seems almost indifferent. She strokes them absently. Peter and Jim's dog, Cloudy, whom she once loved to make much of, now seems to have, for her, the distance and impersonality of an angel. When she sheds tears, softly and for short periods, she hides them with an embarrassment which she no longer feels about any other physical side of herself.

In the old days, she used to weep quite openly, as if it were a form of demonstrable and demonstrated warmth and kindness. Now I find her doing it as if ashamedly, stopping as soon as she sees I have noticed. This is so unlike the past; it is disturbing, too, in another way. It makes me feel she is secretly but fully conscious of what has happened to her and wants to conceal it from me. Can she want to protect me from it? I remember as a child finding my mother crying, and she stopped hastily, and looked annoyed. In Proust, the grandmother has a slight stroke while taking little Marcel for a walk in the park, and she turns her face away so that he should not see it all puckered and distorted.

There are so many doubts and illusions and concealments in any close relationship. Even in our present situation, they can come as an unexpected shock. Iris's tears sometimes seem to signify a whole inner world which she is determined to keep from me and shield me from. There is something ghastly in the feeling of relief that this can't be so; and yet the illusion of such an inner world still there—if it is an illusion—can't help haunting me from time to time. There are moments when I almost welcome it. Iris has always had—must have had—so vast and rich and complex an inner world, which it used to give me immense pleasure *not* to know anything about. Like looking at a map of South America as a child and wondering about the sources of the Amazon, and what unknown cities might be hidden there in the jungle. Have any of those hidden places survived in her?

Showing me a tracing from the most elaborate of the brain scans Iris underwent a year or so ago, the doctor indicated the area of atrophy at the top. The doctors were pleased by the clearness of the indication. I thought then—the old foolish romantic idea of the Amazon—that her brain world had lost its unknown mysteries, all the hidden life that had gone on in it. It had been there, physically and geographically *there*. And now it was proved to be empty. The grey substance that sustained its mysteries had ceased to function, whatever a "function," in there, can possibly mean.

Twice, Iris has said to Peter Conradi that she now feels that she is "sailing into the darkness." It was when he asked her, gently, about her writing. Such a phrase might be said to indicate the sort of inner knowledge that I had in mind. It seems to convey a terrible lucidity about what is going on. But can one be lucid in such a way without possessing the consciousness that can produce such language? And if consciousness can go on producing such words, why not many more, equally lucid?

Were I an expert on the brain, I should find it hard to believe in such flashes of lucidity revealing, as it were, a whole silent but conscious and watching world. It would be as if—to use a clumsy analogy from my hidden city in the jungle—a flash of lightning were to reveal its existence, and then the explorers found that it

didn't exist after all. The words which Iris used with such natural-
ness and brilliance cannot be stacked there silently, sending out an
occasional signal. Or can they? I notice that the eerie felicities
which Iris has sometimes produced, such as "sailing into the darkness" or "I see an angel," seem to come with a little help from her
friends. They are like the things a young child suddenly comes out
with, to the delight and amusement of parents and friends. But it
was the friends or parents who unconsciously did the suggesting.
Must have been.

Iris has heard nothing from a great friend, a novelist whom she
had once befriended and inspired, counselled and consoled. Had
this now famous friend left her, abandoned in her silence? Was it
in resignation or in bitterness of spirit that she spoke those words?
Sailing alone into the dark . . .

In my own daily intercourse with Iris, words don't seem to be
necessary, hardly appear to be uttered. Because we don't talk coherently, and because we talk without seeming to ourselves to be
talking, nothing meaningful gets said. The clear things Iris does
sometimes come out with are intended for public consumption.
They are social statements. They have the air of last remarks before
all the lights go out.

November 30, 1997

I always liked Sunday mornings, but Iris never noticed them. She
still doesn't, but now I find TV a great help. Looking in on her as
I potter about, I am relieved to see her sitting intently, like a good
child, watching the Sunday-morning service. Later, she is still

there; the service has changed to an animated cartoon featuring Bible history, Roman soldiers, and so on, in which she is equally engrossed. Thank goodness for Sunday-morning TV.

There are occasions when I have such a strong wish to remind Iris of something we did or saw that I find myself describing it hopefully, in great detail. I don't say, "You probably don't remember, but . . ." Instead, I now have the feeling that she is trying to follow something I am creating for her. Spring is more vivid when you talk about it in winter, and I find myself telling her about one of our visits with Peter and Jim to Cascob, in Wales, at the end of last May. The small schoolhouse, where twenty or thirty children were once taught, lies on a rising knoll at the end of a steep and narrow valley. It is an old place, a single large high-roofed room. Adjacent to it is the schoolmistress's house, one room up and one down. Although they were once separate buildings, Peter and Jim have joined the two and made some alterations, but the basic structure remains intact. The crown of the hillock on which their home stands slopes sharply down to their pond, with a little island in the middle, thick with alder and willow and with flowers in summer. Just beside the school is an extremely old church, half-buried in green turf nearly up to the window openings on one side, so that the sheep can look in. An immense yew tree, much older even than the church, makes a kind of jungle beside it, dark red with shadows.

On that visit to this enchanting place, we soon found a special routine. A pair of redstarts were nesting just above the back doorway. If we sat motionless in the little courtyard, or looked out of the schoolhouse window, we could see them come and go: small flamelike birds, looking much too exotic to be seen in the British Isles. The breast and tail (*steort* means "tail" in Old English) were bright cinnamon red, the head jet black, with a white ring on the neck. When they hovered near the nest, wary of a possible watcher, they were as jewel-like as hummingbirds.

After watching the redstarts, our ritual was to go round to the churchyard, where we could have quite a different experience. Jim had fixed a nesting box on a great ash tree where the graveyard bordered their copse. He told us a pair of pied flycatchers were nesting there. A fly-catcher is a little bird, even more rare than the redstart, a migrant who now only comes back to the borders of south and central Wales. We stood by a gravestone, watching. Nothing happened for a long time. Suddenly and soundlessly, a neat little apparition in black and pure white appeared by the hole in the nesting box. It was motionless for a moment and then vanished inside. We looked at one another, hardly believing we had really seen it. It seemed like a pure speck of antiquity, robed in the hues of the old religion, almost as if a ghostly emanation from the church itself.

After this, we could not keep away from the grave mound by the edge of the copse, a vantage point only a few feet away from the nest on the ash tree. The little birds seemed unaware of us, just as ghosts would have been. Their busy movements had a soft spirit-like silentness. Peter and Jim told us they did have a small song, but we never heard them make a sound. Although we saw both birds, and identified the male and the female, we could not really believe in their physical existence at all. Like the ghosts in *Macbeth*, they came like shadows, so departed.

In the winter, I find myself telling Iris all this, and she listens with a kind of bemused pleasure and toleration, as if I were making up a fairy story. She doesn't believe it, but she likes to hear it. I myself find that these bird memories, and the whole memory pattern of summer sunshine and green leaves, become subtly different from what it was like at the time. It really is as if I were making the whole thing up.

I remembered that Kilvert, the Victorian parson who once lived not far off in the same part of Wales and had so much loved writing his diary about his days, his walks, and his priestly duties, had once confided to it that what he wrote down was more real to him than what he had actually seen that day or the one before and was now writing about. Only memory holds reality. At least this seems to have been his experience, and that of a lot of other writers, too—romantic souls who, like Wordsworth (worshipped by Kilvert), made the discovery that for them to remember and to write was to create their lives, and their sense of living things. The actual experience was nothing beside it, a mere blur always on the move, always disappearing. Proust or D. H. Lawrence must have felt the same, however much Lawrence himself might protest about "Life—Life" being the great thing. Wordsworth only *really* saw his daffodils when he lay on his couch and viewed them with his inward eye.

Iris's genius as a writer is rather different, I think, more comprehensive. Nor does one think of Shakespeare as creating this wonderful vision after the event. It seems to be a Romantic discovery, this sense that all depends on memory. But like all such generalisations, this is not altogether true: Some writers or artists—Vermeer for instance—create such vanished moments but without bothering to make a song and dance about it.

As I create, or re-create, those birds for Iris, I wonder what is going on in her head. Is she cognisant of an invention, a fairy tale instead of a memory? For a writer of her scale and depth, the power of creation seems so much more important than memory, almost as if it could now continue independent of it. And yet the one seems to depend on the other. So what are we remembering when we invent?

The main thing is, she likes to hear me talk about the birds. They must be just a part, a coming-and-going part, of the me she is always with. Once I was outside her, a reality quite separate from herself, her mind, her powers of being and creating. Not now.

Now I feel us fused together. It appalls me sometimes, but it also seems comforting and reassuring and normal.

Reminded of *The Girl with the Red Hat,* the Vermeer portrait that for me haunted our short but happy stay in The Hague. When we were there, I at once began to have that fantasy about it, which I told to Audi and Iris, separately I think. For Audi, I wanted it to be comic, a comical adventure fantasy, with sinister overtones, which we could laugh at together. Could it be that for Iris I instinctively tried to make it sound a bit like something in her own novels? As if I were trying to remind or inspire, or even carry on the torch by a kind of imitation? However that was, the story I wrote about it does not sound in the least like Iris, except perhaps to me. It came out much more like the fantasy I told Audi, who kindly said she enjoyed it when the book appeared a year later.

Life is no longer bringing the pair of us "closer and closer apart," in the poet's tenderly ambiguous words. Every day we move closer and closer together. We could not do otherwise. There is a certain comic irony—happily, not darkly comic—that after more than forty years of taking marriage for granted, marriage has decided it is tired of this, and is taking a hand in the game. Purposefully, persistently, involuntarily, our marriage is now getting somewhere. It is giving us no choice—and I am glad of that.

Every day, we are physically closer; and Iris's little "mouse cry," as I think of it, signifying loneliness in the next room, the wish to be back beside me, seems less and less forlorn, more simple, more natural. She is not sailing into the dark: The voyage is over, and under the dark escort of Alzheimer's, she has arrived somewhere. So have I.

This new marriage has designed itself, as Darwin once speculated that fish perhaps designed their own eyes, to bring to an end her fearful anxieties of apartness—that happy apartness which marriage had once taken wholly for granted. This new marriage needs us absolutely, just as we need it. To that extent, it is still a question of "taking for granted."

The phrase "taking for granted" was in my head because I had just received a letter from the Japanese psychologist Takeo Doi. Admiring Iris's novels, he had once corresponded with her, and his ideas had interested her. As pen pals, they had got on, and the three of us had once met in Tokyo. He had read a piece of mine on marriage which had been commissioned by *The Times*. The paper had naturally wanted it to be about Iris's Alzheimer's, but I had also made our old point about taking marriage for granted, quoting Iris's character in *A Severed Head* who had lamented that her marriage "wasn't getting anywhere." This had struck the distinguished psychologist, the explorer of *amae*, the taken-for-granted bond which supplies the social cohesion of the Japanese people, and he had titled the essay which he now sent me "Taking for Granted." Japanese husbands and wives, he said, do not make a fuss about marriage, as in the Western style, but take it for granted. I wrote thanking him for the piece, and remarked that marriage was now taking us for granted, rather than we it.

As in the old days, nothing needs to be done. Helplessness is all. Yet it's amusing to contemplate "new marriage." Like New Labour, the New Deal, and so on? Not quite like that. Hard, though, to contemplate one's arrangements without their becoming, at least to oneself, a private form of public relations. I need our closeness now as much as Iris does, but I don't feel I need to cherish it. It has simply arrived, like the Alzheimer's. The best as well as the fullest consciousness of it comes in the early morning, when I am beside Iris in bed, tapping on my typewriter, and feel her hearing it in her doze, and being reassured by it.

In the past, she would have been up and in her study, in her own world. I am in mine, but it seems to be hers, too, because of proximity. She murmurs, more or less asleep, and her hand comes

out from under the quilt. I put mine on it and stroke her finger-
nails for a moment, noticing how long they are, and how dirty. I
must cut them and clean them again this morning. They seem to
grow faster by the month, and I suppose mine do the same.

December 14, 1997

As I am sitting in the kitchen, trying to read something, Iris makes
her mouse noise at the door. She is carrying a Coca-Cola tin
picked up in the street, a rusty spanner—where on earth did she
get that?—and a single shoe.

Single shoes lie about the house as if deposited by a flash flood.
Never a matching pair. Things in odd corners—old newspapers,
bottles covered in dust. A mound of clothing on the floor of the
room upstairs where she used to write. Dried-out capless plastic
pens crunch underfoot. A piece of paper in her handwriting of several years ago with "Dear Penny" on it.

Rubbish becomes relaxing if there is no will to disturb it. It will
see out our time. I think of the autumn in Keats's poem "Hyperion": "But where the dead leaf fell, there did it rest."

An odd parallel between the rubbish on the floor and the
words that fly about the house all day. Words the equivalent of
that single shoe.

Tone is what matters. All is okay with a child or cat or gunga
exclamation. "The bad cat: What *are* we going to do with her?" I
stroke her back or pull her backwards and forwards till she starts
laughing. I imitate the fond way her father used to say in his
mock-exasperated Belfast accent (she told me this long ago),

"Have you got no sense at *all*?" Iris's face always softens if I mention her father in this way. Instead of crying, she starts to smile.

I rely on the bad-child ploy, which can easily sustain some degree of frenzy. "You bad animal! Can't you leave me alone *just for one minute!*" Or sometimes I sound to myself like Hedda Gabler needling her lover. But if I give it the tone of our child talk, Iris always beams back at me.

She never showed any interest in children before. Now she loves them, on television or in real life. It seems almost too appropriate. I tell her she is nearly four years old now—isn't that wonderful?

The Christmas business, it's all come round again. Iris has always enjoyed Christmas, and the socialising that goes with it. The festive season always makes me feel glum, though I go through the motions. Why not get away from it all? In the old days, Iris wouldn't have liked that. Now I am not so sure. Change in one sense means little to her, yet a different scene of any sort can cause her to look around in astonished wonder, like Sleeping Beauty who when she stirred among the cobwebs saw—must have seen, surely—spiders and rats and mice running away in alarm. (I am assuming that the prince who woke her would have stepped tactfully back into the shadows.)

Wonder on the edge of fear. That shows in Iris's face if we go anywhere unfamiliar to her. A momentary relief from the daily pucker of blank anxiety. A change only relieves that anxiety for a few minutes, often only seconds. Then anxiety returns with new vigour. The calmness of routine has more to recommend it. But no choice really—Hobson's choice. Routine needs a change, and change finds some relief again in routine, like the people in Dante's hell who kept being hustled from fire into the ice bucket, then back again.

Well, not as bad as that. The point about Christmas could be that it combines a change with a routine, a routine of custom and ceremony that has at least the merit of a special occasion, of coming but once a year. Years ago, our friend Brigid Brophy and her husband decided to go to Istanbul for Christmas. "To eat our turkey in Turkey," as they explained. Iris then laughed politely, but she was not amused. Indeed, I am not sure she was not really rather shocked. Christmas to her was not exactly holy, but it meant something more important than the opportunity for a witticism about turkey in Turkey.

I think she welcomed at that time the idea of inevitability—something that has to happen. Mary and Joseph in the stable could do nothing about it—why should *we* need to?

Now I must encourage that instinct towards passivity, taking refuge in blest, or at least time-honoured, routines. No point in getting away from it all, nowhere to get away to. Alzheimer's will meet you there, like death at Samarra.

So we'll go to London as usual, visit my brother Michael, have Christmas dinner with him. We'll do all the usual things.

December 25, 1997

It's Christmas morning. And we are doing all the usual things. Routine is a substitute for memory. Iris is not asking the usual anxious questions: "Where are we? What are we doing? Who is coming?"

Someone, or something, is coming. The silence it brings makes no demands. London is uncannily silent on Christmas morning. Nobody seems to be about. If there are churchgoers and church bells, we see none, hear none. The silence and the emptiness seem all the better.

We walk to Kensington Gardens up the deserted street, between the tall stucco façades falling into Edwardian decay, but still handsome. Henry James lived on the left here; Browning farther up on the right. We pass their blue plaques set in the white wall. A few yards back, we passed the great gloomy redbrick mansions where T. S. Eliot had a flat for many years. His widow must be in church now.

Our route on Christmas morning is always the same. We have been doing this for years. As we pass their spectral houses, I now utter a little bit of patter like a guide. Henry James, Robert Browning, T. S. Eliot. On former mornings like these, we used to gaze up at their windows, talk a bit about them. Now I just mention the names. Does Iris remember them? She smiles a little. They are still familiar, those names, as familiar as this unique morning silence. Just for this morning, those writers have laid their pens down, as Iris herself has done, and are taking a well-earned rest, looking forward to their dinners. Thackeray, the gourmet, whose house is just round the corner, would have looked forward to his with special keenness.

Now we can see the park, and beyond it the handsome Williamite façade of Kensington Palace. When Princess Diana died, the whole green here was a mass of cellophane, wrapping withered flowers. And the crowds were silent, too. As quiet, the media said in an awed way, as it is in this morning's calm. The grievers were like good children at bedtime, folding their hands in ritual prayer. It was a tranquil ceremony, like our Christmas, as we wander now vaguely over the deserted road, usually a mass of traffic, and up the expanse of the Broad Walk.

A few dogs here, unimpressed by Christmas, but seeming merrier than usual in contrast with the silence. There is one bell now, tolling somewhere on a sweet high note. Up in the sky, the jet trails move serenely on, seeming more noiseless than usual, their murmur fainter when it comes. Christmas morning in London is always calm and mild and bright. I can only remember one time when it rained, even snowed a bit. I ask Iris if she can remember that Christmas. She smiles. No need to remember, as this ritual that has replaced memory goes on.

The Round Pond. Canada geese standing meditatively, for once making no demands. The same path as usual, downwards, to the Serpentine. Nobody round the Peter Pan statue. Not even a Japanese couple with a camera. One Christmas, we met two middle-aged ladies from New Zealand here, who told us this statue was the one thing they really wanted to see in London.

Young Pan himself, bronze fingers delicately crooked, his double pipe to his lips, has the sublimely sinister indifference of childhood. Captain Hook, his great enemy, was always made nervous by that pose. He considered Peter to have Good Form without knowing it, which is, of course, the best Form of all. Poor Hook was in despair about this. It made Iris laugh when I told her, years ago, before we were married. I read a bit of the book to her (the book is much better, and funnier, than the pantomime play). Iris, I recall, was so amused that she later put the "good form" business into one of her own novels.

Iris's amusement may even have been shared, in a quiet way, by the sculptor himself, who covered the base of the group with elves and rabbits and snails in the Victorian fairy-tale tradition. But at the top, he put the elegant figure of a much more worldly young woman, scrambling determinedly over the plinth to proposition Peter, giving the bystander an agreeable view of her polished bronze derrière. It is clad in a modishly draped and close-fitting Edwardian skirt, and she looks much too old for Peter anyway. Could it be that Sir George Frampton, as well as being an excellent artist and sculptor, had a sense of humour about these matters? It certainly looks like it, on such a quiet, sunny Christmas morning, with real squirrels hopping about all round the statue, vainly soliciting the nuts which the fat little beasts have no trouble in getting from tourists on ordinary, busier days.

As we walk round and admire, I tell Iris that my mother assured me that if I looked hard enough over the railings, into the private dells where the bluebells and daffodils come up in spring, I might see fairies, perhaps even Peter Pan himself. I believed her. I could almost believe her now, with the tranquil sunshine in the park making a midwinter spring, full of the illusion of flowers and fairies as well as real birdsong.

Iris is listening, which she rarely does, and smiling, too. There have been no anxious pleas this morning, no tears, none of those broken sentences whose only meaning is the dread in her voice and the demand for reassurance. Something or someone this morning has reassured her, given for an hour or two what the prayer book calls "that peace which the world cannot give."

Perhaps it is the Christmas ritual. It is going somewhere, but it is also a routine, even though a rare one. It is both. And now it will go on. We shall return to my brother, who has attended matins this morning at Chelsea Old Church, where Sir Thomas More once used to worship. We shall eat sardines and sausages and scrambled eggs together, with a bottle or two of a Bulgarian red wine which goes with everything. The sort of Christmas dinner we all three enjoy, and the only time of the year Michael permits a little cookery to be done in his immaculate and sterile little kitchen. The sardines are routine for him, but the eggs and sausages represent a real concession. I shall do them, with Iris standing beside me, and we shall bring the wine.

A snooze then. Iris will sleep deeply. Later, we listen to carols and Christmas music. And I have the illusion, which fortunate Alzheimer's partners must feel at such times, that life is just the same, has never changed. I cannot imagine Iris any different. Her loss of memory becomes, in a sense, my own. In a muzzy way—the Bulgarian wine, no doubt—I find myself thinking of the Christmas birth, and also of Wittgenstein's comment that death is not a human experience. We are born to live only from day to day. "Take short views of human life—never further than dinner or tea." The Reverend Sydney Smith's advice is most easily taken during these ritualised days. The ancient saving routine of Christmas, which for us today has been twice blessed.

compassion

from

The Dead
by James Joyce

Some intelligent readers are bored or intimidated by the later stylistic experiments of James Joyce (1882–1941). "The Dead" is another matter. In the following selection from that story, the reader finds Gabriel and his wife returning home late at night after a lively dinner party.

G abriel had not gone to the door with the others. He was in a dark part of the hall gazing up the staircase. A woman was standing near the top of the first flight, in the shadow also. He could not see her face but he could see the terracotta and salmonpink panels of her skirt which the shadow made appear black and white. It was his wife. She was leaning on the banisters, listening to something. Gabriel was surprised at her stillness and strained his ear to listen also. But he could hear little save the noise of laughter and dispute on the front steps, a few chords struck on the piano and a few notes of a man's voice singing.

He stood still in the gloom of the hall, trying to catch the air that the voice was singing and gazing up at his wife. There was grace and mystery in her attitude as if she were a symbol of something. He asked himself what is a woman standing on the stairs in the shadow, listening to distant music, a symbol of. If he were a painter he would paint her in that attitude. Her blue felt hat would show off the bronze of her hair against the darkness and the dark panels of her skirt would show off the light ones. *Distant Music* he would call the picture if he were a painter.

The hall-door was closed; and Aunt Kate, Aunt Julia and Mary Jane came down the hall, still laughing.

—Well, isn't Freddy terrible? said Mary Jane. He's really terrible.

Gabriel said nothing but pointed up the stairs towards where his wife was standing. Now that the hall-door was closed the voice and the piano could be heard more clearly. Gabriel held up his hand for them to be silent. The song seemed to be in the old Irish tonality and the singer seemed uncertain both of his words and of his voice. The voice, made plaintive by distance and by the singer's hoarseness, faintly illuminated the cadence of the air with words expressing grief:

O, the rain falls on my heavy locks
And the dew wets my skin,
My babe lies cold . . .

—O, exclaimed Mary Jane. It's Bartell D'Arcy singing and he wouldn't sing all the night. O, I'll get him to sing a song before he goes.

—O do, Mary Jane, said Aunt Kate.

Mary Jane brushed past the others and ran to the staircase but before she reached it the singing stopped and the piano was closed abruptly.

—O, what a pity! she cried. Is he coming down, Gretta?

Gabriel heard his wife answer yes and saw her come down towards them. A few steps behind her were Mr Bartell D'Arcy and Miss O'Callaghan.

—O, Mr D'Arcy, cried Mary Jane, it's downright mean of you to break off like that when we were all in raptures listening to you.

—I have been at him all the evening, said Miss O'Callaghan, and Mrs Conroy too and he told us he had a dreadful cold and couldn't sing.

—O, Mr D'Arcy, said Aunt Kate, now that was a great fib to tell.

Can't you see that I'm as hoarse as a crow? said Mr D'Arcy roughly.

He went into the pantry hastily and put on his overcoat. The others, taken aback by his rude speech, could find nothing to say. Aunt Kate wrinkled her brows and made signs to the others to drop the subject. Mr D'Arcy stood swathing his neck carefully and frowning.

—It's the weather, said Aunt Julia, after a pause.

—Yes, everybody has colds, said Aunt Kate readily, everybody.

—They say, said Mary Jane, we haven't had snow like it for thirty years; and I read this morning in the newspapers that the snow is general all over Ireland.

—I love the look of snow, said Aunt Julia sadly.

—So do I, said Miss O'Callaghan. I think Christmas is never really Christmas unless we have the snow on the ground.

—But poor Mr D'Arcy doesn't like the snow, said Aunt Kate, smiling.

Mr D'Arcy came from the pantry, fully swathed and buttoned, and in a repentant tone told them the history of his cold. Everyone gave him advice and said it was a great pity and urged him to be very careful of his throat in the night air. Gabriel watched his wife who did not join in the conversation. She was standing right under the dusty fanlight and the flame of the gas lit up the rich bronze of her hair which he had seen her drying at the fire a few days before. She was in the same attitude and seemed unaware of the talk about her. At last she turned towards them and Gabriel saw that there was colour on her cheeks and that her eyes were shining. A sudden tide of joy went leaping out of his heart.

—Mr D'Arcy, she said, what is the name of that song you were singing?

—It's called *The Lass of Aughrim,* said Mr D'Arcy, but I couldn't remember it properly. Why? Do you know it?

—*The Lass of Aughrim,* she repeated. I couldn't think of the name.

—It's a very nice air, said Mary Jane. I'm sorry you were not in voice to-night.

—Now, Mary Jane, said Aunt Kate, don't annoy Mr D'Arcy. I won't have him annoyed.

Seeing that all were ready to start she shepherded them to the door where good-night was said:

—Well, good-night, Aunt Kate, and thanks for the pleasant evening.

—Good-night, Gabriel. Good-night, Gretta!

—Good-night, Aunt Kate, and thanks ever so much. Good-night, Aunt Julia.

—O, good-night, Gretta, I didn't see you.

—Good-night, Mr D'Arcy. Good-night, Miss O'Callaghan.

—Good-night, Miss Morkan.

—Good-night, again.

—Good-night, all. Safe home.

—Good-night. Good-night.

The morning was still dark. A dull yellow light brooded over the houses and the river; and the sky seemed to be descending. It was slushy underfoot; and only streaks and patches of snow lay on the roofs, on the parapets of the quay and on the area railings. The lamps were still burning redly in the murky air and, across the river, the palace of the Four Courts stood out menacingly against the heavy sky.

She was walking on before him with Mr Bartell D'Arcy, her shoes in a brown parcel tucked under one arm and her hands holding her skirt up from the slush. She had no longer any grace of attitude but Gabriel's eyes were still bright with happiness. The blood went bounding along his veins; and the thoughts went rioting through his brain, proud, joyful, tender, valorous.

She was walking on before him so lightly and so erect that he longed to run after her noiselessly, catch her by the shoulders and say something foolish and affectionate into her ear. She seemed to him so frail that he longed to defend her against something and then to be alone with her. Moments of their secret life together burst like stars upon his memory. A heliotrope envelope was lying beside his breakfast-cup and he was caressing it with his hand. Birds were twittering in the ivy and the sunny web of the curtain was shimmering along the floor: he could not eat for happiness. They were standing on the crowded platform and he was placing a ticket inside the warm palm of her glove. He was standing with her in the cold, looking in through a grated window at a man making bottles in a roaring furnace. It was very cold. Her face, fragrant in the cold air, was quite close to his; and suddenly she called out to the man at the furnace:

—Is the fire hot, sir?

But the man could not hear her with the noise of the furnace. It was just as well. He might have answered rudely.

A wave of yet more tender joy escaped from his heart and went coursing in warm flood along his arteries. Like the tender fires of stars moments of their life together, that no one knew of or would ever know of, broke upon and illumined his memory. He longed to recall to her those moments, to make her forget the years of their dull existence together and remember only their moments of ecstasy. For the years, he felt, had not quenched his soul or hers. Their children, his writing, her household cares had not quenched all their souls' tender fire. In one letter that he had written to her then he had said: *Why is it that words like these seem to me so dull and cold? Is it because there is no word tender enough to be your name?*

Like distant music these words that he had written years before were borne towards him from the past. He longed to be alone with her. When the others had gone away, when he and she were in their room in the hotel, then they would be alone together. He would call her softly:

—Gretta!

Perhaps she would not hear at once: she would be undressing. Then something in his voice would strike her. She would turn and look at him. . . .

At the corner of Winetavern Street they met a cab. He was glad
of its rattling noise as it saved him from conversation. She was
looking out of the window and seemed tired. The others spoke
only a few words, pointing out some building or street. The horse
galloped along wearily under the murky morning sky, dragging his
old rattling box after his heels, and Gabriel was again in a cab with
her, galloping to catch the boat, galloping to their honeymoon.

As the cab drove across O'Connell Bridge Miss O'Callaghan said:

—They say you never cross O'Connell Bridge without seeing a
white horse.

—I see a white man this time, said Gabriel.

—Where? asked Mr Bartell D'Arcy.

Gabriel pointed to the statue, on which lay patches of snow.
Then he nodded familiarly to it and waved his hand.

—Good-night, Dan, he said gaily.

When the cab drew up before the hotel Gabriel jumped out
and, in spite of Mr Bartell D'Arcy's protest, paid the driver. He
gave the man a shilling over his fare. The man saluted and said:

—A prosperous New Year to you, sir.

—The same to you, said Gabriel cordially.

She leaned for a moment on his arm in getting out of the cab
and while standing at the curbstone, bidding the others good-
night. She leaned lightly on his arm, as lightly as when she had
danced with him a few hours before. He had felt proud and happy
then, happy that she was his, proud of her grace and wifely carriage. But now, after the kindling again of so many memories, the
first touch of her body, musical and strange and perfumed, sent

through him a keen pang of lust. Under cover of her silence he pressed her arm closely to his side; and, as they stood at the hotel door, he felt that they had escaped from their lives and duties, escaped from home and friends and run away together with wild and radiant hearts to a new adventure.

An old man was dozing in a great hooded chair in the hall. He lit a candle in the office and went before them to the stairs. They followed him in silence, their feet falling in soft thuds on the thickly carpeted stairs. She mounted the stairs behind the porter, her head bowed in the ascent, her frail shoulders curved as with a burden, her skirt girt tightly about her. He could have flung his arms about her hips and held her still for his arms were trembling with desire to seize her and only the stress of his nails against the palms of his hands held the wild impulse of his body in check. The porter halted on the stairs to settle his guttering candle. They halted too on the steps below him. In the silence Gabriel could hear the falling of the molten wax into the tray and the thumping of his own heart against his ribs.

The porter led them along a corridor and opened a door. Then he set his unstable candle down on a toilet-table and asked at what hour they were to be called in the morning.

Eight, said Gabriel.

The porter pointed to the tap of the electric-light and began a muttered apology but Gabriel cut him short.

—We don't want any light. We have light enough from the street. And I say, he added, pointing to the candle, you might remove that handsome article, like a good man.

The porter took up his candle again, but slowly for he was

surprised by such a novel idea. Then he mumbled good-night and went out. Gabriel shot the lock to.

A ghostly light from the street lamp lay in a long shaft from one window to the door. Gabriel threw his overcoat and hat on a couch and crossed the room towards the window. He looked down into the street in order that his emotion might calm a little. Then he turned and leaned against a chest of drawers with his back to the light. She had taken off her hat and cloak and was standing before a large swinging mirror, unhooking her waist. Gabriel paused for a few moments, watching her, and then said:

—Gretta!

She turned away from the mirror slowly and walked along the shaft of light towards him. Her face looked so serious and weary that the words would not pass Gabriel's lips. No, it was not the moment yet.

—You looked tired, he said.

—I am a little, she answered.

—You don't feel ill or weak?

—No, tired: that's all.

She went on to the window and stood there, looking out. Gabriel waited again and then, fearing that diffidence was about to conquer him, he said abruptly:

—By the way, Gretta!

—What is it?

—You know that poor fellow Malins? he said quickly.

—Yes. What about him?

—Well, poor fellow, he's a decent sort of chap after all, continued

Gabriel in a false voice. He gave me back that sovereign I lent him and I didn't expect it really. It's a pity he wouldn't keep away from that Browne, because he's not a bad fellow at heart.

He was trembling now with annoyance. Why did she seem so abstracted? He did not know how he could begin. Was she annoyed, too, about something? If she would only turn to him or come to him of her own accord! To take her as she was would be brutal. No, he must see some ardour in her eyes first. He longed to be master of her strange mood.

—When did you lend him the pound? she asked, after a pause.

Gabriel strove to restrain himself from breaking out into brutal language about the sottish Malins and his pound. He longed to cry to her from his soul, to crush her body against his, to overmaster her. But he said:

—O, at Christmas, when he opened that little Christmas-card shop in Henry Street.

He was in such a fever of rage and desire that he did not hear her come from the window. She stood before him for an instant, looking at him strangely. Then, suddenly raising herself on tiptoe and resting her hands lightly on his shoulders, she kissed him.

—You are a very generous person, Gabriel, she said.

Gabriel, trembling with delight at her sudden kiss and at the quaintness of her phrase, put his hands on her hair and began smoothing it back, scarcely touching it with his fingers. The washing had made it fine and brilliant. His heart was brimming over with happiness. Just when he was wishing for it she had come to him of her own accord. Perhaps her thoughts had been running with his. Perhaps she had felt the impetuous desire that was in him and then the yielding mood had come upon her. Now that she had fallen to him so easily he wondered why he had been so diffident.

He stood, holding her head between his hands. Then, slipping one arm swiftly about her body and drawing her towards him, he said softly:

—Gretta dear, what are you thinking about?

She did not answer nor yield wholly to his arm. He said again, softly:

—Tell me what it is, Gretta. I think I know what is the matter. Do I know?

She did not answer a once. Then she said in an outburst of tears:

—O, I am thinking about that song, *The Lass of Aughrim*.

She broke loose from him and ran to the bed and, throwing her arms across the bed-rail, hid her face. Gabriel stood stockstill for a moment in astonishment and then followed her. As he passed in the way of the cheval-glass he caught sight of himself in full length, his broad, well-filled shirt-front, the face whose expression always puzzled him when he saw it in a mirror and his glimmering gilt-rimmed eyeglasses. He halted a few paces from her and said:

—What about the song? Why does that make you cry?

She raised her head from her arms and dried her eyes with the back of her hand like a child. A kinder note than he had intended went into his voice.

—Why, Gretta? he asked.

—I am thinking about a person long ago who used to sing that song.

—And who was the person long ago? asked Gabriel, smiling.

—It was a person I used to know in Galway when I was living with my grandmother, she said.

The smile passed away from Gabriel's face. A dull anger began to gather again at the back of his mind and the dull fires of his lust began to glow angrily in his veins.

—Someone you were in love with? he asked ironically.

—It was a young boy I used to know, she answered, named Michael Furey. He used to sing that song, *The Lass of Aughrim*. He was very delicate.

Gabriel was silent. He did not wish her to think that he was interested in this delicate boy.

—I can see him so plainly, she said after a moment. Such eyes as he had: big dark eyes! And such an expression in them—an expression!

—O then, you were in love with him? said Gabriel.

—I used to go out walking with him, she said, when I was in Galway.

A thought flew across Gabriel's mind.

—Perhaps that was why you wanted to go to Galway with that Ivors girl? he said coldly.

She looked at him and asked in surprise:

—What for?

Her eyes made Gabriel feel awkward. He shrugged his shoulders and said:

—How do I know? To see him perhaps.

She looked away from him along the shaft of light towards the window in silence.

—He is dead, she said at length. He died when he was only seventeen. Isn't it a terrible thing to die so young as that?

—What was he? asked Gabriel, still ironically.

—He was in the gasworks, she said.

Gabriel felt humiliated by the failure of his irony and by the evocation of this figure from the dead, a boy in the gasworks. While he had been full of memories of their secret life together, full of tenderness and joy and desire, she had been comparing him in her mind with another. A shameful consciousness of his own person assailed turn. He saw himself as a ludicrous figure, acting as a pennyboy for his aunts, a nervous well-meaning sentimentalist, orating to vulgarians and idealising his own clownish lusts, the pitiable fatuous fellow he had caught a glimpse of in the mirror. Instinctively he turned his back more to the light lest she might see the shame that burned upon his forehead.

He tried to keep up his tone of cold interrogation but his voice when he spoke was humble and indifferent.

—I suppose you were in love with this Michael Furey, Gretta, he said.

—I was great with him at that time, she said.

Her voice was veiled and sad. Gabriel, feeling now how vain it would be to try to lead her whither he had purposed, caressed one of her hands and said, also sadly:

—And what did he die of so young, Gretta? Consumption, was it?

—I think he died for me, she answered.

A vague terror seized Gabriel at this answer as if, at that hour when he had hoped to triumph, some impalpable and vindictive being was coming against him, gathering forces against him in its vague world. But he shook himself free of it with an effort of reason and continued to caress her hand. He did not question her again for he felt that she would tell him of herself. Her hand was warm and moist: it did not respond to his touch but he continued to caress it just as he had caressed her first letter to him that spring morning.

—It was in the winter, she said, about the beginning of the winter when I was going to leave my grandmother's and come up here to the convent. And he was ill at the time in his lodgings in Galway and wouldn't be let out and his people in Oughterard were written to. He was in decline, they said, or something like that. I never knew rightly.

She paused for a moment and sighed.

—Poor fellow, she said. He was very fond of me and he was such a gentle boy. We used to go out together, walking, you know, Gabriel, like the way they do in the country. He was going to study singing only for his health. He had a very good voice, poor Michael Furey.

—Well; and then? asked Gabriel.

—And then when it came to the time for me to leave Galway and come up to the convent he was much worse and I wouldn't be let see him so I wrote a letter saying I was going up to Dublin and would be back in the summer and hoping he would be better then.

She paused for a moment to get her voice under control and then went on:

—Then the night before I left I was in my grandmother's house

in Nuns' Island, packing up, and I heard gravel thrown up against
the window. The window was so wet I couldn't see so I ran down-
stairs as I was and slipped out the back into the garden and there
was the poor fellow at the end of the garden, shivering.

—And did you not tell him to go back? asked Gabriel.

—I implored of him to go home at once and told him he would
get his death in the rain. But he said he did not want to live. I can
see his eyes as well as well! He was standing at the end of the wall
where there was a tree.

—And did he go home? asked Gabriel.

—Yes, he went home. And when I was only a week in the convent he died and he was buried in Oughterard where his people
came from. O, the day I heard that, that he was dead!

She stopped, choking with sobs, and, overcome by emotion,
flung herself face downward on the bed, sobbing in the quilt.
Gabriel held her hand for a moment longer, irresolutely, and then,
shy of intruding on her grief, let it fall gently and walked quietly
to the window.

She was fast asleep.

Gabriel, leaning on his elbow, looked for a few moments unre-
sentfully on her tangled hair and half-open mouth, listening to her
deep-drawn breath. So she had had that romance in her life: a man
had died for her sake. It hardly pained him now to think how poor
a part he, her husband, had played in her life. He watched her
while she slept as though he and she had never lived together as
man and wife. His curious eyes rested long upon her face and on

her hair: and, as he thought of what she must have been then, in that time of her first girlish beauty, a strange friendly pity for her entered his soul. He did not like to say even to himself that her face was no longer beautiful but he knew that it was no longer the face for which Michael Furey had braved death.

Perhaps she had not told him all the story. His eyes moved to the chair over which she had thrown some of her clothes. A petticoat string dangled to the floor. One boot stood upright, its limp upper fallen down: the fellow of it lay upon its side. He wondered at his riot of emotions of an hour before. From what had it proceeded? From his aunt's supper, from his own foolish speech, from the wine and dancing, the merrymaking when saying good-night in the hall, the pleasure of the walk along the river in the snow. Poor Aunt Julia! She, too, would soon be a shade with the shade of Patrick Morkan and his horse. He had caught that haggard look upon her face for a moment when she was singing *Arrayed for the Bridal*. Soon, perhaps, he would be sitting in that same drawing-room, dressed in black, his silk hat on his knees. The blinds would be drawn down and Aunt Kate would be sitting beside him, crying and blowing her nose and telling him how Julia had died. He would cast about in his mind for some words that might console her, and would find only lame and useless ones. Yes, yes: that would happen very soon.

The air of the room chilled his shoulders. He stretched himself cautiously along under the sheets and lay down beside his wife. One by one they were all becoming shades. Better pass boldly into that other world, in the full glory of some passion, than fade and wither dismally with age. He thought of how she who lay beside him had locked in her heart for so many years that image of her lover's eyes when he had told her that he did not wish to live.

Generous tears filled Gabriel's eyes. He had never felt like that himself towards any woman but he knew that such a feeling must be love. The tears gathered more thickly in his eyes and in the partial darkness he imagined he saw the form of a young man standing under a dripping tree. Other forms were near. His soul had approached that region where dwell the vast hosts of the dead. He was conscious of, but could not apprehend, their wayward and flickering existence. His own identity was fading out into a grey impalpable world: the solid world itself which these dead had one time reared and lived in was dissolving and dwindling.

A few light taps upon the pane made him turn to the window. It had begun to snow again. He watched sleepily the flakes, silver and dark, falling obliquely against the lamplight. The time had come for him to set out on his journey westward. Yes, the newspapers were right: snow was general all over Ireland. It was falling on every part of the dark central plain, on the treeless hills, falling softly upon the Bog of Allen and, farther westward, softly falling into the dark mutinous Shannon waves. It was falling, too, upon every part of the lonely churchyard on the hill where Michael Furey lay buried. It lay thickly drifted on the crooked crosses and headstones, on the spears of the little gate, on the barren thorns. His soul swooned slowly as he heard the snow falling faintly through the universe and faintly falling, like the descent of their last end, upon all the living and the dead.

solitude

from

Rilke on Love and Other Difficulties
by Rainer Maria Rilke
translated and edited by John J. L. Mood

Czech poet and essayist Rainer Maria Rilke's (1875–1976) writing about love is informed by penetrating insight and an exquisite sense of mystery. His notions of love and marriage remain radical today.

I am of the opinion that "marriage" as such does not deserve as much emphasis as it has acquired through the conventional development of its nature. It does not occur to anyone to expect a single person to be "happy,"—but if he marries, people are much surprised if he *isn't*! (And for that matter it really isn't at all important to be happy, whether single or married.) Marriage is, in many respects, a simplification of one's way of life, and the union naturally combines the forces and wills of two young people so that, together, they seem to reach farther into the future than before.— Only, those are sensations by which one cannot live. Above all, marriage is a new task and a new seriousness,—a new challenge to and questioning of the strength and generosity of each partner and a great new danger for both.

It is a question in marriage, to my feeling, not of creating a quick community of spirit by tearing down and destroying all boundaries, but rather a good marriage is that in which each appoints the other guardian of his solitude, and shows him this confidence, the greatest in his power to bestow. A *togetherness* between two people is an impossibility, and where it seems, nevertheless, to exist, it is a narrowing, a reciprocal agreement which robs either one party or both of his fullest freedom and development. But, once the realization is accepted that even between the *closest* human beings infinite distances continue to exist, a wonderful living side by side can grow up, if they succeed in loving the distance between them which makes it possible for each to see the other whole and against a wide sky!

Therefore this too must be the standard for rejection or choice: whether one is willing to stand guard over the solitude of a person and whether one is inclined to set this same person at the gate of one's own solitude, of which he learns only through that which steps, festively clothed, out of the great darkness.

At bottom no one in life can help anyone else in life; this one experiences over and over in every conflict and every perplexity: that one is alone.

All companionship can consist only in the strengthening of two neighboring solitudes, whereas everything that one is wont to call giving oneself is by nature harmful to companionship: for when a person abandons himself, he is no longer anything, and when two people both give themselves up in order to come close to each other, there is no longer any ground beneath them and their being together is a continual falling.

There is scarcely anything more difficult than to love one another. That it is work, day labor, day labor, God knows there is no other word for it. And look, added to this is the fact that young people are not prepared for such difficult loving; for convention has tried to make this most complicated and ultimate relationship into something easy and frivolous, has given it the appearance of everyone's being able to do it. It is not so. Love is something difficult and it is more difficult than other things because in other conflicts nature herself enjoins men to collect themselves, to take themselves firmly in hand with all their strength, while in the heightening of love the impulse is to give oneself wholly away. But just think, can that be anything beautiful, to give oneself away not as something whole and ordered, but haphazard rather, bit by bit, as it comes? Can such giving away, that looks so like a throwing away and dismemberment, be anything good, can it be happiness, joy, progress? No, it cannot. . . . When you give someone flowers, you arrange them beforehand, don't you? But young people who love each other fling themselves to each other in the impatience and haste of their passion, and they don't notice at all what a lack of mutual esteem lies in this disordered giving of themselves; they notice it with astonishment and indignation only from the dissension that arises between them out of all this disorder. And once there is disunity between them, the confusion grows with every day; neither of the two has anything unbroken, pure, and unspoiled about him any longer, and amid the disconsolateness of a break they try to hold fast to the semblance of their happiness (for all that was really supposed to be for the sake of happiness). Alas, they are scarcely able to recall any more what they meant by happiness. In his uncertainty each becomes more and more unjust toward the other; they who wanted to do each other good are now handling one another in an imperious and intolerant manner, and in the struggle somehow to get out of their untenable and unbearable state of confusion, they commit the greatest fault that can happen to human relationships: they become impatient. They hurry to a conclusion; to come, as they believe, to a final decision, they try once and for all to establish their relationship, whose surprising changes have frightened them, in order to remain the same now and *forever* (as they say). That is only the last error in this long chain of errings linked fast to one another. What is dead cannot even be clung to (for it crumbles and changes its character); how much less can what is living and alive be treated definitively, once and for all. Self-transformation is precisely what life is, and human relationships, which are an extract of life, are the most changeable of all, rising and falling from minute to minute, and lovers are those in whose relationship and contact no one moment resembles another. People between whom nothing accustomed, nothing that has already been present before ever takes place, but many new, unexpected, unprecedented things. There are such relationships which must be a very great, almost unbearable happiness, but they can occur only between very rich natures and between those who, each for himself, are richly ordered and composed; they can unite only two wide, deep, individual worlds.—Young people—it is obvious—cannot achieve such a relationship, but they can, if they understand their life properly, grow up slowly to such happiness and prepare themselves for it. They must not forget, when they love, that they are beginners, bunglers of life, apprentices in love,—must *learn* love, and that (like *all* learning) wants peace, patience, and composure!

To take love seriously and to bear and to learn it like a task, this it is that young people need.—Like so much else, people have also misunderstood the place of love in life, they have made it into play and pleasure because they thought that play and pleasure were more blissful than work; but there is nothing happier than work, and love, just because it is the extreme happiness, can be nothing else but work.—So whoever loves must try to act as if he had a great work: he must be much alone and go into himself and collect himself and hold fast to himself; he must work; he must become something!

For believe me, the more one is, the richer is all that one experiences. And whoever wants to have a deep love in his life must collect and save for it and gather honey.

To love is good, too: love being difficult. For one human being to love another: that is perhaps the most difficult of all our tasks, the ultimate, the last test and proof, the work for which all other work is but preparation. For this reason young people, who are beginners in everything, cannot yet know love: they have to learn it. With their whole being, with all their forces, gathered close about their lonely, timid, upward-beating heart, they must learn to love. But learning-time is always a long, secluded time, and so loving, for a long while ahead and far on into life, is—solitude, intensified and deepened loneness for him who loves. Love is at first not anything that means merging, giving over, and uniting with another (for what would a union be of something unclarified and unfinished, still subordinate—?); it is a high inducement to the individual to ripen, to become something in himself, to become world, to become world for himself for another's sake; it is a great exacting claim upon him, something that chooses him out and calls him to vast things. Only in this sense, as the task of working at themselves ("to hearken and to hammer day and night"), might young people use the love that is given them. Merging and surrendering and every kind of communion is not for them (who must save and gather for a long, long time still), is the ultimate, is perhaps that for which human lives as yet scarcely suffice.

But young people err so often and so grievously in this: that they (in whose nature it lies to have no patience) fling themselves at each other, when love takes possession of them, scatter themselves, just as they are, in all their untidiness, disorder, confusion. . . . And then what? What is life to do to this heap of half-battered existence which they call their communion and which they would gladly call their happiness, if it were possible, and their future? Thus each loses himself for the sake of the other and loses the other and many others that wanted still to come. And loses the expanses and the possibilities, exchanges the approach and flight of gentle, divining things for an unfruitful perplexity out of which nothing can come any more, nothing save a little disgust, disillusionment and poverty, and rescue in one of the many conventions that have been put up in great number like public refuges along this most dangerous road. No realm of human experience is so well provided with conventions as this: life-preservers of most varied invention, boats and swimming-bladders are here; the social conception has managed to supply shelters of every sort, for, as it was disposed to take love-life as a pleasure, it had also to give it an easy form, cheap, safe and sure, as public pleasures are.

It is true that many young people who wrongly, that is, simply with abandon and unsolitarily (the average will of course always go on doing so), feel the oppressiveness of a failure and want to make the situation in which they have landed viable and fruitful in their own personal way—; for their nature tells them that, less even than all else that is important, can questions of love be solved publicly and according to this or that agreement; that they are questions, intimate questions from one human being to another, which in any case demand a new, special, *only* personal answer—: but how should they, who have already flung themselves together and no longer mark off and distinguish themselves from each other, who therefore no longer possess anything of their own selves, be able to find a way out of themselves, out of the depth of their already shattered solitude?

They act out of common helplessness, and then, if, with the best intentions, they try to avoid the convention that occurs to them (say, marriage), they land in the tentacles of some less loud, but equally deadly conventional solution; for then everything far around them is—convention; where people act out of a prematurely fused, turbid communion, *every* move is convention: every relation to which such entanglement leads has its convention, be it ever so unusual (that is, in the ordinary sense immoral); why, even separation would here be a conventional step, an impersonal chance decision without strength and without fault.

Whoever looks seriously at it finds that neither for death, which is difficult, nor for difficult love has any explanation, any solution, any hint or way yet been discerned; and for these two problems that we carry wrapped up and hand on without opening, it will not be possible to discover any general rule resting in agreement. But in the same measure in which we begin as individuals to put life to the test, we shall, being individuals, meet these great things at closer range. The demands which the difficult work of love makes upon our development are more than life-size, and as beginners we are not up to them. But if we nevertheless hold out and take this love upon us as burden and apprenticeship, instead of losing ourselves in all the light and frivolous play, behind which people have hidden from the most earnest earnestness of their existence—then a little progress and an alleviation will perhaps be perceptible to those who come long after us; that would be much.

Sex is difficult; yes. But they are difficult things with which we have been charged; almost everything serious is difficult, and everything is serious. If you only recognize this and manage, out of yourself, out of your *own* nature and ways, out of your *own* experience and childhood and strength to achieve a relation to sex wholly your own (*not* influenced by convention and custom), then you need no longer be afraid of losing yourself and becoming unworthy of your best possession.

Physical pleasure is a sensual experience no different from pure seeing or the pure sensation with which a fine fruit fills the tongue; it is a great unending experience, which is given us, a knowing of the world, the fullness and the glory of all knowing. And not our acceptance of it is bad; the bad thing is that most people misuse and squander this experience and apply it as a stimulant at the tired spots of their lives and as distraction instead of a rallying toward exalted moments. Men have made even eating into something else: want on the one hand, superfluity upon the other, have dimmed the distinctness of this need, and all the deep, simple necessities in which life renews itself have become similarly dulled. But the individual can clarify them for himself and live them clearly (and if not the individual, who is too dependent, then at least the solitary man). He can remember that all beauty in animals and plants is a quiet enduring form of love and longing, and he can see animals, as he sees plants, patiently and willingly uniting and increasing and growing, not out of physical delight, not out of physical suffering, but bowing to necessities that are greater than pleasure and pain and more powerful than will and withstanding. O that man might take this secret, of which the world is full even to its littlest things, more humbly to himself and bear it, endure it, more seriously and feel how terribly difficult it is, instead of taking it lightly. That he might be more reverent toward his fruitfulness, which is but *one*, whether it seems mental or physical; for intellectual creation too springs from the physical, is of one nature with it and only like a gentler, more ecstatic and more everlasting repetition of physical delight. "The thought of being creator, of procreating, of making" is nothing without its continuous great confirmation and realization in the world, nothing without the thousandfold concordance from things and animals—and enjoyment of it is so indescribably beautiful and rich only because it is full of inherited memories of the begetting and the bearing of millions. In one creative thought a thousand forgotten nights of love revive, filling it with sublimity and exaltation. And those who come together in the night and are entwined in rocking delight do an earnest work and gather sweetnesses, gather depth and strength for the song of some coming poet, who will arise to speak of ecstasies beyond telling. And they call up the future; and though they err and embrace blindly, the future comes all the same, a new human being rises up, and on the ground of that chance which here seems consummated, awakes the law by which a resistant vigorous seed forces its way through to the egg-cell that moves open toward it. Do not be bewildered by the surfaces; in the depths all becomes law. And those who live the secret wrong and badly (and they are very many), lose it only for themselves and still hand it on, like a sealed letter, without knowing it. And do not be confused by the multiplicity of names and the complexity of cases. Perhaps over all there is a great motherhood, as common longing. The beauty of the virgin, a being that "has not yet achieved anything," is motherhood that begins to sense itself and to prepare, anxious and yearning. And the mother's beauty is ministering motherhood, and in the old woman there is a great remembering. And even in the man there is motherhood, it seems to me, physical and spiritual; his procreating is also a kind of giving birth, and giving birth it is when he creates out of inmost fullness. And pehaps the sexes are more related than we think, and the great renewal of the world will perhaps consist in this, that man and maid, freed of all false feelings and reluctances, will seek each other not as opposites but as brother and sister, as neighbors, and will come together *as human beings,* in order simply, seriously and patiently to bear in common the difficult sex that has been laid upon them.

We are only just now beginning to look upon the relation of one individual person to a second individual objectively and without prejudice, and our attempts to live such associations have no model before them. And yet in the changes brought about by time there is already a good deal that would help our timorous novitiate.

You characterize very well with the term: "living and writing in heat."—*And* in fact artistic experience lies so incredibly close to that of sex, to its pain and its ecstasy, that the two manifestations are indeed but different forms of one and the same yearning and delight. And if instead of heat one might say—sex, sex in the great, broad, clean sense, free of any insinuation of ecclesiastical error, then art would be very grand and infinitely important. Poetic power is great, strong as a primitive instinct; it has its own unyielding rhythms in itself and breaks out as out of mountains.

But it seems that this power is not always honest and without pose. Where, as it rushes through his being, it comes to the sexual, it finds not quite so pure a man as it might require. Here is no thoroughly mature and clean sex world, but one that is not sufficiently *human,* that is only *male,* is heat, intoxication and restlessness, and laden with the old prejudices and arrogances with which man has disfigured and burdened love. Because he loves as man *only,* not as human being, for this reason there is in his sexual feeling something narrow, seeming wild, spiteful, time-bound, uneternal.

The girl and the woman, in their new, their own unfolding, will but in passing be imitators of masculine ways, good and bad, and repeaters of masculine professions. After the uncertainty of such transitions it will become apparent that women were only going through the profusion and the vicissitude of those (often ridiculous) disguises in order to cleanse their own most characteristic nature of the distorting influences of the other sex. Women, in whom life lingers and dwells more immediately, more fruitfully and more confidently, must surely have become fundamentally riper people, more human people, than easygoing man, who is not pulled down below the surface of life by the weight of any fruit of his body, and who, presumptuous and hasty, undervalues what he thinks he loves. This humanity of woman, borne its full time in suffering and humiliation, will come to light when she will have stripped off the conventions of mere femininity in the mutations of her outward status, and those men who do not yet feel it approaching today will be surprised and struck by it. Some day (and for this, particularly in the northern countries, reliable signs are already speaking and shining), some day there will be girls and women whose name will no longer signify merely an opposite of the masculine, but something in itself, something that makes one think, not of any complement and limit, but only of life and existence: the feminine human being.

This advance will (at first much against the will of the out-stripped men) change the love-experience, which is now full of error, will alter it from the ground up, reshape it into a relation that is meant to be of one human being to another, no longer of man to woman. And this more human love (that will fulfill itself, infinitely considerate and gentle, and kind and clear in binding and releasing) will resemble that which we are preparing with struggle and toil, the love that consists in this, that two solitudes protect and border and salute each other.

appreciation

20
by Clint Willis

Clint Willis is a writer, poet and editor; he also is my husband. We married young, and have worked hard to stay connected to one another as we each explore the evolving nature of love, marriage and family. He presented me with this poem on the occasion of our twentieth wedding anniversary.

A garden is a handy metaphor
But more than that it is a plot of land
Complete with dirt
That's populated by—I read this in a book—
Countless living things.
Countless; and for the most part hard to see
Unless you know exactly how to look
And even then the most of them invisible.

I have in mind one garden in particular:
The one behind the breakfast room.
You broke the ground and planted it some six or seven years ago
When we'd been living in this house a year or two
And it seemed likely that we'd stay
At least for long enough for it to get the way
That gardens get when they become familiar;

So that one can hardly tell the difference
From one day to another and another
Except when one remembers to recall
What it looked like—for example—when the garden wasn't there.

At first I didn't notice much about it
No: That isn't true:
I saw you out there on your elbows and your knees;
You look in memory like this:
As if some subtle message
Finds its way from down beneath the dirt into your hands
When you take off your gloves
To set your bony fingers naked to their work
While you think of—I don't know—of lunch
Or it might be that you notice without noticing
The evening shapes made on the day-flecked ground by your
    straw hat
How black or yellow something is:
A bug's wing or a scrap of leaf;
A thing like that.

Above you, in my memory, black branches etch the sky;
The sky is white, perhaps a snowy tint of blue;
The branches and the leaves they sometimes carry shade the
    ground
Thereby making sure that certain flowers do not live to grow
And thereby making room for flowers that can find the sun;

That know a way to drink the blades
That flit between the shadows
On the brightest or the darkest day that anyone has made.

Ah, dear: that you could know the secrets that I wish to know
And tell them to me;
But a secret is a secret maybe just because it cannot be discerned
We cannot learn what water knows (to flow)
Or grow in knowledge by some massive long-term feat of finding
    out:
Whatever I may yearn to say to you I must discover
With the aid of sense or memory that's mine alone
And tells me that I love and will have loved you through your
    flesh
And to your very bone.

separation

from

The Marriage Sabbatical
by Cheryl Jarvis

Journalist Cheryl Jarvis at age 48 took a 'marriage sabbatical'—a temporary time out from her ordinary role as a wife and mother— which she hoped would strengthen and renew those relationships. Her book draws on that experience and on interviews with dozens of other women who took their own marriage sabbaticals, with surprising and sometimes inspiring results.

I'm sitting at the dining-room table making phone calls, struggling to get a job in a city where creative opportunities are limited. The right side of my neck aches from my prolonged, hunched-over position. A pain shoots its way down my arm. I'm longing for a shoulder rub when the phone rings. It's the senior producer of the television show I worked on before it moved east. The producer who replaced me isn't working out, he says, and her successor can't start for a few months. Will I come to Connecticut to fill in?

By the time I'm off the phone, I've forgotten the pain. I start to feel light-headed as I think about how luxurious it would be to focus on the job without feeling pulled in all directions. Before, when I was at work, I was thinking of home; when I was at home, I was thinking of work, my loyalties divided always. Rushing in late to the office, after negotiating breakfasts and schedules and last-minute school projects, racing out early for baseball games, tennis matches, music lessons, I always had the nagging feeling that the single producers on staff were putting in longer hours, achieving more. I think of the shows I could create if I weren't constantly worrying about who or what I was neglecting. My thoughts meander to living alone for three months, to having Sundays just for me. I fantasize about long walks in the New England countryside. Guilty pleasure suffuses my body like an endorphin high.

At dinner I barely touch my food as I talk excitedly about my opportunity. My husband says little; after years of practicing psychotherapy, he is well trained to listen, well trained not to react. The boys, ten and fourteen, ask a few questions: When would you leave? How long would you be gone? Later that evening, I'm reading in bed, psychologically already airborne, when my younger son walks in, closes the door behind him, and sits on the edge of the bed. "I don't want you to go," he says. "School will be starting then. What if I have a problem? I need you when school starts. You can go another time. Please don't go now." Later, my older son comes in, closes the door, and sits at the same spot on the edge of the bed. Same plea, different reason.

Feelings whirl through me: sureness that I won't accept the offer; dejection, now that my chance to live and work alone for a few months has vanished; elation that my sons need me. But something significant has happened. I have admitted to myself how much I long to go.

I was thirty-eight then. Over the next ten years, I celebrated my twenty-fifth wedding anniversary, sent two boys to college at opposite ends of the country, and navigated through five different jobs. Every time I saw single coworkers take off for Chicago or Los Angeles or New York, I felt a pang for the path not taken. Many of them, I knew, looked at married colleagues and longed for a couple's steady intimacy the way I looked at them and longed for their freedom. Is it just human nature that after fulfilling our desire for one, we yearn for the other? Or is it that we really crave both at once? Each time I helped one of our sons pack—for Outward Bound, for a summer in Oregon, for a semester in Spain—I envied his going away on an adventure by himself. I'd take him to the airport, feeling his life widening, mine narrowing, a sense of time and opportunity slipping away. Somewhere in the goodbyes, amid smiles and hugs and admonitions to call/be careful/stay safe, I'd utter what had become my standard line: "In my next life."

The year I turned forty-eight, something clicked. What next life?. . .

. . .Where was it written that I couldn't take a solo adventure, that because I was married I couldn't take time off, time away, time alone? What did one have to do with the other? And where were these emotions coming from?

I had no answers to these questions because I didn't know any married women who had done what I wanted to do. For the first seventeen years of my marriage I didn't imagine it. Once I imagined it, I couldn't voice it. Growing older, however, meant I came increasingly to believe that if I felt something strongly, there must be other women who felt the same way. I wrote this book to find these women, women who had successfully left home to pursue a dream, women in good marriages who could explain the journey and support me along the way. I wrote this book because I needed answers to my questions. Subconsciously, I needed permission to leave.

I began by confiding my thoughts hesitantly to an older friend, who told me her story. She led me to other women, who told me theirs. And then I came to realize what was missing from our culture: a new narrative for marriage. And when I found the narrative, I discovered the grace within the tension: a way to reconcile my desires for both commitment and freedom, a way to honor both my marriage and myself. Rooted in language that goes back two thousand years, the narrative is contemporary, the model ancient.

The Bible tells us that after God created the heavens and the earth, "he rested on the seventh day from all his work which he had done." And then he blessed the day. Honoring the Sabbath (from *shabbat,* to rest) became one of the Ten Commandments and a distinguishing feature of the Jewish faith. Today, most religions of the world honor periods of rest. The ancient Hebrews extended the principle to agriculture: According to Mosaic law, the land and vineyards were to lie fallow every seventh year "as a Sabbath to the Lord." The belief was that fields could be grazed for only so long without losing nutrients. They needed replenishing. The Hebrews called the respite a "sabbatical year."

Modern interpretations give the word a deeper dimension. Theologians have defined the Sabbath as spirit in the form of time, a day of re-creation or reconnection. One Jewish scholar believes it is intended to be an invigorating experience, focused on human fulfillment. With its theological underpinnings, the concept spread to the secular world: If God needed to rest from the work of creation, then surely mortal men and women needed to rest, too. In 1880, Harvard University became the first American institution to grant sabbaticals to its faculty. While today the practice is most widespread in the teaching profession, sabbaticals can be found in journalism, medicine, law, government, and business. The connotation has remained essentially the same over the last hundred years: time off from daily routines to develop intellectually, focus creatively, renew physically. The parameters, however, have changed considerably. Sabbaticals today are accelerated, shortened, and variable. One college offers them after just three years; another offers faculty development leaves over six-week short terms. Some companies require that sabbaticals be spent on social service. Others urge employees to go after a dream. A paid sabbatical in business typically lasts four to six weeks.

Yet in marriage—one of the world's oldest institutions, one of life's greatest challenges, a relationship which can be as emotionally intense as any job, which even conventional wisdom calls *hard work*—there is no development leave, no ritual rest. It may not be coincidence that in biblical times the land was to lie fallow every seventh year and that the average length of marriage at the time of divorce in this country is 7.4 years, making "the seven-year itch" more than a catchphrase. What would happen if we looked to nature and let our marriages rest for a while in order to regenerate?

What would happen if we took time out for an invigorating experience, focused on human fulfillment?

Sabbaticals have actually been taking place in marriage under other guises for centuries. In the Middle Ages, wealthy married women who wanted time alone retreated to convents. In Victorian times, the treatment for hysteria, a psychiatric condition characterized in part by excessive anxiety, was a sea voyage, a long journey, a move from town to country—anything to stimulate the nervous system. Among the prescribed treatments for neurasthenia, a mental disorder characterized by inexplicable exhaustion and irritability, was separation from family and familiar surroundings. Water-cure establishments, sanitariums, and other retreats proliferated during this era.

No wonder these illnesses were considered predominantly female. No wonder they were overdiagnosed. No wonder they were found only in the middle and upper classes, those who could afford a retreat or sea voyage. No wonder these "treatments" usually brought relief. Getting sick was one of the few acceptable ways women could get time for themselves.

Today, many marriages have built-in separations from commuter jobs, travel-dependent professions, military service, and company relocations. When a man gets transferred and his wife waits a year to join him because she's putting the house on the market or when a man takes a few months to follow his wife, who has moved to a new position in another city, whether they are conscious of it or not, the relationship is getting a rest.

But what about couples whose jobs don't provide such opportunities for renewal? What makes a sabbatical an idea worth examining today is our longer life expectancy and its corollary, a longer marriage expectancy. At the turn of the century, few people lived to see all their children grown. Most were dead by fifty. Today at fifty, we have another thirty years to go. At the same time that we're looking at a longer and healthier life span than any other time in history, we're having fewer children and, therefore, spending fewer years raising all of them. We're also living in a society that's changing faster than we are. A world in which people can, or must, reinvent their lives at forty, fifty, and sixty is a world in which marriage for life becomes an increasing challenge. With the rise in gender equality has come another cultural shift: a revolution in marital expectations. How many of us enter marriage expecting our spouse to be our lover, best friend, parenting partner, recreational companion, and spiritual soul mate? That's a lot of psychic weight to place on one relationship—given that nearly half of all couples divorce, more weight than it apparently can bear. A time when many are wondering how to make their marriages thrive over a long stretch of years is a time to examine sabbaticals in marriage not as pathology but as promise.

A marriage sabbatical is as relevant for men as it is for women. The more men I talked with, the more I struggled with focusing only on women's journeys. But while the emotions are universal, cultural realities and expectations are not. Four specific realities make taking a sabbatical a bigger issue for women than for men.

Marriage disproportionately benefits men. Pioneer marital researcher Jessie Bernard said it in 1972, and both male and female researchers say it today. Married women suffer more depression than married men—twice the rate, in fact, over the last three decades. When compared to their single counterparts, married women have more stress, less sense of mastery, and lower self-esteem. Married men, on the other hand, are healthier and happier and live longer than single men. A study led by social psychologist Marjorie Fiske Lowenthal found early warning signs: Newlywed women think about death more often than the middle-aged and the elderly, while newlywed men think about it the least. The Victorians anticipated that women's health would decline after they married, and it was this belief, historians say, that fueled the rise of sanitariums and water-cure retreats. What was assumed in the nineteenth century, researchers proved in the twentieth: Marriage carries greater health hazards for women than for men.

A sabbatical is a greater issue for women because it is harder for women to leave. In spite of men's increasing involvement in family life, women still outnumber men in all caregiving roles. Studies overwhelmingly show that in families of two working parents, women still put in longer hours with children and household tasks. When a child of two working parents gets sick, it is still the mother who most often stays home. Women spend significantly more time than men taking care of elderly relatives, and this time is destined to increase. An American working woman today can expect to spend more years caring for an aging parent than she will for a dependent child. And as women themselves grow older, they are

more likely to take care of their husbands than their husbands are
to take care of them.

Sabbaticals are also a bigger issue for women because of psychological gender differences. As behavioral psychologist Carol Gilligan
theorized in her groundbreaking work *In a Different Voice,* women are
conditioned to be more relational than men and while men develop
their identity through separation and autonomy, women develop
their identity through relationship with others. Because women are
raised to invest more in relationship, because their sense of self is
organized around affiliation, it is psychologically more difficult for
them to move away from the relationships in their lives.

Swiss psychiatrist Carl Jung proposed a different theory of psychological development, but equally relevant. Historically, our culture has suppressed what we once called "male" characteristics
(power and independence) in women and "female" characteristics
(emotional expressiveness and nurturing) in men. The task of the
second half of life, said Jung, is to claim our contrasexual energies—
in other words, to find our missing selves. To fulfill this task, "to
become whole," men who need to discover their "feminine" side are
pulled inward, toward home and family life, while women who need
to develop their "masculine" traits are pulled outward, away from
home and family life. Although increasing numbers of women find
personal power in their twenties and thirties, those who spend the
first half of their adult life raising children often don't discover this
power until their middle and later years.

And finally, sabbaticals are a bigger issue for women because
women have fewer role models. In the classroom, we grew up on

male archetypes. *The Odyssey* was the world's first story that combined wanderlust with married love, but it was the Greek hero Odysseus who traveled the world while his wife Penelope stayed at home. His ten-year sea voyage after the Trojan War was a journey of self-discovery; her ten-year wait, a model of virtue. Homer wrote his epic prose poem more than 2,700 years ago, yet the marital myth of men's mobility and women's rootedness still predominates on the screen. Whether the Knights of the Round Table ride into forests to search for the Holy Grail, soldiers cross continents to fight for a cause, or adventurers dare oceans, mountains, and skies just for the challenge, our cinematic history is filled with images of men leaving and returning home.

When women leave home, however, the movies tell a different story. In *Fatal Attraction,* when the wife leaves *for the weekend,* all hell breaks loose. Her husband commits adultery with a woman so deranged that she stalks him, terrorizes his family, and finally ends up dead in their bathtub, murdered by the wife whose absence started it all. In *Thelma and Louise,* Thelma leaves her husband to go on a two-day road trip and ends up driving off the edge of the Grand Canyon. If women who leave home aren't punished, it's a sure thing they're not coming back. When the heroine of *Shirley Valentine* leaves her house in London for an island in Greece, she stays in Greece. Why wouldn't she? Her marriage is stifling, her husband both tyrant and bore. When Billy Crystal leaves home in *City Slickers,* however, he leaves a likable and sympathetic wife and two engaging children. He not only returns, he comes back with new energy for life, for love, for work. Why hasn't a movie been made about a married woman who leaves home and returns a stronger person to a loving family? The problem with these stereotyped images is that they shape our perceptions, and then they shape our lives.

Many of us grew up seeing our fathers go off—on hunting, fishing, golfing trips—but how many of us over forty have memories of our mothers leaving home for anything but a visit to relatives or a stay in the hospital? How many of us had a mother who went off for herself alone? Men have always had permission to leave, but of women's leaving we have two dominant images: Edna walking into the ocean in Kate Chopin's *The Awakening,* and Nora walking out the door in Ibsen's *A Doll's House.* A self submerged or a relationship severed. Either way, sinking or bailing, a permanent disconnect.

There is no paradigm for a married woman's leaving home *for a while* for personal growth. There is no paradigm for a married woman's returning at all, much less fulfilled, energized, maybe newly in love with her husband. If women lack role models, if women are suffering in marriage, if women are increasingly the ones choosing to dismantle in court what they once yearned to wreathe in ceremony, then it's women who need to write a new script. . .

. . .How do I define sabbatical? I use the term the same way it is used in professional life: a personal time-out from daily routines for creative, professional, or spiritual growth, for study, reflection, or renewal. It is not a prolonged visit with friends or an emergency leave to care for an ailing parent. It is not summers with the children at the lake, with husbands arriving on the weekend. The sabbaticals . . . are solo journeys in which women voluntarily leave all that is familiar and comfortable and safe to venture into the unknown.

What time frame constitutes a sabbatical in marriage? The more I tried to contain the duration, the more elastic it became. It's whatever a woman needs to re-create her life or fulfill a dream, which means it's different for each woman. What's important about the duration is less the time spent, more the stretch and the effect. A five-week leave for one woman can be a more difficult and transformative act than a five-month leave for another.

. . . A sabbatical is biblical, historical, archetypal. A time to lie fallow. It may be an atypical narrative for marriage, but it is one narrative, and it needs to be told.

. . . In relationships, there is always tension, always a struggle between the desire for intimacy and the yearning for independence, between what Thomas Moore calls "the soul of attachment and the spirit of detachment." A sabbatical is not a universal panacea, but it is one way to embrace both sides of life.

The advantages of a sabbatical in academia and business are widely understood: a time to develop one's mind, focus one's creativity, renew physically and spiritually. The value in leaving one's ordinary world for an extraordinary one is not only in what we discover but also in what we return with: a renewed self, with a dedication to engage in work on a higher level—more conscious, deliberate, and open. The assumption behind sabbaticals is that employees return stronger individuals, with greater insight and broader perspective—resources that will enhance the environment to which they return. Where a sabbatical is valued in the workplace, the benefits can be dramatic and far-reaching.

Where there is a foundation of trust and commitment, a sabbatical in relationships can be equally powerful. I am not suggesting, however, that every married woman—and man—take off alone for distant shores. While it's easy to fall into the trap of evangelical thinking, that if something transformed your life, it will transform everyone's, the reality is we are all vastly different individuals, trailing different histories, harboring different dreams. And with these differences we form marriages radically diverse in expectations and needs. Some women's dreams can be fulfilled in their hometowns; some women's, right at home. Some men hate to travel, aren't adventuresome. Not everyone craves solitude. Some couples are so burdened with financial expenses and caretaking that the problems a sabbatical would entail seem far greater than potential gains. Others with growing children don't want to be anywhere but involved daily with those children's lives. Some women have spent many years alone or in unsatisfying first marriages, and now that they've found their soul mates have no desire to be apart. In relationships where infidelity has proven to be the marital issue, a sabbatical is probably not a wise choice. Some couples already know that continual togetherness works best for them. Marriage is not a one-size-fits-all concept.

And I'm not advocating a one-size-fits-all solution. I'm advocating a broadening of our ideas about what's possible in the marriage of the future. What's universal about marriage is not the answer we find but the question we ask: How do we stay married to one person for a long time when the only constant in life is change? Today's messages promoting stricter divorce laws and a return to the traditional model for marriage focus on making it more difficult to divorce. Why not make it easier to stay married?

The place to begin is with a new definition. We need to view marriage as something other than an institution with all that word's constrictive connotations—public in character, traditional in practice, committed to the status quo. The goals of an institution invariably work against the needs of the individual.

We could view marriage as a laboratory, for example, with all that word's positive implications for breakthroughs and progress. With this definition, marriage becomes a safe place to challenge assumptions, remedy problems, risk new forms of relationship, legitimize experimentation. With this definition, marriage becomes a dynamic state of consciousness, a partnership in progress. Sabbaticals symbolize forward movement.

We could view marriage as an energy system, requiring individual solutions for individual landscapes. With this definition, couples attend to neglected resources, look for new and renewable sources of power, link the conventional with the unconventional, and sometimes reverse paths. When marriage becomes an energy system, the goal is a steady exchange of fresh air—comfort, warmth, and electricity year-round. Sabbaticals bring energy to a relationship.

We could view marriage as an artistic creation, where we invest as much time into composing a partnership as we invest in designing a home, where we're less concerned with adapting to an older model than in innovating a new one. With this definition, marriage becomes a canvas we approach with an open mind, a creative spirit, and a feeling the possibilities are inexhaustible. To bring the canvas to life with color and texture and emotional impact, we need to stay inspired, continually see the world anew. A long-term marriage then becomes an artistic evolution, an unfolding of the multiple selves that exist in us all. With each unfolding we can come to our marriage as a new individual—same body, changed spirit. During times we wish our partners were different people, instead of looking for someone else, first we should see if we can become someone else. Sabbaticals provide space to recreate ourselves, time to see the world anew.

We could view marriage as a mutual personal-growth contract, a launching pad to self-discovery rather than a utility ride to the grocery store. Just as corporations founder when they don't pay attention to the psychic needs of their employees, so do marriages. The increasing number of women in midlife filing for divorce, citing as a reason "self-development," should be a wake-up call to view independent acts in marriage not as threats but as the self-development women obviously need. When we see marriage as a personal-growth contract, we commit ourselves to nurturing our own development just as we nurture our partner's. Marriage then becomes an incubator not just for raising families but for realizing dreams, for seeking defining experiences that connect us to who we are at our core. As we age, these defining experiences become increasingly important if we are to continue to be engaged in life. One of the advantages of a sabbatical is that it is a defining experience focused on self-development.

Finally, we can view marriage as a journey of the spirit. My sister-in-law, who is a minister, says that in the 1970s when she helped couples write their wedding vows, many of them wanted to leave out the phrase "for worse." But as any long-married couple knows, it's holding on through the "for worse" that makes a marriage endure. Marriage can be great fun when the jobs are good, the kids are thriving, and the money is rolling in. The real test comes when life blindsides us at four in the morning, when our partners lose their jobs, their health, their hope, when we become depressed or grief-stricken, when the relationship ebbs, as it inevitably will. When we have to put our needs on hold because someone we love has a greater need, the challenge is not just staying the course but doing so with a modicum of grace. Since marriage sabbaticals can be a "for worse" for the partner left behind, they can also be one aspect of a couple's spiritual journey together.

Whatever definition resonates, we need to be more concerned with the essence of relationship and less concerned with form. We need to let go of outdated ideas about how marriage *ought* to be and, instead, look for new ideas about how marriage *might* be.

A marriage sabbatical sounds like a discordant idea to many couples, maybe most, in their early years together. It never occurred to me when I was twenty-one to ask the man with whom I planned to spend the rest of my life how much time alone he needed. It didn't occur to me to wonder about my needs for solitude, either. But as

I've learned, the togetherness/separateness dynamic is critical in a relationship, so critical that when couples in love talk about where they want to live and whether they want children, they should add to the conversation: How much time alone do you need? How important is it to you to have solo adventures? How will you feel if I want to go off by myself for a while? In her 1972 treatise *The Future of Marriage,* researcher Jessie Bernard wrote that in the past, the goal for committed relationships was stability. In committed relationships of the future, she predicted, "the emphasis, among both men and women, may well be on freedom."

Sabbaticals are one way to build freedom into marriage, to give it softer edges and wider spaces—to transform it from within.

Looking back, some days I feel my experience was as surreal as a Remedios Varo painting. Did I really go away like that, I wonder, or did I just dream it? I who have been fear-ridden, guilt-laden most of my life, who have stayed married to one man for twenty-nine years, who pulled out of the workforce to stay home with my children when they were little—how is it I came to do something that others see as radical? Other days, I ask myself what all the fuss was about. Why was it such a big deal that I had to sit down to write a book on the subject?

At times like these, I think nothing changed. I still have arguments in my head, just new ones. My routines are the same: I write most days, teach one or two classes a semester. When there's a phone message from one of our sons, Jim returns the call when it's convenient for him to return it, whereas—even if a deadline is looming—I still respond to the call so quickly, so automatically, that the wires feel like an electronic umbilical cord.

Then there are days I think everything changed. We're moving from our home in the suburbs to a co-op in the city—shedding a shell. Jim leaves the house now as much as I do. The boys call him more often. A book on writers' retreats around the world is by my bed. I know I'll be going to them again, maybe every year for a month or so. The time will be mine to nurture myself, revalue my work, a time, also, to miss my husband, sharpen the chemical edge, remember not to take him or his love for granted. Next time, I hope I can go without guilt.

Everything changed and nothing changed. As I finish this book, one year later, these thoughts linger.

I left for three months, the same length of time as one summer vacation when I was a child—just a pixel, really, on the computer screen of a marriage. But during those months I fulfilled three dreams. Not long ago, Jim said, "I just want you to know it's fine with me if you want to do that nine-month master's program in New York. I know we'll be okay." The most important thing I learned by leaving was that it wasn't marriage that held me back. All the barriers to the life I wanted were within myself. And when I realized that, I fell in love with my husband all over again.

I never imagined that I could leave for three months yet stay married. When I discovered that I could, life began to feel wide again, expansive with time, rich with possibility, stretched out before me like the sage-scented fields of Montana.

intimacy

Summoning Venus:

An Interview with Thomas Moore on Sex and the Soul

by Genie Zeiger

Thomas Moore has written many books about what he calls "soul". They include *Care of the Soul* (1993), *Soul Mates* (1994) and *The Soul of Sex* (1998). Moore contends that "our sexuality is connected to the way we live, to the sensuality, pleasure and beauty in life." Here, Genie Zeiger interviews him for *The Sun*.

Zeiger: *Soul* is a word that appears again and again in your books. How do you understand that word and its meaning in our culture now?

Moore: I think soul is a mysterious word, and I want to keep that mystery, rather than explain it away. The phrase "care of the soul" was used over and over in the medieval world. Today, it suggests a different approach to life, the opposite of our usual notions of "improving ourselves": going to doctors and thera-pists to get our problems figured out so we can get back on track and "function" better. Marsilio Ficino, a philosopher who lived in Florence in the fifteenth century, described the soul as being midway between mind and body, or spirit and matter, linking them and restraining them from excess. The soul is involved partly in time and partly in eternity, he said. He believed that the worlds of nature and culture have souls, and recommended making a beautiful world and drawing soul from it—a method he called "natural magic."

Zeiger: There is so much talk about "spirituality" nowadays. Is there a difference between the soul and the spirit?

Moore: Generally, the spirit is the driving force that pushes us forward, while the soul is rich in reverie and memory, with a tendency to reflect, ponder, create, and express. Spiritual people are interested in climbing up a ladder. There are many such images in spiritual literature: The "seven steps to success," for example. With spirit, we're trying to get to someplace higher—higher consciousness, elevated states. (No one talks about steps going down, which is the way I'd probably go.) Spirituality creates hierarchies of people, rules by which they can measure how well they are doing: titles, colored belts, initiations.

The soul unfolds in ways you'd never predict. It's vegetative, like a plant, and goes down, like roots. The concerns of the soul are home, family, place, intimacy, and beauty. The concerns of the spirit, on the other hand, are: How quickly can I become enlightened? Where can I find a great teacher? How can I have great sex? [Laughs.]

People say that all meaning in life comes from the spiritual realm, but I don't think so. In fact, there is a lot that goes on in the spiritual realm that I think is an escape from life. There is a tendency in much spiritual activity to withdraw from ordinary life, the body, and the world. You don't find these sentiments in the best spiritual writings, but they're there in much of the literature. I think anyone pursuing a spiritual life should be careful not to try to force the body into an ideal condition with yoga and fitness, or to force the emotions into an ideal condition with moralism. Spirituality works only if it is connected to the deep soul—to family, body, emotion, ordinary life, failure, ignorance, and imperfection. This is spirituality in tune with the human condition, not perfectionist, and not escapist.

Zeiger: You've said that the greed and materialism of our culture taint our spiritual pursuits.

Moore: Yes, they create *spiritual* greed and ambition. The same people who are out running and trying to get their bodies in shape are often the ones buying books and tapes about spirituality, but spirituality reduced to a kind of "fitness" loses its awesome depth and sublimity. Spirituality isn't a matter of individuals becoming perfect. It has to do with living a holy life, being motivated by profound compassion, and feeling wide and deep love and sense of community. Whether we're "fit" or not is irrelevant. Physically ill and emotionally unsettled people can be holy.

Zeiger: What is the relationship between sexuality and soul?

Moore: Soul shows itself in many aspects of life, but particularly in sex. This is because, to use the Jungian term, sex is the "archetype" of life. In sex, we are dealing intimately with such essentials as self-expression, primal relatedness to one another, and the sense of being alive.

Zeiger: In *The Soul of Sex,* you talk about sex as something woven into the fabric of life and the senses; you say that nurturing one's sexuality, in the broadest sense, means living through the senses.

Moore: I do think that everything in life is sexual. All the things we do, big or small, involve the ingredients of our sexuality: body, desire, fantasy, pleasure, frustration, sensuousness, relatedness.

These ingredients can, of course, be considered singly and separately, but they may be better thought of as part of a larger whole: the erotic life. For example, I'm responding to your questions now partly from a rational standpoint, but also because I take pleasure from it. I find sensuous joy in making myself clear, in relating to the public, and in choosing my words carefully. In this sense, conversation is a type of sexual act. So our sexuality is not restricted to one corner of life, but suffuses the whole.

Let me give you another example: When I was a therapist, I'd say that well over half of my clients came to me to talk about sexual issues. Now, you could say that these people just had problems with sex, but I think it was deeper than that. As we work out our sexuality, we are working out our lives. Our sexuality is, in its most complete sense, connected to the way we live, to the sensuality, pleasure, and beauty in life. All the qualities you see in sex—beauty, body, intimacy, pleasure—form the sexual dimension of our everyday life.

Zeiger: You've also said that many couples came to therapy because of an attraction outside the marriage.

Moore: I've never objected to married people fantasizing about having sex with others, because the soul wants more life, more freedom, and less guilt. But I don't recommend acting on all these desires or casually breaking marriage vows. Sometimes, when we yield to desire, we find it doesn't satisfy our longing.

I think, however, that if we allowed ourselves more freedom to fantasize, we wouldn't have such widespread sexual confusion and emotional pain. Also, the urge to have sex outside the marriage might be satisfied in some other way—say, by finding work that involves pleasure, sensuality, and intimacy, or by living in a place with those qualities. We are confused: we think that another person has to be the love object, because we understand sex only as an act between two *people*.

Zeiger: Why are Americans so mixed up about sex?

Moore: One reason is that, despite the ever-present sexual images in our culture, we don't live very sexual lives. We repress our deeper sexuality, and when you repress something, it becomes a monster in your face. Our society is oversexed precisely because we haven't really grappled with sex and made it our own.

We believe we're being moral when we repress our sexuality, and are perhaps even proud of having conquered our desires. In turn, we are quick to judge others for not being so in control. Recall the unbelievable hypocrisies on display during the Clinton impeachment trial. But if we could admit to our own desires and deal honestly with our complex sexual lives, then we might be more tolerant of others as they grapple with theirs.

In addition, our lives are too fast paced and too focused on productivity. A sensuous life requires that one slow down, but we're not willing to do that, because we tend to justify our existence through work. And look at the places where we work. Go to the fanciest office buildings in New York City. They are not sensuous. You walk into the lobby and find high ceilings, marble walls, no place to sit, no place for the body. And now, with so many of us working in front of computer screens all day, we don't even look at each other.

We are culturally induced to find meaning in acquiring new and better gadgets and machines. As a result, we're making our living environments more efficient and less beautiful. So many of the beautiful old buildings are being torn down. I travel a lot on book tours—Atlanta, Denver, Chicago—and as soon as I get into town, people say, "Please come help us fight to save this great old building." All this beauty is being destroyed in favor of homogeneous boxes; you can't even tell one building from the next. We don't realize that, in destroying old buildings, we are also destroying our sexuality.

Zeiger: A friend of mine who teaches at a girls' prep school worries about how sexualized her thirteen-year-old students are, with their revealing halter tops and tight pants. Yet they don't know the first thing about sex. She tells me that they are unabashedly engaging in oral sex and, like Bill Clinton, saying that it's *not* sex. Their bodies have become commodities that they exchange. It's scary.

Moore: It is scary. I don't want to reduce sexual behavior to simple explanations, but here is one thought that might speak to what you've described: We have created a society with many spirited entertainments but few deep pleasures. For most, work is not a pleasure, family pleasures seem to have been lost, and beauty has given way to function and profit. In this wasteland—just visit any small town and walk the strip of fast-food restaurants and gas stations—sex becomes exaggerated and problematic. It takes the place of all those other pleasures.

We don't have the daily physical activity that people in another time had in the normal course of their lives, so sex is now our primary avenue to the body. In what other arena can those kids you describe explore their bodies and get away from the flatness of daily life? And what cultural images do they have to help them deepen their sexuality: Movies full of symptomatic sexuality? Television programs about the extremes of sexual behavior? Songs that take sex to its painful limits?

Zeiger: You emphasize the importance of marriage, family, and kids as the arena in which we work out our lives.

Moore: It seems to me that marriage is a holy state. It's never easy, but it polishes away our narcissism and deepens our capacity to love. Living with and caring for children does the same. Children are very demanding, but they give us remarkable perspectives on all aspects of life.

That is not to say, however, that the single, childless life is soulless. I've been a celibate monk, I've been single, I've been married, and I've gone through divorce. I'm a father and a stepfather. All these ways of life are full of soul. I focus particularly on marriage because marital sex is often felt to be limited and not as exciting as nonmarital sex. To me, sex in marriage can be particularly intense, valuable, and satisfying because it can bring the whole of life together, whereas, when engaging in sex with a relative stranger, one tends to separate one's heart and emotions from the lovemaking. It is in long-term relationships—marriage and family and children—that we really work out our lives.

Zeiger: You say that we work too hard, that this detracts from the sensuousness of our lives. Is there a positive correlation between sexuality and loafing or leisure?

Moore: Trying to make life productive and profitable is the American way, but it has a negative effect on sexuality. The wish to be productive is a highly *spiritual* intention, whereas sex is made mostly of soul stuff: deeper, closer to the emotions, less goal oriented. We can be so preoccupied with justifying our lives through hard work and busyness that we don't allow enough room for sex, pleasure, and sensuality. We might make room in our hectic schedules for entertainment and days off, but this kind of leisure only supports our busy way of life. So I don't think leisure is the answer, but rather a slower, less goal directed, more relaxed way of life overall.

Zeiger: Now that I'm in my fifties, I notice that my contemporaries and I are slowing down a bit. Being slower and more present to your life can be challenging, and even frightening. Often, frantic work serves as a diversion from the ghosts and the feelings you haven't wanted to face.

Moore: Yes, allowing soul into our everyday life can be hard for a number of reasons. One is that the whole spiritual realm looks so bright and wonderful. People want to transcend their everyday lives, not be more *in* them. People don't want to grow old and face the concerns of the soul. I think our American society, if you could put it on the psychiatrist's couch, would reveal the psychology of a very young person.

Zeiger: An adolescent?

Moore: Very much an adolescent. Look at this man who has somehow been elected president. George Bush reminds me of the college kids I taught in Texas. I know his type well. I have to wonder: do we want to turn this country over to an adolescent, whatever his age?

Zeiger: Will America ever grow up?

Moore: There are no signs of it. We've had more than two hundred years. How long is it going to take? I think we are an eternally young society, and what happens to eternally young people is that, instead of maturing, they burn out. To prevent that, we need to cultivate the imagination and develop our own philosophies of life, rather than unconsciously live the life that advertisers and big business want us to lead. To find our own way, we have to have intellectual and historical background. That's why my books are full of quotes from great writers of the past.

Zeiger: Speaking of that, could you say more about the philosopher Ficino, whom you mentioned earlier? I understand his work has been a great influence on you.

Moore: It has. Ficino lived from 1433 to 1499. As a young man, he became a translator for Cosimo de' Medici, a wealthy political leader in Florence. Ficino was a royal scholar. He learned Latin and Greek, studied philosophy, and became a priest in his forties. He translated Plato and the Neoplatonists from Greek into Latin, making them more widely accessible, and wrote commentaries about their work.

At one point, the Church held a council in Florence, and the Greeks attended, bringing with them books full of magic and spells and ancient philosophy that no one in Italy had ever seen before. When Medici heard about this, he said to Ficino, "Stop what you're doing and translate these magical texts for me." And so Ficino did. He took the Greek traditions of astrology and the magical use of music, imagery, stones, and jewelry, put all of this together with his Neoplatonic philosophy, and created his own unique blend—a fascinating mixture of the Neoplatonists' soul-centeredness and a way of being in the world in which music and the use of color and wood and other materials are important. This room is modeled on Ficino's principles: for instance, putting quotations in Latin above the doorways.

Zeiger: What does that one say?

Moore: It's from Nicholas of Cusa: it says, "Wherever I turn, you are there." The "you" he refers to is God, but it could also be the *anima mundi,* the soul of the world. Ficino's work encourages us to create a life that nurtures the soul, a physical life, a concrete life in our home and our physical surroundings—not just a life of ideas.

Zeiger: You've said the soul can be a way out of the dualistic manner in which we perceive most things: mind versus body, thought versus feeling.

Moore: What I mean is that, even when we're in the mind—in other words, being very rational and intent upon understanding things—there's still a large unconscious undercurrent there; for example, the fantasies we have as we converse with someone. Even when we're trying to be completely rational, the imagination is there. The primary activity of the soul is imagination: dream, poetry, art, painting. Can I read you something? [Reaches for a book.] "If there are only two things in the universe, on one side the intellect and on the other side the body, but no soul, then the intellect would never be attracted to the body, and the body would never be drawn to the intellect, but if the soul, conforming to both, lies between them, an attraction will easily occur from one to the other." That's Ficino.

Zeiger: You also often quote the poet Rainer Maria Rilke, who says that the things of the world have souls and want us to notice them. We think of a bottle of water, a book, or a wall as just an object, but Rilke would say that they need us to see them.

Moore: Yes, Rilke's view overcomes the split between the world out there and the me in here. If the world has its own soul, individuality, and will, then we have a basis for dialogue with it, and we do not consider ourselves superior to it. Most of us today, though, seem to feel that the world is a commodity with which we can do as we please.

The things of the world have much to offer us, if we would only listen to what they have to say. Artists can help us do this. A still-life painting or a poem can show us that things have souls.

Zeiger: In our culture, it's hard even to talk about *people* having souls. For example, I often feel the presence of my parents, who have died, and that presence speaks to the part of me that I would call soul. But I'm careful whom I tell about this.

Moore: Of course, if you live in a soulful world, then you know that the end of this life is not the end of the relationship, nor of the connection. Mysteriously, the intimacy becomes even greater than it was before.

Zeiger: You've referred to depression and illness as a "gift." This, too, is an unusual point of view in our society.

Moore: My take on depression is influenced primarily by late-medieval and early-Renaissance medical writings on the subject. Ficino thought he was a melancholic person from birth and said that Saturn, which represents depression, is poisonous and dangerous, yet also valuable and necessary. People used to talk about being "in Saturn": depression as a mood or a state of being that takes you to a faraway place. When you're depressed, you withdraw from the world around you. And in that faraway place of emotion and imagination, you see what the average person cannot. The melancholic artist can make paintings or write poetry or compose music that is valuable to others because the artist has gone to a painful, disturbing place, but one that is closer to reality than most other emotional places we visit. Today we see depression only as a disease. We don't appreciate what it has to offer.

Zeiger: I like the idea of depression as a place you are in, rather than something you are.

Moore: Our clinical and medical language is often a worse problem than the depression itself. [Laughs.] I don't want to make light of depression, but to give it a context. Along with all that pain and suffering, there's actually something working for you, and you have to be open to that. But in America today, we see cheerfulness and positive thinking as a sign of health, and depression as an illness.

There are many kinds of depression, and I don't encourage cultivating any of them, but they can be a means of liberation from the tyranny of cheerfulness and the religion of positive thinking. Through depression, we can deepen our character and discover new things about ourselves and the world. If, on the other hand, we go out of our way to avoid depression or combat it, I think we run the risk of developing an unrealistic view of the world.

Zeiger: You've also written somewhat favorably about another subject with many negative associations: pornography.

Moore: Most people think that pornography isn't art, but I think of it as a special formula characterized by dumb scripts, an extreme focus on the genitals, and the absence of romantic love. For some, at least, that formula is appealing. To a degree, pornography is the opposite of what we consider to be the appropriate attitude toward sex: that we should be educated and intelligent about it, focus on the whole person, and use sex to express love. I suspect that, when we require sex always to have those qualities, we defend ourselves unduly against the other sides of our sexuality. I don't think we should drop our defenses entirely, because sex is a powerful force of the human soul, but we might be more tolerant of pornography if we admitted to our defensiveness.

Zeiger: You've called pornography "the return of the repressed, the religious nature of sex presenting itself in dark instead of bright colors."

Moore: Religion and sex can be powerful partners or powerful enemies. Many religions have used sex as part of initiation rites or used sexual imagery to represent contact between the divine and the human. The great Roman and Greek statues of the deities, for example, recognize the deep tie between religion and sexuality, and some famous Indian temples are packed with images of lovemaking couples. (Of course, many people in India are repressed sexually, but that doesn't contradict the wisdom of the erotic temples.) Sexual images are numinous—that is, possessed with great power to attract and disturb—because they address some of the same issues that religion struggles with, especially the craving for vitality.

When we don't allow any real religious power into our secular society, that power gets pushed into the extremes of sexuality. While the churches try to keep sex within strict bounds, ministers and priests are defrocked for their sexual transgressions, and their parishioners commit adulteries and keep bizarre pornography sites flourishing on the Internet. If we could ever get to the point where our spirituality didn't contradict our sexuality, and our sexuality completely embraced our spirituality, then we would be in the right place.

Zeiger: Where is your work taking you now?

Moore: In the book I'm just finishing, I'm dipping back into my Catholic roots much more, trying to show that what I'm doing now is really an evolution of my early life as a monk, though the Catholic press sometimes sees my work as apostasy, heresy.

I should say that not all the press is critical. Several Catholic publications have published my writing and have interviewed me with considerable understanding. But the conservative wing doesn't like my work, partly because I don't use the usual, accepted language. I also refer positively to the Greek gods and goddesses, and any suggestion that paganism has value bothers them. For some Christians, pagan religion still represents evil and temptation. I think, too, that my references to other world religions trouble some Catholics. And maybe they pick up on the fact that I have no intention of subjecting myself to the authoritarianism and mind-control attempts of the church hierarchy. At this point in my life, such rules and threats can't touch my Catholicism or my spirituality.

Zeiger: You've been accused of focusing too much on the individual and not enough on political efforts to improve the soul of society. Is it self-centered to talk only about the individual soul?

Moore: I have never said that caring for the soul is an entirely individual matter, and I have always tried to push beyond the ego.

In almost all my books, I try to offer a deeper understanding. *The Soul of Sex,* for example, is largely about living in the social, concrete world more erotically. When I write, I'm motivated by the suffering I see everywhere in the world, but I want to get to the root of the problems. If I think the merely social approach doesn't go deep enough, that doesn't mean I advocate navel-gazing.

Zeiger: You write a great deal about the marriage bed. What is your marriage bed like?

Moore: My marriage bed is quite ordinary. I admire the way some of my friends surround their beds with mirrors or silky red drapes, but my wife and I prefer simple décor. I do like the bed to be secluded from the rest of the house. The bed's importance and sanctity come from what goes on there rather than from its appearance.

To me, the marriage bed is the altar to Venus, a sacred place. The Romans said that adultery offends the bed, not the couple, because the bed is the holy, sacramental object that represents the marriage. Care of the bed and other things having to do with sex is similar to caring for a chapel.

The goal of our sexuality—especially in our thinking about lovemaking—should be to evoke the spirit of Venus. That's really what it's about. It's not about the modern idea of people trying to communicate with each other. Nor is it just instinct, nor biology. In *The Soul of Sex,* I set out to write about sex in a way that was not biological, not psychological, and not sociological. I came to the conclusion that summoning the spirit of sex—which the Greeks called Aphrodite and the Romans called Venus—is still what sex is about, and is what we need to do in today's world.

The spirit of Venus is a combination of sexuality, beauty, and desire, as well as their shadow elements: jealousy, possessiveness, and obsession. All of these nurture the soul. You must evoke the spirit physically, concretely, so that you have the sense of devoting yourself to it. If that spirit is not evoked, then you can't have a satisfying sexual life, nor a sensuous society.

indulgence

At a Summer Villa
by Anton Chekhov

Anton Chekhov (1860–1904) remains one of the most influential writers in Western literature. His eye for detail, the clarity of his emotional vision and the directness of his wit are evident in this story about a married couple and their secrets.

I love you. You are my life, my happiness—everything to me! Forgive the avowal, but I have not the strength to suffer and be silent: I ask not for love in return, but for sympathy. Be at the old arbour at eight o'clock this evening . . . . To sign my name is unnecessary I think, but do not be uneasy at my being anonymous. I am young, nice-looking . . . what more do you want?"

When Pavel Ivanitch Vyhodtsev, a practical married man who was spending his holidays at a summer villa, read this letter, he shrugged his shoulders and scratched his forehead in perplexity.

"What devilry is this?" he thought. "I'm a married man, and to send me such a queer letter! Who wrote it?"

Pavel Ivanitch turned the letter over and over before his eyes, read it through again, and spat with disgust.

"'I love you'" . . . he said jeeringly. "A nice boy she has pitched on! So I'm to run off to meet you in the arbour! . . . I got over all such romances and *fleurs d'amour* years ago, my girl. . . . Hm! She must be some reckless, immoral creature. . . . Well, these women are a set! What a whirligig—God forgive us!—she must be to write a letter like that to a stranger, and a married man, too! It's real demoralisation!"

In the course of his eight years of married life Pavel Ivanitch had completely got over all sentimental feeling, and he had received no letters from ladies except letters of congratulation, and so, although he tried to carry it off with disdain, the letter quoted above greatly intrigued and agitated him.

An hour after receiving it, he was lying on his sofa, thinking:

"Of course I am not a silly boy, and I am not going to rush off to this idiotic rendezvous; but yet it would be interesting to know who wrote it! Hm. . . . It is certainly a woman's writing. . . . The letter is written with genuine feeling, and so it can hardly be a joke. . . . Most likely it's some neurotic girl, or perhaps a widow . . . widows are frivolous and eccentric as a rule. Hm. . . . Who could it be?"

What made it the more difficult to decide the question was that Pavel Ivanitch had not one feminine acquaintance among all the summer visitors, except his wife.

"It is queer . . ." he mused. "'I love you!' . . . When did she manage to fall in love? Amazing woman! To fall in love like this, apropos of nothing, without making any acquaintance and finding out what sort of man I am. . . . She must be extremely young and romantic if she is capable of falling in love after two or three looks at me. . . . But . . . who is she?"

Pavel Ivanitch suddenly recalled that when he had been walking among the summer villas the day before, and the day before that, he had several times been met by a fair young lady with a light blue hat and a turn-up nose. The fair charmer had kept looking at him, and when he sat down on a seat she had sat down beside him. . . .

"Can it be she?" Vyhodtsev wondered. "It can't be! Could a delicate ephemeral creature like that fall in love with a worn-out old eel like me? No, it's impossible!"

At dinner Pavel Ivanitch looked blankly at his wife while he meditated:

"She writes that she is young and nice-looking. . . . So she's not old. . . . Hm. . . . To tell the truth, honestly I am not so old and plain that no one could fall in love with me. My wife loves me! Besides, love is blind, we all know. . . ."

"What are you thinking about?" his wife asked him.

"Oh . . . my head aches a little . . ." Pavel Ivanitch said, quite untruly.

He made up his mind that it was stupid to pay attention to such a nonsensical thing as a love-letter, and laughed at it and at its authoress, but—alas!—powerful is the enemy of mankind! After dinner, Pavel Ivanitch lay down on his bed, and instead of going to sleep, reflected:

"But there, I daresay she is expecting me to come! What a silly! I can just imagine what a nervous fidget she'll be in and how her *tournure* will quiver when she does not find me in the arbour! I shan't go, though. . . . Bother her!"

But, I repeat, powerful is the enemy of mankind.

"Though I might, perhaps, just out of curiosity . . ." he was

musing, half an hour later. "I might go and look from a distance
what sort of a creature she is. . . . It would be interesting to have a
look at her! It would be fun, and that's all! After all, why shouldn't
I have a little fun since such a chance has turned up?"

Pavel Ivanitch got up from his bed and began dressing. "What
are you getting yourself up so smartly for?" his wife asked, noticing
that he was putting on a clean shirt and a fashionable tie.

"Oh, nothing. . . . I must have a walk. . . . My head aches. . . . Hm."

Pavel Ivanitch dressed in his best, and waiting till eight o'clock,
went out of the house. When the figures of gaily dressed summer
visitors of both sexes began passing before his eyes against the
bright green background, his heart throbbed.

"Which of them is it? . . ." he wondered, advancing irresolutely.
"Come, what am I afraid of? Why, I am not going to the rendezvous! What . . . a fool! Go forward boldly! And what if I go into
the arbour? Well, well . . . there is no reason I should."

Pavel Ivanitch's heart beat still more violently. . . . Involuntarily,
with no desire to do so, he suddenly pictured to himself the half-
darkness of the arbour. . . . A graceful fair girl with a little blue hat
and a turn-up nose rose before his imagination. He saw her,
abashed by her love and trembling all over, timidly approach him,
breathing excitedly, and . . . suddenly clasping him in her arms.

"If I weren't married it would be all right . . ." he mused, driving
sinful ideas out of his head. "Though . . . for once in my life, it
would do no harm to have the experience, or else one will die
without knowing what. . . . And my wife, what will it matter to her?
Thank God, for eight years I've never moved one step away from

her. . . . Eight years of irreproachable duty! Enough of her. . . . It's positively vexatious. . . . I'm ready to go to spite her!"

Trembling all over and holding his breath, Pavel Ivanitch went up to the arbour, wreathed with ivy and wild vine, and peeped into it. . . . A smell of dampness and mildew reached him. . . .

"I believe there's nobody . . ." he thought, going into the arbour, and at once saw a human silhouette in the corner.

The silhouette was that of a man. . . . Looking more closely, Pavel Ivanitch recognised his wife's brother, Mitya, a student, who was staying with them at the villa.

"Oh, it's you . . ." he growled discontentedly, as he took off his hat and sat down.

"Yes, it's I" . . . answered Mitya.

Two minutes passed in silence.

"Excuse me, Pavel Ivanitch," began Mitya: "but might I ask you to leave me alone?? . . . I am thinking over the dissertation for my degree and . . . and the presence of anybody else prevents my thinking."

"You had better go somewhere in a dark avenue . . ." Pavel Ivanitch observed mildly. "It's easier to think in the open air, and, besides, . . . er . . . I should like to have a little sleep here on this seat. . . . It's not so hot here. . . ."

"You want to sleep, but it's a question of my dissertation . . ." Mitya grumbled. "The dissertation is more important."

Again there was a silence. Pavel Ivanitch, who had given the rein to his imagination and was continually hearing footsteps, suddenly leaped up and said in a plaintive voice:

"Come, I beg you, Mitya! You are younger and ought to consider me. . . . I am unwell and . . . need sleep. . . . Go away!"

"That's egoism. . . . Why must you be here and not I? I won't go as a matter of principle."

"Come, I ask you to! Suppose I am an egoist, a despot and a fool . . . but I ask you to go! For once in my life I ask you a favour! Show some consideration!"

Mitya shook his head.

"What a beast! . . ." thought Pavel Ivanitch. "That can't be a rendezvous with him here! It's impossible with him here!"

"I say, Mitya," he said, "I ask you for the last time. . . . Show that you are a sensible, humane, and cultivated man!"

"I don't know why you keep on so!" . . . said Mitya, shrugging his shoulders. "I've said I won't go, and I won't. I shall stay here as a matter of principle. . . ."

At that moment a woman's face with a turn-up nose peeped into the arbour. . . .

Seeing Mitya and Pavel Ivanitch, it frowned and vanished.

"She is gone!" thought Pavel Ivanitch, looking angrily at Mitya. "She saw that blackguard and fled! It's all spoilt!"

After waiting a little longer, he got up, put on his hat and said:

"You're a beast, a low brute and a blackguard! Yes! A beast! It's mean . . . and silly! Everything is at an end between us!"

"Delighted to hear it!" muttered Mitya, also getting up and putting on his hat. "Let me tell you that by being here just now you've played me such a dirty trick that I'll never forgive you as long as I live."

Pavel Ivanitch went out of the arbour, and beside himself with rage, strode rapidly to his villa. Even the sight of the table laid for supper did not soothe him.

"Once in a lifetime such a chance has turned up," he thought in agitation; "and then it's been prevented! Now she is offended . . . crushed!"

At supper Pavel Ivanitch and Mitya kept their eyes on their plates and maintained a sullen silence. . . . They were hating each other from the bottom of their hearts.

"What are you smiling at?" asked Pavel Ivanitch, pouncing on his wife. "It's only silly fools who laugh for nothing!"

His wife looked at her husband's angry face, and went off into a peal of laughter.

"What was that letter you got this morning?" she asked.

"I? . . . I didn't get one. . . ." Pavel Ivanitch was overcome with confusion. "You are inventing . . . imagination."

"Oh, come, tell us! Own up, you did! Why, it was I sent you that letter! Honour bright, I did! Ha ha!"

Pavel Ivanitch turned crimson and bent over his plate. "Silly jokes," he growled.

"But what could I do? Tell me that. . . . We had to scrub the rooms out this evening, and how could we get you out of the house? There was no other way of getting you out. . . . But don't be angry, stupid. . . . I didn't want you to be dull in the arbour, so I sent the same letter to Mitya too! Mitya, have you been to the arbour?"

Mitya grinned and left off glaring with hatred at his rival.

Acknowledgments

Many people made this anthology.

At Marlowe & Company and Avalon Publishing Group:
Neil Ortenberg and Susan Reich offered vital support and expertise.
Sue Canavan designed a beautiful book. Maria Fernandez cheerfully
and skillfully oversaw production with the help of Paul Paddock and
Simon Sullivan. Proofreader Rick Willet caught our slip-ups.
My gratitude is due to Will Balliett and Matthew Lore for their friend-
ship and guidance.

At the Thomas Memorial Library in Cape Elizabeth, Maine:
Thanks to all the librarians, but especially to Susan Sandberg, for working hard to find and borrow books from around the country.

At The Writing Company:
Thanks to Nate Hardcastle for keeping me on task and managing those
oh-so-important details that make all the difference.

At Shawneric.com:
Thanks to Shawneric Hachey for securing permissions for the selections
in this book, and going that extra mile for me when needed.

Among family and friends:
Thanks to all the friends and family who have helped me to learn about
love over the course of my lifetime.

A special thanks to my husband of over 20 years, Clint Willis, who has
been so brave in his pursuit of love and truth.

Finally, I am grateful to the writers whose work appears in this book.

378

Excerpt from *Teachings on Love* by Thich Nhat Hanh. Copyright © 1998 by Thich Nhat Hanh. Reprinted by permission of Parallax Press, Berkeley, California, www.parallax.org. ❋ Excerpt from *Gift from the Sea* by Anne Morrow Lindbergh. Copyright © 1955 by Anne Morrow Lindbergh. Reprinted by permission of Pantheon Books, a Division of Random House, Inc. ❋ Excerpt from *Journey of the Heart* by John Welwood. Copyright © 1990 by John Welwood. Reprinted by permission of HarperCollins Publishers, Inc. ❋ "Just Married" from *The Solace of Open Spaces* by Gretel Ehrlich. Copyright © 1985 by Gretel Ehrlich. Used by permission of Viking Penguin, a division of Penguin Putnam Inc. ❋ "Ciudad Juàrez" from *Honey* by Elizabeth Tallent. Copyright © 1993 by Elizabeth Tallent. Used by permission of Alfred A. Knopf, a division of Random House, Inc. ❋ From *Everyday Blessings* by Myla and Jon Kabat-Zinn. Copyright © 1997 Myla Kabat-Zinn and Jon Kabat-Zinn. Reprinted by permission of Hyperion. ❋ Excerpt from *Passionate Marriage: Love, Sex, and Intimacy in Emotionally Committed Relationships* by David Schnarch. Copyright © 1997 by David Schnarch. Used by permission of W.W. Norton & Company, Inc. ❋ "Love" from *The Collected Stories* by Grace Paley. Copyright © 1994 by Grace Paley. Reprinted by permission of Farrar, Straus & Giroux, LLC. ❋ Excerpt from *Sexual Detours* by Holly Hein. Copyright © 2000 by Holly Hein. Reprinted by permission of St. Martin's Press, LLC. ❋ "The Anniversary" from *The Anniversary and Other Stories*. Copyright © 1999 by Louis Auchincloss. Reprinted by permission of Houghton Mifflin Company. All rights reserved. ❋ Excerpt from *Soul Mates* by Thomas Moore. Copyright © 1994 by Thomas Moore. Reprinted by permission of HarperCollins Publishers. ❋ Excerpts from *100 Love Sonnets: Cien Sonetos de Amor* by Pablo Neruda, translated by Stephen Tapscott. Copyright © 1959 by Pablo Neruda and Fundación Pablo Neruda.

Bibliography

The selections used in this anthology were taken from the editions listed below. In some cases, other editions may be easier to find. Hard-to-find or out-of-print titles can often be acquired through inter-library loan services or through Internet booksellers.

Auchincloss, Louis. *The Anniversary and Other Stories*. New York: Houghton Mifflin Company, 1999.

Bayley, John. *Elegy for Iris*. New York: St. Martin's Press, 1999.

Chekhov, Anton (translated by Constance Garnett). *Love and Other Stories*. New York: Ecco Press, 1987.

Ehrlich, Gretel. *The Solace of Open Spaces*. New York: Viking Penguin, 1985.

Hanh, Thich Nhat. *Teachings on Love*. Berkeley, CA: Parallax Press, 1998.

Hein, Holly. *Sexual Detours*. New York: St. Martin's Press, LLC, 2000.

Jarvis, Cheryl. *The Marriage Sabbatical*. New York: Basic Books, 2001.

Joyce, James. *Dubliners*. New York: Viking Books, 1967.

Kabat-Zinn, Myla and Jon Kabat-Zinn. *Everyday Blessings*. New York: Hyperion Books, 1997.

Lindbergh, Anne Morrow. *Gift from the Sea*. New York: Signet Books, 1962.

Moore, Thomas. *Soul Mates*. New York: HarperCollins Publishers, 1994.

Neruda, Pablo (translated by Stephen Tapscott). *100 Love Sonnets: Cien Sonetos de Amor*. Austin, TX: University of Texas Press, 1986.

O. Henry. *The Gift of the Magi*. New York: Dover Publications, 1992.

Paley, Grace. *The Collected Stories*. New York: Farrar, Straus & Giroux, LLC, 1994.

Rilke, Rainer Maria. *Love and Other Difficulties*. New York: W.W. Norton & Company, 1993.

Schnarch, David. *Passionate Marriage: Love, Sex, and Intimacy in Emotionally Committed Relationships*. New York: W.W. Norton & Company, Inc., 1997.

Tallent, Elizabeth. *Honey*. New York: Alfred A. Knopf, 1993.

Welwood, John. *Journey of the Heart*. New York: HarperCollins Publishers, Inc., 1990.

Willis, Clint. "20". Unpublished work.

Zeiger, Genie. "Summoning Venus". Originally appeared in *The Sun*, June 2001, issue 306.